LABOR POLICY OF THE
FEDERAL GOVERNMENT

THE BROOKINGS INSTITUTION

The Brookings Institution—Devoted to Public Service through Research and Training in the Social Sciences—was incorporated on December 8, 1927. Broadly stated, the Institution has two primary purposes; the first is to aid constructively in the development of sound national policies; and the second is to offer training of a super-graduate character to students of the social sciences.

The responsibility for the final determination of the Institution's policies and its program of work and for the administration of its endowment is vested in a self-perpetuating board of trustees. It is the function of the trustees to make possible the conduct of scientific research under the most favorable conditions, and to safeguard the independence of the research staff in the pursuit of their studies and in the publication of the results of such studies. It is not a part of their function to determine, control, or influence the conduct of particular investigations or the conclusions reached; but only to approve the principal fields of investigation to which the available funds are to be allocated, and to satisfy themselves with reference to the intellectual competence and scientific integrity of the staff. Major responsibility for "formulating general policies and co-ordinating the activities of the Institution" is vested in the president. The by-laws provide also that "there shall be an advisory council selected by the president from among the scientific staff of the Institution."

BOARD OF TRUSTEES

LABOR POLICY
OF THE
FEDERAL GOVERNMENT

BY

HAROLD W. METZ

THE BROOKINGS INSTITUTION
WASHINGTON, D.C.
1945

Printed in the United States of America
George Banta Publishing Company
Menasha, Wisconsin

AUTHOR'S ACKNOWLEDGMENTS

With great pleasure I acknowledge the assistance of Kurt Braun during the early stages of this undertaking. As a research assistant he brought intelligence, thoroughness, and resourcefulness to the task of gathering material. A considerable portion of the material used in Chapters III, IV, and VI was gathered by him. In addition to the assistance rendered the author by a co-operating committee composed of Lewis Meriam, Meyer Jacobstein, and E. G. Nourse, the manuscript had the benefit of a careful reading by Professor William M. Leiserson of Johns Hopkins University, who offered a number of constructive and helpful suggestions. The author, however, assumes full responsibility for all issues of fact or evaluation.

HAROLD W. METZ

The Brookings Institution
September 1945

The study upon which this book is based was made possible by funds granted by The Maurice and Laura Falk Foundation of Pittsburgh. However, the Falk Foundation is not the author, publisher, or proprietor of this publication and is not to be understood as approving or disapproving by virtue of its grant any of the statements and views expressed herein.

CONTENTS

INTRODUCTION

In many separate pieces of legislation and through a multitude of administrative activities, the federal government has taken an active hand in determining the position and shaping the fortunes of wage earners. The policy implied in these various statutes and administrative acts points in one general direction—improving the economic and social lot of the working men and women. Nevertheless there are cases where the policy set forth in one law or administered by one agency proves to be more or less inconsistent with that of another statute or other administrators. Sometimes a piece of labor legislation designed to attain one objective actually is being used to attain another goal.

Since labor policies have been embodied in different laws not directly related to each other, and since many separate agencies have been administering these laws, there have been few systematic studies of similar problems presented under different laws. Some studies have been made of the attitude of the National Labor Relations Board toward collective bargaining, but nothing has been done to relate its treatment of this problem to the way the several phases of the problem have been handled under the Railway Labor Act. Again, some studies have been made of wage fixing under the Fair Labor Standards Act and others of wage determination under other laws, but no one has published a general analysis of the principles applied by the several agencies dealing with wage determination.

The failure to develop a unified labor policy has been due partly to the Constitution. It is a fundamental principle of American constitutional law that the national government can exercise only those powers that are specifically granted to it, together with such other powers as are necessary and proper to carry out the granted powers. Since the Constitution makes no direct grant of authority to the national government to regulate labor, it is only through relatively limited channels that it can act in this field. As a result, its labor policy has sometimes been expressed indirectly and always in a fragmentary manner. Thus to illustrate, it is mainly through its specific power to regulate interstate commerce and through its power to spend money to promote the general welfare that the federal government can guarantee to workers the right to organize and can encourage the development of labor organizations. Indirectly the federal government can enunciate a policy as to the desirability of collective action, through the power of the courts to hold state laws unconstitutional, especially on the ground that they deprive a person of life, liberty, and property without due process of law in violation of the Fourteenth Amendment. Finally, since the federal courts have jurisdiction over cases involving diversity of citizenship, they can by adjudication, at least to a limited extent, express an attitude toward concerted activities of workers.[1]

From its power to regulate interstate commerce, the federal government derived its authority to control concerted activities of workers by such laws as the Sherman Anti-Trust Act or the National Labor Relations Act. Since Congress has the power to control the jurisdiction and procedure of the federal courts, by the Norris-LaGuardia Act it could make unenforceable in the federal courts any contract whereby an employee agreed not to join a union. Because the federal courts have jurisdiction over cases between parties who are citizens of different states and over cases involving the validity of state laws under the federal Constitution, they have been able to express views on the desirability and legality of picketing.

Our federal form of government further complicated the development of a unified labor policy. All powers not specifically granted to the national government belong to the states, unless the Constitution specifically denies them to the states. Hence many problems of labor relations that the national government has not or cannot touch are within the power of the states, should they care to exercise their authority. In many instances the federal government actually assumes that the states have exercised their authority in fields that are beyond the jurisdiction of the national government.

Thus although by federal law, workers have a right to organize unions, the legal basis of such labor organizations springs entirely from state statute or common law. Employers have an obligation under national law to engage in collective bargaining, but the legal enforceability of the agreement arrived at by the collective bargaining process is determined by state law. Under federal law it may be legal for a trade union and an employer to enter into a closed shop contract,

---

[1] This is definitely restricted by the decision in *Erie Railroad Co.* v. *Tompkins,* 304 U.S. 64 (1938).

but the right of a specific worker to join a union and the power of that union to expel a worker are determined not by the United States, but by the laws of the several states.

Partly because of these constitutional limitations, the powers of the national government in the field of labor are embodied in many unrelated laws enacted at different times to attain various objectives and shaped by diverse forces. When policy is embodied in many separate laws, inconsistencies and incongruities are likely to develop. Varied and dissimilar devices frequently are used to implement similar policies. Thus we shall see that the methods used to enforce labor's right to organize are diverse. Under the Railway Labor Act, judicial methods are used, while under the National Labor Relations Act, only administrative remedies are provided. Again, we shall see that some rights are derived directly from the Constitution (the right to picket), while others are derived only from statutes (as labor's right to organize free from employer interference). In other cases the task of stating policy is made difficult because the statutory authorization is only partial and indirect (as for instance the policy of encouraging the peaceful settlement of labor disputes).

In this process of description and analysis, an effort will be made to determine what are the basic objectives of our labor policy. The division of constitutional authority, piecemeal legislation, and many independent administrative agencies make it possible for the government to pursue diverse objectives at the same time. Consequently it is necessary to analyze the objectives of the different laws as actually applied so that we may judge whether they supplement one or another, or whether inconsistent objectives are being pursued.

This study will attempt to survey the general labor policy of the federal government in a systematic, analytical manner. The attitude of the government toward labor will be taken up on a subject matter basis, not on the basis of the individual statutes or agencies involved. The policy on a given topic will be considered irrespective of the agency that formulates it or carries it out. The attitude of the government is the primary issue; the major interest is not the laws, regulations, and decisions embodying the policy, nor is it the institutions that apply it. An effort will be made to find policy by considering what agencies actually do, not merely what they say they do. No attempt will be made to present the federal labor policy in all of its details and ramifications. The basic underlying issues will be stressed. Only within the last twelve years has the federal government manifested a major interest in this field; therefore the emphasis will be placed on the policy existing in this period.

Some specific activities of the federal government in the labor field have not been included. Unemployment insurance is not considered, because it is being adequately covered in a study of social security shortly to be published by the Brookings Institution. The attitude of the government toward technological changes and their consequences to labor and toward union-management co-operation is not described, because the evidence bearing upon its handling of these problems is so scattered and fragmentary that it is difficult to discover any definite attitude of the government toward these questions.

Likewise some general aspects of the activities of the government in the field of labor have not been analyzed. Limitations of time and space have prevented a consideration of the political and economic forces that have shaped the policies in this field. The administrative machinery that implements and applies the various policies is touched upon only in an incidental manner. Although it is believed that the machinery of administration can be studied only in connection with the actual subject matter that it is administering, here again limitations of time and space made such an analysis impossible.

Above all, it should be remembered that this study attempts to describe and analyze only the actual labor policy of the government. It is not concerned with the desirability of the objectives of the policy, and it does not seek to discover whether any given policy is successful in attaining its objectives.

In the following chapters the major aspects of federal labor policy will be considered. An attempt will be made to determine what are the objectives of the government, the methods of attaining these goals, and the standards that are actually applied. Consistencies and inconsistencies in objectives, principles, and methods will be indicated.

In Chapter I there will be presented a brief survey of the development of labor legislation and of the institutions designed to carry out such legislation. It is hoped that this discussion will indicate the piecemeal development of labor law and administration.

To secure better terms of employment, workers attempt to increase their power to bargain with employers by engaging in various forms of concerted action; these include the formation of unions, strikes, picketing, and boycotts. The attitude of the government toward the efforts of workers to increase their bargaining power will be considered in Chapter II.

Collective bargaining is the outstanding manifestation of concerted action. Actually workers join unions to make such bargaining possible, and strike and picket as a means of making it effective. The steps the government has taken to assist workers in collective bargaining will be discussed in Chapter III. The purpose of this process is to negotiate a collective agreement. The nature of these agreements and the rights and duties arising under them will also be summarized in this chapter.

In attempting to assist the concerted action of workers, the government has influenced the form and organization of unions. If employers are to bargain collectively with their employees, they must be able to know the groups of employees with which they must bargain. Consequently several government agencies designate appropriate bargaining units in different fields. How do these agencies influence the organization of the labor unions that workers join? In several other ways the government influences the form of labor organizations. These problems will be considered in Chapter IV.

In addition to the bargaining power of the workers, the condition of the labor market affects the terms of employment. The attitude of the government toward the labor market will be investigated in Chapter V. Its attempts to influence the supply of labor will be considered, together with its efforts to distribute information on the conditions of the market.

The bargaining power of labor and the condition of the labor market are not the only factors that determine the conditions of employment. The government also attempts to influence or even dictate some of the terms of employment. Whether or not an employee must be a union member is an important item in the employment contract. In Chapter VI the attitude of the government toward various forms of union preference and assistance that might be made a part of the labor contract will be analyzed.

What the government does to determine the wages of workers will be summarized in Chapter VII.

The efforts of the national government to control the hours of employment, to regulate child labor, and to maintain safe working conditions will be examined in Chapter VIII.

When employers and employees fail to arrive at mutually satisfactory terms of employment, a labor dispute develops. The government's attempts to settle labor disputes without resort to strikes will be investigated in Chapter IX. The methods and policies of the different agencies engaged in conciliation and arbitration will be described.

The special agencies established during World War II to facilitate the peaceful settlement of labor disputes will be discussed in Chapter X.

Against the background of diverse and piecemeal legislation, separate administrative agencies, basic principles that are not entirely harmonious, and a division of the field between the different levels of government, an attempt will be made in Chapter XI to consider the policy of the federal government toward these different problems in the field of labor relations.

CHAPTER I
THE DEVELOPMENT OF NATIONAL
LABOR POLICY

Because there are many different laws and numerous separate administrative agencies dealing with labor, a summary of the development of the government's attitudes and activities in this field will give some perspective to an analytical discussion. As a result of this summary, it is hoped the reader will understand that federal labor legislation and administrative agencies developed piecemeal and were designed to meet specific problems. First we shall survey the activities of the government in the field of labor before 1933. This broad survey will be followed by a brief historical summary of the developments during the past twelve years; legislation, administrative institutions, and judicial attitudes will be considered.

I. GENERAL DEVELOPMENT OF GOVERNMENT INTEREST IN LABOR BEFORE 1933

For a century and a quarter the national government did little in the labor field other than gather limited amounts of information. Practically nothing was done during the first hundred years of our national history. Only in 1884, after thirteen years of agitation by labor groups, did Congress create a Bureau of Labor in the Department of the Interior.[1] The duty of this Bureau was to collect data concerning wages and hours of employment and information on the "means of promoting their [workers'] material, social, intellectual, and moral prosperity." Its function was solely to gather information; it had no regulatory powers. Four years later Congress changed the name of this establishment to the Department of Labor, and thereby it became an independent establishment, although not of cabinet rank.[2] Upon the request of President Theodore Roosevelt, Congress in 1903 established a Department of Commerce and Labor.[3] The old Department of Labor was transferred to the newly created Department. The Office of the Commissioner-General of Immigration was also transferred to the new Department from the Treasury. By the

[1] Act of June 27, 1884, 23 Stat. 60.
[2] Act of June 13, 1888, 25 Stat. 182.
[3] Act of Feb. 14, 1903, 32 Stat. 825.

7

Act of April 9, 1912, a Children's Bureau was established in this Department to study and report on the special problems of children.[4]

Not until 1913 was a Department of Labor
established with a head of Cabinet rank.

Labor pressure led Congress on March 4, 1913, again to establish a separate Department of Labor but this time with a head of Cabinet rank.[5] The purpose of the Department was declared to be "to foster, promote, and develop the welfare of the wage earners of the United States, to improve their working conditions, and to advance their opportunities for profitable employment."[6] The Bureau of Labor, renamed the Bureau of Labor Statistics, was transferred to the new Department along with the Children's Bureau and the Immigration Bureau. This latter agency was divided into two sections—a Bureau of Immigration and a Bureau of Naturalization. The Secretary of Labor was directed to attempt to mediate labor disputes.[7] This was the only new function given to the Department.

About 1915 as a result of the Secretary's power to mediate labor disputes, the Conciliation Service developed into a separate division.[8] From some activities of the Bureau of Immigration, the United States Employment Service emerged during World War I.[9] After that war, it functioned as a co-operative organization partly financed by state and municipal funds. In 1920 Congress created the Women's Bureau to study and report on the special economic and social problems of women.[10] This Bureau was an outgrowth of the Women in Industry Division created in 1918 by the Secretary to deal with problems of women in wartime employment.[11]

Former trade union officials headed the Department of Labor from 1913 to 1933. The first Secretary, William B. Wilson, had been Secretary-Treasurer of the United Mine Workers of America. He had also been a member of Congress, where he was Chairman of the House Committee on Labor. His appointment had the approval of

[4] 37 Stat. 79.
[5] 37 Stat. 736.
[6] The same, Sec. 1.
[7] The same, Sec. 8.
[8] John Lombardi, *Labor's Voice in the Cabinet* (1942), p. 98.
[9] The same, pp. 142-60.
[10] 41 Stat. 987.
[11] Lombardi, *Labor's Voice in the Cabinet*, p. 309.

the American Federation of Labor. James J. Davis, who succeeded to the position in 1921, had been an official of the Amalgamated Association of Iron, Steel, and Tin Workers of America. President Harding had cleared his appointment with the American Federation of Labor in advance. When Mr. Davis went to the Senate in 1930, President Hoover appointed W. N. Doak. He had been Vice President of the Brotherhood of Railroad Trainmen, and at one time headed the Labor Division of the Republican National Committee. The A.F. of L. did not approve of his appointment, and it even asserted that the President should select the Secretary of Labor from a panel of names submitted by it.[12]

*Before 1933 few important
labor laws were enacted.*

Little actual regulatory activity in the general field of labor was attempted by the federal government before 1933. The Anti-Trust Act of 1890 was probably the first positive federal law that had a restrictive effect on labor.[13] It prohibited any restraint on interstate commerce in the form of an agreement, contract, or trust. The Supreme Court held that it applied to concerted acts of workers such as strikes and boycotts when designed to restrain interstate commerce.[14] In 1914 labor organizations prevailed upon Congress to include in the Clayton Act several provisions which the unions believed would remove labor activities from the Anti-Trust Law.[15] But the Supreme Court held that "it was but declaratory of the law as it stood before" its enactment.[16] By the Norris-LaGuardia Anti-Injunction Act of 1932, Congress again attempted to free labor from the Anti-Trust law.[17] By this law the federal courts are prohibited from issuing injunctions in labor disputes, and as applied by the Supreme Court, it effectively freed labor from the limitations of the Anti-Trust law.[18] This act contained the first general legislative statement that it is desirable for labor to organize and to bargain collectively.

[12] E. Pendleton Herring, *Public Administration and the Public Interest* (1936), p. 285.
[13] Act of July 2, 1890, 26 Stat. 209.
[14] *Loewe* v. *Lawlor*, 208 U.S. 274 (1908).
[15] Act of Oct. 15, 1914, 38 Stat. 730, Secs. 6 and 20.
[16] *Duplex Printing Press Co.* v. *Deering*, 254 U.S. 443 (1921).
[17] Act of Mar. 23, 1932, 47 Stat. 70.
[18] *United States* v. *Hutcheson*, 312 U.S. 219 (1940).

*Railroad labor problems
received special attention.*

Since the national government has almost exclusive control over interstate commerce, Congress at a relatively early date gave special attention to the problems of railroad labor. In 1888[19] Congress enacted the first measure to facilitate the peaceful settlement of labor disputes on railroads. This act made provision for voluntary arbitration to settle such disputes, and it authorized the President to establish special temporary commissions composed of two members to investigate railroad disputes that were not settled by other means. Only one special investigating commission was ever appointed by a President under the law. The failure of this statute to avert labor difficulties led to new legislation in 1898.[20] In that year the Erdman Act was passed; it provided for voluntary arbitration and mediation.[21] The chairman of the Interstate Commerce Commission and the Commissioner of Labor were constituted a special commission with authority to attempt to mediate railroad labor disputes. The act made it illegal for any party accepting voluntary arbitration to engage in a strike or a lockout for a period of three months after the award, unless he gave thirty days' notice of his intention to do so. This law apparently worked well, for "every significant dispute between 1906 and 1912 was peacefully adjusted under its provisions."[22] After a strike of conductors and trainmen in 1913, Congress enacted the Newlands Act to strengthen the existing arbitration and mediation machinery.[23] A Board of Mediation and Conciliation was established. This Board consisted of a commissioner of mediation and conciliation appointed by the President with the confirmation of the Senate and not more than two other employees of the government who had been appointed in the same manner. The Board was directed to attempt to mediate any railroad labor dispute when requested, and if an interruption of traffic appeared imminent, it could intervene on its own motion. If mediation failed, it could urge arbitration. If both parties were willing to arbitrate, machinery for selecting an arbitral board was provided. Arbitration resulted in an award enforceable judicially.

[19] 25 Stat. 501.
[20] H. G. Moulton and Associates, *The American Transportation Problem* (1933), p. 195.
[21] 30 Stat. 424.
[22] Moulton and Associates, *The American Transportation Problem*, p. 195.
[23] 38 Stat. 103.

During World War I after the government took over the carriers and in order to adjust disputes, there was created a Railway Wage Board and subsidiary boards of adjustment. These boards successfully handled many disputes, but their tasks were made easier because the government, as employer in wartime, was willing to be more lenient than the carriers themselves. When the roads were returned to private ownership, it was necessary to create new machinery to assist in the settlement of the disputes arising under these new circumstances.

The Transportation Act of 1920[24] established a Railroad Labor Board composed of seven members appointed by the President. It was given authority to adjust and decide all disputes not settled by mediation or arbitration; and to "establish rates of wages, salaries and standards of working conditions [for every class of employees] which in the opinion of the Board are just and reasonable." But Congress provided no machinery for the enforcement of the Board's decisions. The failure of certain carriers as well as some labor organizations to abide by the Board's decisions led to its abolition in 1926.

The Railway Labor Act of 1926 drastically modified the machinery for the settlement of railway labor disputes. It established a permanent Board of Mediation composed of five members appointed by the President by and with the advice and consent of the Senate. This agency was directed to attempt to settle by mediation any dispute that was not adjusted through direct bargaining by the parties concerned, and where mediation failed, the Board was directed to urge the parties to submit the dispute to arbitration.[25] If arbitration was accepted, it resulted in a binding award enforceable in the courts. If a dispute was not settled by mediation or arbitration, the President was given the power to appoint a special emergency board to investigate it and to make a public report concerning the dispute and its settlement. For thirty days after the emergency board has been appointed and for an additional thirty days after it has rendered its report, the parties are not supposed to modify the terms of employment. The act also provides that both the rail carriers and their employees should have the right to select bargaining representatives, "without interference, influence, or coercion exercised by either party over the self organization or designation of representatives by the other." This was

[24] 41 Stat. 469.
[25] 44 Stat. 576.

the first congressional declaration of the right of employees to organize without employer interference or coercion.

Since 1893 the regulation of the conditions of employment on railroads has been a subject of federal legislation. That year Congress first required the installation of safety devices for the protection of railroad employees and passengers.[26] To prevent accidents, the hours of work were limited in 1907 to not more than 16 a day.[27] Because the workers threatened a nationwide transportation strike in 1916 to secure a wage increase, Congress provided that for the purpose of the payment of wages, eight hours shall constitute a day's work in the railroad industry.[28] This was an effective means of providing a wage increase, since most railroad employees worked more than eight hours a day.

Child labor, vocational education, and public works
employment were subjects of legislation.

In the field of child labor the federal government made two unsuccessful attempts at regulation. In 1916 Congress prohibited the transportation in interstate commerce of goods made by child labor.[29] When this act was held unconstitutional,[30] Congress tried to put an end to child labor by imposing a tax on all goods produced by such workers,[31] but the Supreme Court also held the second act unconstitutional.[32] In 1924 Congress submitted to the states for ratification a constitutional amendment granting to the federal government the power to regulate child labor;[33] but it has never been ratified by three-fourths of the states.

Vocational education, workmen's compensation for longshoremen, and the hours and wages of employees on public works projects have been considered by Congress. In 1917 financial assistance was offered to the states to enable them to provide vocational education.[34] Various attempts to bring longshoremen and harbor workers under state

[26] Act of Mar. 2, 1893, 27 Stat. 531.
[27] Act of Mar. 4, 1907, 34 Stat. 1415.
[28] Act of Sept. 3, 1916, 39 Stat. 721.
[29] 39 Stat. 675.
[30] *Hammer* v. *Dagenhart*, 247 U.S. 251 (1918).
[31] Act of Feb. 24, 1919, 40 Stat. 1138.
[32] *Bailey* v. *Drexel Furniture Co.*, 259 U.S. 20 (1922).
[33] 43 Stat. 670.
[34] Act of Feb. 23, 1917, 39 Stat. 929.

workmen's compensation encountered constitutional difficulties;[35] accordingly, Congress enacted a federal workmen's compensation law applicable to these employees. This law is administered by the same board that is responsible for the enforcement of the comparable acts applicable to employees of the federal government and to workers in the District of Columbia.[36] By a series of laws, Congress fixed the hours of work of employees of contractors engaged in the construction of federal public works,[37] and in 1931 it provided that the wages paid by contractors engaged in erecting public buildings must not be less than the prevailing rate of pay.[38]

II. OUTLINES OF DEVELOPMENT, 1933-44

Because the labor policy of the government has evolved so rapidly since 1933, special attention will be given to its development during this period. Legislation, administrative organization, and the change of judicial attitude toward labor will be considered.

A. Legislation

In 1932 President Roosevelt and a majority of both houses of Congress were elected on a platform that pledged the enactment of legislation regulating wages and hours and establishing unemployment insurance and old-age pensions. Because of dissatisfaction resulting from the depression of 1929, public opinion favored legislation long desired by labor. Instead of merely tolerating labor, Congress inaugurated a program of positive assistance to workers.

A large amount of labor legislation
has been enacted since 1933.

In 1933 Congress enacted the National Industrial Recovery Act,[39] providing for the general regulation of all industry by voluntary codes or by government licenses. For a large segment of industry these codes fixed minimum wages and maximum hours; many of them limited child labor, and often they contained safety regulations. The act also guaranteed to workers the right to organize and to bargain

---

[35] *The Employers' Liability Cases,* 207 U.S. 463 (1908); *Knickerbocker Ice Co.* v. *Stewart,* 253 U.S. 149 (1920); *Washington* v. *Dawson and Co.* 264 U.S. 219 (1924).

[36] Act of Mar. 4, 1927, 44 Stat. 1424.

[37] The first was the Act of Aug. 1, 1892, 27 Stat. 340.

[38] Act of Mar. 3, 1931, 46 Stat. 1494.

[39] Act of June 16, 1933, 48 Stat. 195.

collectively. The same year the Employment Service Act provided for a reorganized and expanded United States Employment Service financed on a grant-in-aid basis and administered co-operatively by the federal government and the states.[40]

To carry out the provision of the NIRA that granted to workers the right to organize, in 1934 Congress empowered the President to establish labor relations boards.[41] These agencies were given only limited power to enforce their decisions. The same year a railroad retirement law was enacted which established a system of old-age pensions for railway employees.[42] Congress also created a new National Mediation Board to mediate railway labor disputes and a board to arbitrate controversies arising out of the interpretation of existing collective agreements.[43]

Legislation guaranteeing to workers the right to engage in concerted action, establishing social security, and dealing with the special problems of soft coal mining was enacted in 1935. The National Labor Relations Act guarantees to workers the right to organize, and it prohibits employers from engaging in unfair labor practices.[44] Employers are required to bargain with the representatives chosen by a majority of their workers. To determine whether an employer has engaged in an unfair labor practice and to designate the true representatives of a majority of the workers in a bargaining unit, Congress established a National Labor Relations Board composed of three members appointed by the President, with Senate approval. Its decisions are subject to appeal to a Circuit Court of Appeals and, after approval by the Court, they can be enforced by contempt proceedings. If an employee is discharged in violation of the act, the Board can order his reinstatement with back pay.

By the Social Security Act of 1935, Congress provided for old-age benefits, public assistance, and unemployment compensation, all administered by a Social Security Board composed of three members appointed by the President.[45] The first Bituminous Coal Conservation Act permitted bituminous mine owners to combine to fix minimum

---

[40] Act of June 6, 1933, 48 Stat. 113.
[41] Act of June 19, 1934, 48 Stat. 1183.
[42] Act of June 27, 1934, 48 Stat. 1283.
[43] Act of June 21, 1934, 48 Stat. 1185, 1195.
[44] Act of July 15, 1935, 49 Stat. 449.
[45] Act of Aug. 14, 1935, 49 Stat. 620.

prices for coal.[46] It also guaranteed to their employees the right to organize. It provided that the wage fixed by collective agreement in any district was to be the minimum wage for all workers in that area if such agreement covered both a certain percentage of the miners employed and a designated portion of the coal produced in the area. There was a similar provision for the determination of the maximum hours of employment.

The Public Contracts Act was the only major piece of labor legislation enacted in 1936.[47] This law regulates the working conditions of persons employed in the production of goods on government contracts where the order is for $10,000 or more. Such workers can be employed only eight hours a day, they have to be paid at least the prevailing minimum wage, and child labor is prohibited. The administration of this law is vested in the Secretary of Labor.

In May 1937 President Roosevelt requested Congress to enact legislation establishing minimum wages and maximum hours in almost all types of work. He also desired that child labor should be restricted. A year later, legislation was enacted prohibiting child labor and providing for a maximum 40-hour week by 1940 and a minimum wage of 40 cents an hour by 1945.[48] Its administration was vested in a Wage and Hour Administrator in the Department of Labor.

Government determination of maximum wages and the first limitation on union activity came as wartime measures during World War II. As a part of the price-control program, the act of October 2, 1942 gave to the President authority to control all changes in wages for a limited period.[49]

The first restrictive labor legislation enacted by Congress in more than 50 years became law over the President's veto on June 25, 1943.[50] This statute legalized the National War Labor Board previously created by the President by executive order. It prohibited the calling of strikes in plants operated by the government, and it provided that in a plant engaged in defense production a strike could be called only after a vote of the employees. Campaign contributions by labor unions were prohibited during the war.

[46] Act of Aug. 30, 1935, 49 Stat. 991.
[47] Act of June 30, 1936, 49 Stat. 2036.
[48] Act of June 25, 1938, 52 Stat. 1064.
[49] 56 Stat. 765.
[50] 57 Stat. 163.

B. Administrative Development

At least four permanent and a like number of temporary agencies are primarily concerned with the administration of labor problems. Of these agencies, the Department of Labor has the widest field of action. The Department was created "to foster, promote, and develop the welfare of the wage earners of the United States, to improve their working conditions and to advance their opportunities for profitable employment." It is essentially a department *for* labor, organized to promote its interests primarily as envisaged by organized labor.

*The Labor Department seeks to
promote the interests of labor.*

Both through educational and regulatory activity the Department has sought to promote the interests of labor. The Secretary said in the Annual Report of the Department for 1939:

Two types of activity are appearing clearly in the work of the Department: one, the investigation of situations that appear unfavorable to working people, reporting upon these findings and devising a program with consultation and advice to overcome the disadvantages found under the investigation. For these services the Department's personnel should be sympathetic, alert, and imaginative to find and foresee those conditions which are adverse to the life of wage earners and can be corrected. The other type of activity lies in the field of the enforcement of the statute—the Public Contracts Act, the Davis-Bacon Act, the Wages and Hours Act, the Immigration law. . . .[51]

The Department has formulated a labor program, and it has been actively working for its general adoption. Broadly, the Department has continued to promote and assist in developing a program of—

1. Reasonably short hours of labor;
2. Adequate annual income from wages;
3. Safe and healthful conditions of work;
4. Practical industrial relations based on—
    a. Collective bargaining;
    b. Conciliation, mediation, and arbitration through government agencies;
5. Elimination of child labor.[52]

Not only has the Department tried to secure the adoption of this program on the national level, but it has been trying to promote state

[51] *Annual Report of the Secretary of Labor* (1939), pp 13-14.
[52] The same (1937), p. 4.

action to implement it. In 1934 a Division of Labor Standards was established. Its function is to draft model state labor legislation and to assist the states in securing the enactment of these model bills. It also seeks to promote industrial safety.

Three other bureaus of the Department are engaged primarily in investigating the problems of labor and in informational activities designed to educate the people concerning those problems: the Bureau of Labor Statistics, the Children's Bureau, and the Women's Bureau. In addition to their promotional activity, the latter two establishments administer certain grants-in-aid to the states under the Social Security Act. The Children's Bureau also enforces the child labor provisions of the Fair Labor Standards Act.

Two divisions were created in the Department primarily to perform regulatory functions, the Public Contracts Division and the Wage and Hour Division. The former was created by the Secretary in 1936 to carry out the functions imposed upon the Department by the Public Contracts Act of 1936. Congress created the Wage and Hour Division by the Fair Labor Standards Act of 1938.[53] This division has been fixing minimum wages under that act as well as enforcing most of its other provisions.[54]

The Public Contracts Division and the Wage and Hour Division performed similar functions—determining minimum wages and enforcing maximum hour and minimum wage standards. Both required branch offices and field inspectors. The activities of the two divisions were parallel if not overlapping. Early in 1942 one man was appointed to head both divisions, and later that year, after the House Committee on Appropriations recommended it, the Public Contracts Division and the Wage and Hour Division were combined.[55]

The Department of Labor has lost
several important functions.

The importance of the Department of Labor in developing and implementing labor policy has been reduced by the establishment of new agencies. The personality of Frances Perkins, the Secretary of Labor from 1933 to 1945, may have contributed to this. Previously

---

[53] Act of June 25, 1938, 52 Stat. 1061, Sec. 4 (a).
[54] The same.
[55] *Department of Labor-Federal Security Agency Appropriation Bill for 1944,* Hearings before the Subcommittee of the House Committee on Appropriations, Pt. 1, 78 Cong. 1 sess., p. 143.

she was a social worker and also Industrial Commissioner in New York State. Her appointment was not entirely satisfactory to organized labor, possibly because she had not been a labor leader, and possibly because of her social worker background. She was not an exceedingly forceful Secretary, and her attempts to bring new labor agencies under her jurisdiction met with failure. She desired to have the National Labor Relations Board, the National Mediation Board, and the Social Security Board placed in the Department of Labor, but Congress saw fit to set them up as independent organizations. She also desired that the United States Employees' Compensation Commission be transferred to the Department.[56] Not only did the Department of Labor fail to secure these new functions, but it lost to other departments and agencies several long-established divisions.

The Employment Service and the Immigration Service were taken from the Department by the President under his authority to reorganize the executive branch of the government granted by Congress in 1939.[57] Under this same grant of power the President established the Federal Security Agency.[58] The United States Employment Service was transferred to it, and the Social Security Board was placed under its jurisdiction. It was logical that these two organizations should be in the same establishment, because the Social Security Act requires that any state unemployment system, to receive federal assistance must provide for the payment of benefits through public employment offices.[59] In 1940 the Immigration and Naturalization Service was transferred from the Department of Labor to the Department of Justice.[60]

Although the main function of the Federal Security Agency is in the field of welfare, it performs a number of functions that fall within the labor field. Since 1933[61] the Office of Education, which was subsequently transferred to the Federal Security Agency from the Department of Interior, has administered the federal grants-in-aid to the states for vocational education and vocational rehabilitation. As will be shown later these two programs have a bearing upon the supply of labor.

[56] *Annual Report of the Secretary of Labor* (1934), p. 11.
[57] Act of Apr. 3, 1939, 53 Stat. 561.
[58] *Reorganization Plan No. 1*, Apr. 25, 1939, 53 Stat. 1424, Sec. 201.
[59] Act of Aug. 24, 1935, 49 Stat. 626, Sec. 303 (a) (2).
[60] *Reorganization Plan No. 5*, May 22, 1940, 54 Stat. 1238.
[61] Executive Order No. 6166, June 16, 1933.

Two agencies by different means
help workers organize and bargain.

The National Labor Relations Board and the National Mediation Board are the other two important permanent agencies dealing with labor. To administer the National Labor Relations Act, Congress provided a board of three members to be appointed by the President with Senate confirmation. Since broad discretion to interpret and apply the act is vested in the Board, its composition is important. As first constituted, it consisted of J. Warren Madden, a former professor of law, who had specialized in domestic relations, J. W. Carmody, formerly a member of the National Mediation Board, and Edwin M. Smith, a former member of the old National Labor Relations Board (under the NRA) and Commissioner of Labor and Industry of Massachusetts. In 1936 Mr. Carmody was succeeded by D. W. Smith of Pennsylvania. All these men were active protagonists of organized labor. In the period from 1935 to 1940 the Board was vigorously attacked from many quarters; employers charged it with being pro-labor, and the A.F. of L. charged it with being pro-CIO.

By a change of membership of the Board, some of the causes of criticism were eliminated. When D. W. Smith's term expired in 1939, Mr. William Leiserson came from the National Mediation Board to take his place, and Harry A. Millis, Professor of Labor at the University of Chicago, succeeded J. Warren Madden in 1940. The next year Edwin Smith was followed by C. D. Reilly, formerly solicitor of the Department of Labor. Early in 1943 Mr. Leiserson returned to the National Mediation Board and John M. Houston, a defeated member of Congress from Kansas, succeeded him. This change in membership has caused the Board to modify some of its decisions that were a cause of criticism.[62]

The Railway Labor Act of 1934 provided for the abolition of the Board of Mediation and the creation of a new National Mediation Board, composed of three members to be appointed by the President, with Senate approval. This Board designates appropriate bargaining units for railway labor, and it mediates disputes concerning the negotiation of new collective agreements in this field. Since the act was drafted largely by the carriers and the railway unions, it is not surprising that the parties subject to it have been generally satisfied with

[62] See "New Personnel and New Policies of the National Labor Relations Board," 55 *Harvard Law Review* 269 (1942).

it. During most of the life of the present Board, William Leiserson was the dominant figure on it.

Four temporary agencies were organized to
handle special war labor problems.

To handle the special labor problems arising out of World War II, the President established the War Production Board, the War Manpower Commission, the National War Labor Board, and the Committee on Fair Employment Practice. When the National Defense Advisory Commission was created in May 1940, Sidney Hillman, President of the Amalgamated Clothing Workers of America, was made a member. Labor supply, training, and industrial peace were his special functions. When the Office of Production Management was created early in 1941, he became a co-director general. And a year later when the War Production Board followed it, his labor functions were given to it. Finally when the War Manpower Commission was set up in April 1942, most, but not all, of the functions of the labor division of the WPB were transferred to it. The WPB still attempts to mediate labor disputes in war industries.[63]

In the spring of 1942 the mobilization of man power for war purposes became such a pressing problem that the War Manpower Commission was created by executive order. All its power was vested in the Chairman, Paul V. McNutt.[64] The Employment Service and much of the labor division of the WPB were transferred to it.[65] As originally established its functions were purely advisory. In December 1942 other agencies, including Selective Service, were transferred to it.[66] At the same time it was given authority to control all hiring in certain areas,[67] and in February 1943 it was indirectly given authority to regulate the hours of employment in labor shortage areas.[68]

In the spring of 1941 strikes in defense production became prevalent, and consequently the President set up a National Defense Mediation Board composed of representatives of labor, management, and

---

[63] *National War Agencies Appropriation Bill, 1945*, Hearings before the House Committee on Appropriations, Pt. 1, 78 Cong. 2 sess., pp. 690-702.

[64] Executive Order No. 9139, Apr. 18, 1942, *Federal Register*, Vol. 7, p. 2919.

[65] Executive Order No. 9247, Sept. 17, 1942, *Federal Register*, Vol. 7, p. 7279.

[66] Subsequently Congress removed the Selective Service from the War Manpower Commission. Act of Dec. 5, 1943, 57 Stat. 598, Sec. 3.

[67] Executive Order No. 9279, Dec. 5, 1942, *Federal Register*, Vol. 7, p. 10177.

[68] Executive Order No. 9301, Feb. 9, 1943, *Federal Register*, Vol. 8, p. 1825.

the public.[69] It was to consider all labor disputes affecting defense production that could not be settled by the Conciliation Service. It was to settle them by mediation, or by special recommendations, but it was given no direct power to enforce its decisions. When the United Mine Workers of America refused to abide by one of its decisions, the CIO members of the Board resigned, and its usefulness was over. The President set up in place of it the National War Labor Board similarly constituted and equally limited in powers.[70] Acting under the Economic Stabilization Act, the President in October 1942 conferred upon this Board the task of regulating the wages of all persons receiving less than $5,000 a year.

A Committee on Fair Employment Practice was created by the President to put an end to the discrimination against workers because of race, color, religion, or country of national origin. This committee was first set up by executive order in June 1941.[71] It was reorganized in May 1943.[72] It is supposed to end discrimination in training facilities financed with federal funds and in employment in war industries and government establishments. It has no direct power to enforce its decisions and its authority has been limited by Congress.[73] The Committee is composed of a chairman and six other members.

C. Change in the Judicial Attitude Toward Labor

Within the past eight years the Supreme Court has become much more sympathetic toward labor than it had ever been before. No attempt will be made to present anything approximating a complete picture of the development of the law of labor in the decisions of the Supreme Court during recent years. Here the only objective is to show that a tremendous change has occurred in the attitude of that Court.

*A change in judicial attitude made
possible a new federal labor policy.*

The Supreme Court had long recognized that unions were desirable,[74] but in the very decision recognizing this, it placed stringent

---

[69] Executive Order No. 8617, Mar. 19, 1941, *Federal Register*, Vol. 6, p. 1552.
[70] Executive Order No. 9017, Jan. 12, 1942, *Federal Register*, Vol. 7, p. 237.
[71] Executive Order No. 8802, June 25, 1941, *Federal Register*, Vol. 6, p. 3109.
[72] Executive Order No. 9346, May 27, 1943, *Federal Register*, Vol. 8, p. 7183.
[73] Act of June 28, 1944, Public Law No. 372.
[74] *American Steel Foundries Co.* v. *Tri-City Central Trades Council*, 257 U.S. 184 (1921).

limits on a union's right to carry on concerted action. In 1908 the
Court held that Congress could not prohibit an interstate railroad
from discriminating against employees who were union members.
This section of the law was found to interfere with the carrier's
liberty and property guaranteed by the Fifth Amendment.[75] Such an
interference with rights of the carrier was not considered to be justified as a necessary and proper exercise of Congress' power to regulate
interstate commerce. Seven years later, largely on the basis of this
decision, the Court held unconstitutional a state law prohibiting all
employers in the state from discriminating against employees because
they were union members. This enactment was held to violate the
employer's liberty and property that were protected against state en-
croachment by the Fourteenth Amendment.[76]

It had been permissible for an employer to require his employees
to agree not to join a union.[77] Such a contract was considered a valu-
able property right, and therefore a union could be enjoined from
attempting to solicit members among employees who had signed the
agreement. The Supreme Court held that concerted labor activity,
such as a strike or a boycott constituted a violation of the Anti-Trust
Act if it were designed to restrict interstate commerce to a substantial
degree.[78] This problem of labor and the Anti-Trust law will be considered in greater detail in the following chapter. Picketing was not
considered illegal providing it was carried on peacefully,[79] but the
Court held that a state that prohibited its courts from enjoining disorderly picketing deprived employers of liberty and property without
due process of law, since the employer had a property right in the
business picketed.[80] The Court took no account of the picket's comparable liberty to make known his grievance.

Neither the power of the federal government to regulate interstate
commerce[81] nor its authority to levy taxes[82] were considered to be
sufficiently broad to permit Congress to enact laws regulating child
labor. No government, state or national, had the authority to regulate

[75] *Adair* v. *United States,* 208 U.S. 161.
[76] *Coppage* v. *Kansas,* 236 U.S. 1 (1915).
[77] *Hitchman Coal and Coke Co.* v. *Mitchell,* 245 U.S. 229 (1917).
[78] *Loewe* v. *Lawlor,* 208 U.S. 274 (1908); *Coronado Coal Co.* v. *U.M.W.A.,*
268 U.S. 295 (1925).
[79] *American Steel Foundries Co.* v. *Tri-City Trades Council,* 257 U.S. 184 (1921).
[80] *Truax* v. *Corrigan,* 257 U.S. 312 (1921).
[81] *Hammer* v. *Dagenhart,* 247 U.S. 257 (1918).
[82] *Bailey* v. *Drexel Furniture Co.,* 259 U.S. 20 (1922).

wages.[83] In May 1936 the Supreme Court held that the power of Congress to regulate interstate commerce did not authorize it to regulate wages, hours, and labor relations in bituminous coal mining, even though it was contended that the free flow of goods in interstate commerce was impeded by low wages, long hours of work, and the employer's unwillingness to deal with labor organizations.[84] A year earlier it held that the power of Congress to regulate interstate commerce did not include the authority to establish old-age pensions for employees of interstate railroads.[85] Generally the Court strictly construed the legislative powers of Congress as they related to labor, but it construed broadly the guarantees of personal liberty contained in the Fifth and Fourteenth Amendments.

In 1930 came the first intimation of a change of attitude in the Supreme Court toward the power of the government to enact labor legislation. The Court held in *Texas and New Orleans R.R.* v. *the Brotherhood of Railroad and Steamship Clerks*[86] that because of Congress' power over interstate commerce, it could prohibit railroads from interfering with and coercing their employees in the choice of their own bargaining representatives. The power of Congress over interstate commerce extended to the enactment of legislation designed to reduce disputes that might interfere with such commerce. The Court said that Congress was entitled to believe that this legislation, enacted to protect the workers' right to organize free from employer interference, might facilitate the amicable settlement of disputes. This decision was a manifestation of the first indication of a change of attitude toward labor law. But before the Court again evidenced a comparable attitude toward labor, it handed down a significant number of decisions, already mentioned, that strictly limited the power of the federal and state governments to enact legislation for the benefit of the working man.

Early in 1937 the Court definitely began to manifest a general and far-reaching change of attitude toward labor legislation. In March 1937 the Court reversed a decision of the previous year and held that the states could establish minimum wages for women.[87] A month later

---

[83] *Adkins* v. *Children's Hospital*, 261 U.S. 525 (1923); *Morehead* v. *New York ex rel Tipaldo*, 298 U.S. 587 (1936).
[84] *Carter* v. *Carter Coal Co.*, 298 U.S. 238 (1936).
[85] *Railroad Retirement Board* v. *Alton R. Co.*, 295 U.S. 330 (1935).
[86] 281 U.S. 548.
[87] *West Coast Hotel Co.* v. *Parrish*, 300 U.S. 379 (1937).

it held that Congress has the power to regulate labor relations of all persons engaged in interstate commerce, thus reversing the position it had taken the previous year.[88] Consequently Congress could prohibit employers from discriminating against union members, and it could require employers to bargain collectively with their employees. The establishment of a general system of unemployment compensation and of old-age benefits was also held to be unconstitutional.[89] Subsequently the Supreme Court held that Congress can fix maximum hours of work and minimum wages, and that it could prohibit child labor,[90] thus sustaining the constitutionality of the Fair Labor Standards Act. The Court has defined interstate commerce more broadly and has permitted the government to exercise more extensive powers over it.

As a result of the Court's interpretation of the Norris-LaGuardia Anti-Injunction Act, labor unions appear at the present time to enjoy virtual freedom from the restraints of the Anti-Trust Act.[91] Not only is picketing permissible, but the Court has held that workers have a constitutional right to picket under the guarantee of freedom of speech in the First Amendment and the right to liberty under the Fourteenth Amendment.[92]

Without this general change of attitude on the part of the Supreme Court, the present labor policy of the federal government would not be possible in a constitutional sense. We are not here concerned with how or why this change in the viewpoint of the Court took place.

In endeavoring to get a view of the actual state of labor policy in the United States, it is at once evident (1) that there is no clear division of authority between the federal government and the states; (2) that Congress has enacted many separate laws dealing with the different aspects of the problem of labor and its organized activities; (3) that these laws have been subject to interpretation and application by a considerable number of independent administrative agencies and the courts. This situation makes extremely difficult any attempt to discover what is in fact "the labor policy" of the United States.

[88] *NLRB* v. *Jones and Laughlin Steel Co.,* 301 U.S. 1 (1937).
[89] *Carmichael* v. *Southern Coal and Coke Co.,* 301 U.S. 495 (1937).
[90] *United States* v. *Darbey,* 312 U.S. 100 (1941).
[91] *United States* v. *Hutcheson,* 312 U.S. 219 (1941).
[92] *Thornhill* v. *Alabama,* 310 U.S. 88 (1940).

CHAPTER II

THE GOVERNMENT AND CONCERTED ACTION OF EMPLOYEES

Three broad stages in the development of the public attitude toward collective action can be distinguished: *suppression, toleration,* and *encouragement.* At least since 1842 most of the states have generally regarded trade unions as legal. The federal government has taken little part in the direct suppression of concerted action. Only after the enactment of the Sherman Anti-Trust Act in 1890 was the legality of concerted activities considered in the federal courts. As actually applied by the courts, this act limited the right of unions to engage in various forms of collective action where such activities were regarded as constituting restraints on interstate commerce. The attitude of tolerance toward concerted action can be seen in the Railway Labor Act of 1926. The policy of encouragement developed even more recently: the Norris-LaGuardia Anti-Injunction Act of 1932, the National Industrial Recovery Act, and the National Labor Relations Act of 1935 are examples.

It is not the purpose of this chapter to describe the evolution of public policy toward concerted activities of workers. Here we shall deal only with the attitude of the government toward the right to organize, to strike, to picket, and to boycott; and collective responsibility for the exercise of those rights will be considered. The right to bargain collectively will be treated in another chapter.

I. THE RIGHT TO ORGANIZE

The formation of unions is the precursor of collective action. Unions are primarily partnerships or associations, and as such their rights and duties are determined by state law.[1] They are voluntary organizations without limited liability and are generally without a personality apart from that of their individual constituent members. Only rarely have trade unions been incorporated. Although from 1886 to 1932 a federal law permitted them to be organized as federal corporations, few unions sought incorporation.[2] Colorado is the only state that requires

[1] *Steele* v. *Louisville and Nashville R.R. Co.,* 323 U.S. 192 (1944).
[2] *Monthly Labor Review,* Vol. 40 (1935), pp. 38-43.

trade unions to be incorporated.[3] In Kansas they must register with the Secretary of State.[4]

*Suppression of unions soon
gave way to toleration of them.*

Previous to 1842 trade unions were generally regarded by the states as illegal, either as conspiracies or organizations in restraint of trade. Since the federal government never has had a common law upon the basis of which such decisions could be made, and since it had no applicable statute until 1890, it took no part in the general policy of suppression. The use of the conspiracy doctrine declined after the Supreme Judicial Court of Massachusetts held it inapplicable in *Commonwealth* v. *Hunt* in 1842.[5] Only with the enactment of the Sherman Act in 1890, could the federal courts consider certain union activities as constituting restraints of trade. The federal government has never considered that the mere existence of a union constituted a restraint of trade;[6] only certain specific activities of unions were considered as improper restraints of trade.

In 1898 the federal government first extended some assistance to one type of workers in their efforts to organize. This was under the Erdman Act, which established machinery to facilitate the settlement of railroad labor disputes. It provided that no interstate railroad could require that a prospective employee agree not to join a labor organization, and also that the carrier could not discharge or otherwise discriminate against an employee because he belonged to a union. Criminal penalties could be imposed on an employer who violated this law.[7] As was noted in Chapter I, the Supreme Court held this act unconstitutional in 1908 in *Adair* v. *United States*.[8] The Court said that membership in a union had nothing to do with the movement of goods in interstate commerce. The fitness and diligence of an employee were not increased by membership in a labor organization. Thus

[3] Act of Apr. 1, 1943, *Session Laws of Colorado for 1943*, p. 413.
[4] Laws of 1943, Chap. 10, Sec. 4. Several states require that union organizers must register with the state government. A Texas law requiring the registration of union organizers was held unconstitutional by the U.S. Supreme Court on the basis of the facts presented. *Thomas* v. *Collins*, 323 U.S. 516 (1945).
[5] 45 Mass. 111.
[6] Labor feared that some decisions of the Supreme Court might possibly be so construed; see Act of Oct. 15, 1914, 38 Stat. 731, Sec. 6.
[7] Act of June 1, 1898, 30 Stat. 424, Sec. 10.
[8] 208 U.S. 161.

under this decision, Congress could not prohibit employers in interstate commerce from discriminating against union members.

For a short period during World War I, the executive branch of
the government adopted the policy that employees should have the
right to join unions free from employer discrimination, coercion, or
domination. In January 1918 the Secretary of Labor called upon
twelve representatives of management and labor to formulate a wartime labor policy. The resulting statement of the War Labor Conference Board declared that workers had a right to organize and that
employers should not discriminate against them for so doing. It
specifically declared,

The right of workers to organize in trade-unions and to bargain collectively, through chosen representatives, is recognized and affirmed. The
right shall not be denied, abridged, or interfered with by the employers
in any manner whatsoever. . . . Employers should not discharge workers
for membership in trade unions, nor for legitimate trade union activities.[9]

In April 1918 President Wilson appointed the same twelve men
as a National War Labor Board to settle labor disputes in accordance
with the policy statement of principles set forth by the War Labor
Conference Board. The War Labor Board had no power to enforce
its decisions, and its authority terminated shortly after the end of
hostilities. While it was operating, it handed down numerous decisions
declaring that workers had the right to organize, and that employers
could not interfere with this right. Workers could not be discharged
for union membership or for participation in strikes. Employers could
not dominate or otherwise interfere with the organization of unions.[10]
When the Board terminated its work, the practice of protecting the
workers' right to organize came to an end.

Chief Justice Taft summed up the attitude of the federal government in 1922 toward labor's right to organize unions: "Labor unions
are recognized as legal when instituted for mutual help and lawfully
carrying out their legitimate objects."[11] Thus it was conceded that
laborers could organize if they desired, but employers could discriminate against them if they did so organize. Before 1933 employers
generally could refuse to employ workers because they belonged to a

[9] Bureau of Labor Statistics, *National War Labor Board*, Bulletin 287 (1922) p. 32.
[10] The same, pp. 52-64.
[11] *American Steel Foundries* v. *Tri-City Central Trades Council*, 257 U.S. 184.

union. Before 1932 workers (with the exception of those on railroads after 1926) could at will contract away their right to organize. They could make agreements with their employers promising not to join unions. Neither Congress nor the states could interfere with the right to make such contracts, because the Supreme Court considered such legislation would have been an unconstitutional interference with the right to contract.[12] An attempt to induce a worker to join a union in violation of such an agreement could be enjoined.[13]

In 1926 Congress gave limited assistance to railroad workers in their effort to form unions free from employer interference. The Railway Labor Act enacted in that year provided that railroad employees had the right to select collective bargaining representatives "without interference, influence or coercion" by the employer.[14] In a case involving an attempt by the Texas and New Orleans Railroad to discourage membership in the Brotherhood of Railway and Steamship Clerks and to promote a company union, the Supreme Court held that this statute was constitutional and consequently enjoined its violation by the carrier.[15] In upholding the statute, Chief Justice Hughes said, "The legality of collective action on the part of employees . . . is not to be disputed. . . . Such collective action would be a mockery if representation were made futile by interferences with freedom of choice." By protecting this right Congress facilitates the peaceful settlement of disputes that might otherwise disrupt interstate commerce. This decision represents a far different attitude toward the right to organize than did the opinion in *Adair* v. *United States*. But instead of reversing that decision, the Court in this opinion said it was not applicable to this situation.

For more than a decade unions have been
encouraged by the federal government.

The increase in the bargaining power of the workers is the primary but not the exclusive reason for encouraging unions. The Norris-LaGuardia Act of 1932 contains the following declaration:

[12] *Adair* v. *United States*, 208 U.S. 161 (1908); *Coppage* v. *Kansas*, 236 U.S. 1 (1915).
[13] *Hitchman Coal and Coke Co.* v. *Mitchell*, 245 U.S. 229 (1917).
[14] Act of May 20, 1926, 44 Stat. 578, Sec. 2 (third).
[15] *Texas and New Orleans R.R.* v. *Brotherhood of Ry. and S.S. Clerks*, 281 U.S. 548, 570 (1930).

Whereas under prevailing economic conditions, developed with the aid of governmental authority for owners of property to organize in the corporate and other forms of ownership association, the individual unorganized worker is commonly helpless to exercise actual liberty of contract and to protect his freedom of labor, and thereby to obtain acceptable terms and conditions of employment, wherefore, though he should be free to decline to associate with his fellows, it is necessary that he have full freedom of association, self-organization, and designation of representatives of his own choosing, to negotiate the terms and conditions of his employment. . . . [16]

Thus Congress has said that unions must be assisted to equalize the bargaining power of workers. As we shall see later, this is not the exclusive reason for encouraging unions, but it is the primary one for doing so.

The Norris-LaGuardia Act specifically gave some assistance to workers in the exercise of their right to organize. It declared that any agreement entered into by an employee not to join a labor union was contrary to the public policy of the United States, and it prohibited the federal courts from enforcing such agreements.[17] By this law Congress did not make such agreements illegal; it only limited the remedies that can be used to enforce them.

The National Industrial Recovery Act of 1933 was the first law that generally guaranteed to all workers the right to organize.[18] It declared that workers had the right to form unions free from employer domination, interference, or coercion. One of the leading supporters of this legislation asserted that the depression was caused by the maldistribution of income and that this could be best corrected by increasing the bargaining power of labor.[19] Other proponents of the law believed that industrial planning would prevent depressions. Consequently they contended that if employers were given the right to organize to facilitate such planning, then the employees also should have a comparable right. For these reasons it was considered desirable to increase the workers' bargaining power.

The proponents of the National Labor Relations Act asserted in 1935 that government protection of collective bargaining was needed

[16] Act of Mar. 23, 1932, 47 Stat. 70, Sec. 2.
[17] Sec. 3.
[18] 44 Stat. 195, Sec. 7a.
[19] Statement of Senator Robert Wagner, *National Industrial Recovery Act*, Hearings before the Senate Committee on Finance, 73 Cong. 1 sess., pp. 1, 8.

to increase the purchasing power of the nation. Mr. Lloyd Garrison, a member of the Labor Relations Board created under the NRA, made the clearest statement of this position:

> . . . As costs decrease and profits increase it is absolutely essential that the level of wages should be increased if the mass of the consumers are to have the necessary purchasing power to keep industry going. The wage level cannot be maintained and increased as it should be merely by legislative enactment. All that you can do by law is to provide for the barest minimum wages. Over and above that it is essential to have collective bargaining, preferably through industry-wide agreement between organized labor and organized management. In no other way will the wage structure of the country be maintained at a proper level. . . .[20]

The Senate Committee report on the bill placed major emphasis on the need for increasing the bargaining power of workers in order to increase their purchasing power. It assumed that the depression was caused by a maldistribution of purchasing power. The Committee felt it was better to bring about a redistribution of purchasing power through increasing the workers' bargaining power than to rely upon minimum wage and maximum hour legislation.[21] As another justification, Section 1 of the act states that it is necessary to free interstate commerce from the burdens of strikes and other forms of labor disturbances.[22]

In the hearings on the National Labor Relations Act, much evidence was introduced to show that it was necessary for the government to protect and assist unions if such organizations were to become effective devices for increasing the bargaining power of employees. Employers actively resisted the formation of unions. Members of labor organizations frequently were discharged or discriminated against by other means.[23] Spies were often employed to inform employers of union activities.[24] Workers who took part in strikes were

---

[20] Lloyd K. Garrison, *National Labor Relations Board*, Hearings before the Senate Committee on Education and Labor, 74 Cong. 1 sess., p. 125; also Francis Biddle, the same, p. 76.

[21] *National Labor Relations Board*, S. Rept. 573, 74 Cong. 1 sess., pp. 3-4.

[22] This second justification was advanced primarily to help sustain the act's constitutionality. This was the main ground on which the Supreme Court upheld its constitutionality; *NLRB* v. *Jones and Laughlin Corp.*, 301 U.S. 1, 33 (1937).

[23] William Green in *National Labor Relations Board*, Hearings before the Senate Committee on Education and Labor, p. 104.

[24] John L. Lewis, *To Create a National Labor Board*, Hearings before the Senate Committee on Education and Labor, 73 Cong. 2 sess., p. 142.

discharged. As a result of such actions of employers, there were entire industries in which practically no union members were employed.[25] Where such discriminatory methods did not succeed in preventing the development of labor organizations, an employer not infrequently encouraged the formation of an independent, or so-called company union, that could be dominated or controlled by him.[26] Collective bargaining with a labor organization actually controlled by the employer could be nothing but a sham.

The workers' right to organize is protected
by both criminal penalties and administrative remedies.

By a number of devices the federal government has encouraged the development of unions.

1. The Railway Labor Act imposes criminal penalties on railroads that attempt to interfere with their workers' right to organize. The act contains a general declaration that the employees have this right;[27] and it provides that no employer shall in any way question the right of his employees to join, organize, or assist in organizing a labor organization. It is unlawful for the employer to interfere with the organization of his employees, or to induce them to join or not to join any organization, or to use any funds to maintain or assist any labor organization.[28] These guarantees are enforced in two ways. Any person convicted of violating the provisions can be punished by a fine of from $1,000 to $20,000 and imprisonment for not more than six months or both.[29] Such violations are prosecuted by United States Attorneys just like any other crimes. Second, the employees or their representatives can enjoin employers from violating these rights by a proceeding in an appropriate court.[30] The National Mediation Board has no authority to enforce these provisions of the Railway Labor Act.

2. The National Labor Relations Act confers comparable rights on all persons employed in interstate commerce or in pursuits that affect such commerce.[31] But here the rights are enforced by administrative

[25] The same, p. 152.
[26] Senator Robert Wagner, the same, pp. 39-43.
[27] Sec. 2, third.
[28] Sec. 2, fourth.
[29] Sec. 2, tenth.
[30] *Texas and N.O. Railroad Co.* v. *Brotherhood of Railroad and SS Clerks,* 281 U.S. 548 (1930).
[31] Act of July 5, 1935, 49 Stat. 449.

means. Section 7 of the National Labor Relations Act grants to employees the right of self-organization and the right to engage in concerted activities for the purpose of collective bargaining. Section 8 obligates employers to respect these rights. Employers are prohibited from interfering with labor organizations and from discriminating against union members in fixing the terms of employment. Cease and desist orders of the National Labor Relations Board direct employers to cease violating these rights, and the orders can be enforced by an appeal to a Circuit Court of Appeals. A violation of the decision of such a tribunal can be punished as a contempt of court. The Board can require the employer to recompense employees for any loss of earnings suffered as a consequence of a discharge or discrimination in violation of the act, and it can require the reinstatement of an employee improperly discharged.

3. Attempts have been made to prevent the award of public contracts to employers who do not permit their employees to organize and to bargain collectively. Thus the Bituminous Coal Act of 1937 provided that if the administrator of the Division found that an operator of a bituminous coal mine had denied his employees the right to organize and bargain collectively, he was not to be permitted to sell coal to the government.[32] In only two instances did the Administrator make such a determination.[33] The National Labor Relations Act does not prohibit the award of government contracts to employers who have committed an unfair labor practice, but the NLRB has repeatedly sought to accomplish this objective. It has tried to persuade government procurement agencies to refrain from awarding contracts to low bidders who have violated the act. The Board has even attempted to prevent the placing of contracts with producers who only had been charged with violating the law and before these charges had been proved.[34]

4. The Department of Labor has always promoted and encouraged unions by publicity and other propaganda devices.[35]

---

[32] Act of Apr. 26, 1937, 50 Stat. 1, 87, Sec. 9.

[33] 11 LRR 531, and 5 LRR 273.

[34] *Final Report of the Special Committee to Investigate the National Labor Relations Board*, H. Rept. 3109, 76 Cong. 3 sess., pp. 32-35; the minority report admits that this happened, Intermediate Report . . . H. Rept. 1902, Pt. 2, 76 Cong. 3 sess., pp. 48-51.

[35] See *Fourth Annual Report of the Secretary of Labor* (1916), pp. 48-49.

The National Labor Relations Act is now the
workers' chief protection of the right to organize.

Since the National Labor Relations Act is of wide application, and since the NLRB has given the most definite content to the right to organize, our attention will be concentrated on its interpretation of the right. Only the general principles underlying its decisions will be considered.

Section 7 of the National Labor Relations Act provides:

Employees shall have the right to self-organization, to form, join, or assist labor organizations, to bargain collectively through representatives of their own choosing, and to engage in concerted activities, for the purpose of collective bargaining or other mutual aid or protection.

And Section 8 goes on to declare the following to be unfair labor practices:

(1) To interfere with, restrain, or coerce employees in the exercise of the rights guaranteed in Section 7.

(2) To dominate or interfere with the formation or administration of any labor organization or contribute financial or other support to it. . . .

(3) By discrimination in regard to hire or tenure of employment or any term or condition of employment to encourage or discourage membership in any labor organization. . . .[36]

All persons working for employers covered by the act have the right to organize and to engage in concerted action. Even supervisory employees such as foremen are included.[37]

The first paragraph of Section 8, which prohibits any restraint, coercion, or interference with the right of self-organization, is broad enough to embrace all other paragraphs of the section. An employer cannot do anything to hinder or interfere with the free right of his employees to organize. Neither he nor his agents can use violence against union members.[38] He cannot employ spies to report to him on union activities.[39] A threat to shut down a plant or to move it to another location in order to discourage organizational activities is a violation of Section 8 (1).[40] The Board has also held that in some

[36] Sec. 8 (4) prohibits discrimination against employees who have filed charges under the act; and Sec. 8 (5) makes it an unfair labor practice for an employer to refuse to bargain collectively.
[37] *Soss Mfg. Co.*, 56 NLRB 348 (1944).
[38] *Dow Chemical Co.*, 13 NLRB 993 (1939).
[39] *Agwilines, Inc.*, 2 NLRB 1 (1936).
[40] *Triplett Electrical Instrument Co.*, 5 NLRB 635 (1938).

instances he must permit union agents to enter upon his property to contact his employees, and he cannot prohibit union solicitation upon his property outside of working hours.[41] For an employer to give a wage increase to his employees is an unfair labor practice if there is any evidence that his purpose might have been to discourage organizational activities.[42]

An employer cannot engage in bribery to influence the attitude of his employees toward a union or to coerce union officials. It is an unfair labor practice for an employer to offer vacations with pay to employees who promise that in a representation election they will vote against an outside union.[43] In another case an employer offered to give a building to two union employees and suggested that they go into business themselves.[44] Another employer was found to have violated the law by offering a union representative a good position "at a high salary provided he would desert the union."[45]

Section 8 (1) as actually applied tends to limit the employer's right to comment concerning unions, their desirability, and rights. The Board has said that the effect of an employer's statements concerning a union is to be determined "by an evaluation of the natural consequences of such statements made not by one equal to another, but by an employer to those dependent upon it for their continued employment and livelihood."[46] The Board has held that an employer cannot call a union "cut throat,"[47] nor can he tell the employees that the union can do nothing to improve their conditions of employment.[48]

Any statement of employer preference for one of two rival unions is considered coercive.[49] The Board has held that an admittedly correct statement of the employees' rights under the National Labor Relations Act is a violation of Section 1 (1).[50]

[41] *Seas Shipping Co.*, 4 NLRB 757 (1938); *Harlan Fuel Co.*, 8 NLRB 25 (1938); *Carter Carburetor Co.*, 48 NLRB 354 (1943); *Republic Aviation Co.*, 54 NLRB 539 (1944).

[42] *Indianapolis Power and Light Co.*, 25 NLRB 163 (1940); *West Texas Utility Corp.*, 22 NLRB 522 (1940). See also *Appalachian Electric Power Co.*, 47 NLRB 102 (1943), reversed 140 Fed. (2d) 217 (1944).

[43] *McNeely and Price Co.*, 6 NLRB 800 (1937).

[44] *Stackpole Carbon Co.*, 6 NLRB 177 (1937).

[45] *Carlisle Lumber Co.*, 2 NLRB 248 (1936).

[46] *Yale and Towne Mfg. Co.*, 17 NLRB 69 (1939).

[47] *Jones and Laughlin Steel Corp.*, 1 NLRB 503 (1936).

[48] *Yale and Towne Mfg. Co.*, 17 NLRB 69 (1939).

[49] *Continental Box Co.*, 19 NLRB 860 (1940).

[50] *Mock Gadson Voehbenger Co.*, 8 NLRB 133, 136 (1938).

The Supreme Court has held that for any statement of an employer to constitute a violation of the act, coercion must be evident either in the language used or in some of the surrounding circumstances. In the case of the Virginia Electric and Power Company,[51] the employer had posted a bulletin, saying that it had been free from union organization for fifteen years. It went on to say, "The Company recognizes the right of every employee to join any union that he may wish to join, and such membership will not affect his position with the Company." It added that no law requires him to join any union. Concerning this statement the Board said: "We find that by posting the Bulletin the Respondent interfered with, restrained, and coerced his employees." But the Supreme Court held in an opinion written by Mr. Justice Murphy that the employer had the right to express his views on any side in an industrial controversy provided that no coercion was involved.

If the total activities of an employer restrain or coerce his employees in their free choice, then those employees are entitled to the protection of the Act. And in determining whether a course of conduct amounts to restraint or coercion, pressure exerted vocally by the employer may no more be disregarded than pressure exerted in other ways.

Thus where the language used is not of itself coercive, the coercion can be inferred from other circumstances, but the Board must make a determination of coercion based upon the utterances or their background. The Court found that these utterances were not of themselves coercive, and since the Board did not relate them to their background, it found that the act had not been violated.[52]

After this decision the Board retried the case. In its second opinion it found that the Bulletin previously mentioned, when taken in connection with anti-union activities of the company and certain discriminatory discharges, constituted coercion and therefore violated the law.[53] This decision was affirmed by the Supreme Court which said: "While the Bulletin of April 26 and the speeches of May 24 are still stressed, they are considered not in isolation but as part of a pattern of events adding up to" domination, interference, and coercion.[54]

[51] 20 NLRB 911, 920 (1940).
[52] *NLRB v. Virginia Electric Power Co.*, 314 U.S. 469, 477 (1941).
[53] 44 NLRB 404 (1942).
[54] *Virginia Electric and Power Co. v. NLRB*, 319 U.S. 533, 539 (1943).

These decisions of the Court have only a limited significance, since the Board is generally able to find the existence of coercion by considering employer utterances in connection with his other actions.[55]

Even where a union has taken a public stand against the very existence of the employer's business, for him to call this fact to the attention of his employees is a violation of Section 8 (1), although no finding of coercion was made by the Board.[56] An employer has an interest in seeing that the union his employees are about to join is not fundamentally antagonistic to his business and that it is responsible, especially since he cannot discharge an employee for joining a union, and since he may have to bargain with that organization.

The second provision of Section 8 prohibits interference by an employer with the formation and administration of unions. The Board has said: "The formation and administration of labor organizations are the concern of the employees and not of employers."[57] Thus it was designed as a prohibition against the establishment of so-called company unions; its full import will be considered in Chapter IV, which deals with the influence of the government on the organization of unions.

Probably the classic case involving the application of this section is that of the International Harvester Company.[58] Here the employer had established an industrial council plan, wherein representatives of the workers selected by the members of the employees' association met with representatives of management to consider conditions of employment. The program was initiated by the employer, who financed both the industrial council and the employees' association. The Company urged all new employees to join the association. The council could not make a decision contrary to the wishes of management.

Representatives of management and employees sit in solemn council, discuss and debate matters of mutual concern, and decide such matters by a vote in which the strength of each is equal, one vote to each side. But obviously, the management representatives do not exercise a judgment independent of that of their superior, the Superintendent.

---

[55] *American Tube Bending Co.*, 44 NLRB 120 (1942), reversed, 14 LRR 647; *Leach Relay Corp.*, 45 NLRB 112 (1942); *Anderson Mfg. Co.*, 58 NLRB 271 (1944).

[56] *Ohio Greyhound Lines, Inc.*, 21 NLRB 751, 757; *Pacific Greyhound Lines, Inc.*, 2 NLRB 431 (1937).

[57] *Third Annual Report of the National Labor Relations Board* (1938), p. 125.

[58] 2 NLRB 310, 348 (1936).

Changes in the terms of employment were made by management alone, the role of the employees was only to make suggestions. The industrial council was found to be employer dominated, and the Board ordered its disestablishment.

It is a violation of Section 8 (2) for an employer to discharge or to threaten to discharge an employee, because of his unwillingness to join an unaffiliated union.[59] An employer cannot give any positive assistance to a labor organization; he cannot draft its constitution nor can he give it financial assistance.[60] Thus the employer cannot pay the wages of an employee who spends most of his time organizing a union.[61] The act obviously prohibits actual employer domination of a union, but the Board even considers that an unsuccessful attempt at domination is an unfair practice.[62]

It is immaterial that all the members of an allegedly dominated organization joined it for reasons not connected with the attempted domination.[63] Even though all the members joined the union of their own free will and prefer it to any other organization, the attempted domination is illegal and the union will be disestablished.[64] The act on its face prohibits only an actual domination of a union by an employer. But the Board has interpreted this provision to constitute a prohibition against any attempted interference with the right to organize.

An employee cannot be discriminated against because of union activities.

Section 8 (3) prohibits employers from encouraging or discouraging union membership by discriminating against union members. In hiring workers and in fixing the terms and tenure of employment, the employer cannot discriminate against an employee because he is a union member.[65]

[59] *Titan Metal Mfg. Co.*, 5 NLRB 577, 582 (1938); *Philips Packing Co.*, 5 NLRB 272, 280-83 (1938).

[60] An employer is guilty of giving financial assistance to a union if he permits it to receive the commission from a concession selling milk in the plant, even though the employer never received any income from the concession. *General Dry Batteries, Inc.*, 27 NLRB 102 (1940).

[61] *Swift and Co.*, 11 NLRB 809 (1939).

[62] *Canvas Glove Mfg. Co., Inc.*, 1 NLRB 519 (1936).

[63] *Donnelly Garment Co.*, 21 NLRB 164 (1940).

[64] *Hicks Body Co.*, 33 NLRB 858 (1941); *Norman H. Stone*, 33 NLRB 1014 (1941).

[65] Under the National Labor Relations Act an employer can discriminate in favor of the members of one union if he has signed a valid closed shop contract with that

A person discharged because of union membership can be reinstated by order of the Board with back pay. Likewise a refusal to hire a person because of union membership entitles that person to a position with the discriminating employer, with back pay from the time of such original refusal to hire.[66] To some this ruling may be a little surprising, but if the objective is to prohibit discriminatory hiring, it is an effective device to attain that objective.

The prohibition in the act against discrimination specifically provides: "It shall be an unfair labor practice for an employer ... by discrimination in regard to hire or tenure of employment ... to encourage or discourage membership in any labor organization." This language would appear to mean that discrimination would be improper if it actually would either discourage or encourage union membership. But the Board has not so construed this provision. According to the Board: "It forbids the employer to affect or change an employment relationship because of the employee's union membership or activity."[67] Consequently if the Board finds that any action was taken by the employer on the basis of union membership, it practically always assumes the existence of the intent to discriminate. Such an interpretation certainly makes the prohibition much broader in actual application than the words of the statute seem to warrant.

Obviously it would be improper for an employer to discharge a worker on the sole ground that he is a union member or engaged in union activity.[68] If several union leaders are the only employees discharged at a given time, there is an inference that the dismissal was discriminatory.[69] The same thing is true if only employees active in the formation of a union are discharged at a given time.[70] An employee cannot be discharged if the employer alleges that he was released both because of his union activities and for other legitimate causes. If at any time the employer has given evidence of opposition to unions, the Board generally finds that the dismissal of an employee was due to union activity, even though other good reasons for the discharge actually existed and were alleged, and although there was

union. Under the Railway Labor Act the employer cannot discriminate against a worker either because he is or is not a member of a union. Closed Shop contracts will be considered in Chap. 6.

[66] *Phelps Dodge Co.* v. *NLRB*, 313 U.S. 177 (1941).
[67] *Third Annual Report of the National Labor Relations Board* (1938), p. 81.
[68] *Washington, Virginia, and Maryland Coach Co.*, 1 NLRB 769 (1936).
[69] *Arcadia Hosiery Co.*, 12 NLRB 467 (1939).
[70] *Ross Packing Co.*, 11 NLRB 934 (1939).

no direct evidence that the action was taken because of the employee's participation in union activities.[71] The Supreme Court has held that this practice of the Board is improper,[72] but nevertheless the Board has continued to follow it.[73] If a discriminatory discharge is alleged by the Board and some evidence of union opposition is presented, the employer then has the burden of proving that the discharge was not a consequence of union activities.[74]

The obligation not to discriminate has been construed by the Board as a positive obligation to protect union employees against nonunion workers. Where nonunion employees, without the knowledge or approval of the employer, forcibly evicted union workers, the employer was held to be guilty of engaging in discrimination, because he did not give positive protection to the union members.[75]

As applied by the Board, Section 8 (3) tends to make it difficult for an employer to discipline workmen who refuse to obey orders. Employees cannot be discharged because they refuse to take a job formerly held by a union official who had been discharged. This refusal to work was considered to be union activity, and the discharge constituted discrimination against the employees because of their union membership.[76] Employees cannot be discharged for threatening to strike to secure the discharge of a foreman who is not liked,[77] or for refusing to work on Labor Day.[78]

The reinstatement of employees discriminatorily discharged involves difficulties. If the employer should discharge a person who previously had been reinstated by an order of the Board, or if he should discharge a union organizer or official, it would be difficult to prove that such discharge was for good and sufficient cause. In addition the reinstatement of discharged employees may have detrimental effects upon productive efficiency. To justify the potential interference with productive efficiency, one must assume that the absolute eradication of discrimination against labor is more important

[71] *Hearst Consolidated Publications,* 10 NLRB 1299; *Arcade Sunshine Co.,* 12 NLRB 259 (1939).
[72] *NLRB v. Sands Mfg. Co.,* 306 U.S. 332 (1939).
[73] *Arcade Sunshine Co.,* 12 NLRB 259 (1939).
[74] *Reliance Mfg. Co. v. NLRB,* 125 Fed. (2d) 311 (1941).
[75] *Riverside Mfg. Co.,* 20 NLRB 394 (1941), modified, 119 Fed. (2d) 302.
[76] *Niles Fire Brick Co.,* 30 NLRB 426 (1941); *Williamson Dickis Mfg. Co.,* 35 NLRB 1220 (1941).
[77] *Pittsburgh Standard Envelope Co.,* 20 NLRB 516 (1940).
[78] *Good Coal Co.,* 12 NLRB 136 (1939); affirmed 110 Fed. (2d) 501 (1940).

to the community than the maintenance of efficiency. Of course reinstatement with back pay is a simple and direct way of punishing discrimination and of ensuring that employees will not suffer as a result of it.

If an employer is being injured by inter-union warfare carried on among his employees, he cannot attempt to end it by discharging the members of one of the unions. Such action would constitute a discrimination prohibited by Section 8 (3). Thus if the employees in a plant belong to two different unions, and the members of one of these unions refuse to work if members of the other organization continue to be employed, it is a violation of the act for the employer to dismiss the persons who were objected to by the first union even to prevent a strike.[79] Discrimination is forbidden though the members of the objecting union engage in a sit-down strike, which is illegal under the act.[80] Under such circumstances, if the employer does not wish to violate the law, he must permit his business to be disrupted by a strike.

With widespread rival unionism, this prohibition against discriminatory discharges places the employer in a most difficult position if he has employees belonging to rival unions. If one union threatens to strike unless the members of the other are discharged, the employer cannot discharge the members of the other group in order to prevent the strike. He is placed in a position of violating the law or having his business damaged by a strike, and as will be seen later he cannot take any effective steps to combat such a strike. Strikes by rival organizations also are injurious to the rights of properly recognized unions. But here the legitimate union is in the same position as the employer; it cannot prevent the rival organization from interfering with its rights. The framers of the act were not concerned with the problems of rival unionism, because the split in the labor movement developed after the enactment of the National Labor Relations Act.

II. STRIKES

The right to strike includes not only the right of a group of workers to quit work, but also their right to return to work if and when they so desire. The National Labor Relations Act specifically confers the

---

[79] *NLRB* v. *Star Publishing Co.*, 97 Fed. (2d) 465 (1938).

[80] *New York and Puerto Rico Steamship Co.*, 34 NLRB 1028 (1941); *Great Steel Co.*, 38 NLRB 65 (1942); *Isthmian Steamship Co.*, 22 NLRB 689 (1940); *Mooremack Gulf Lines*, 28 NLRB 869 (1941).

right to strike[81] Under its terms, strikers are employees, and striking is recognized as a legitimate form of concerted activity.[82] The Railway Labor Act carefully states that nothing in it is to be construed as restricting the right to strike.[83] The Norris-LaGuardia Act of 1932 limited the remedies that can be utilized against strikes, but it does not in any way modify the right to strike. We will consider first what constitutes a legal strike under federal law, and then the rights of strikers and the duties of their employers.

*The Anti-Trust Act now does not
limit the right to strike.*

The anti-trust laws formerly constituted some limitation on the right of workers to strike, but as now interpreted they constitute no restraint on strikes or other forms of concerted action. The Sherman Anti-Trust Act prohibits all contracts, combinations, and conspiracies in restraint of interstate commerce.[84] As a means of enforcement it provides for criminal penalties, civil damages, and injunctive relief. The courts have applied this law to various forms of concerted labor activities, but for any concerted action of labor to be a violation of the Sherman Anti-Trust Act, there must have been an intent to restrict interstate commerce, and the restraint must have been unreasonable and not merely incidental. Thus a strike for the establishment of a union shop is not improper if there is no intent to restrict interstate commerce unreasonably.[85] A refusal to work on nonunion materials does not constitute a violation of the act where there was no intention to restrain the flow of interstate commerce and where all acts occurred at the place of original production.[86]

In 1914 by the Clayton Act Congress made certain amendments to the Sherman Act. According to some of their congressional supporters, these amendments were designed to remove labor activities from the anti-trust law, but the courts held that this legislation was only a restatement of the existing law.[87]

Recently the Supreme Court almost completely removed all forms

---

[81] Sec. 13.
[82] Sec. 2 (3).
[83] Sec. 2 (tenth).
[84] Act of July 2, 1890, 26 Stat. 209. In 1908 the Supreme Court in *Loewe* v. *Lawlor*, 208 U.S. 274, first held that this law was applicable to labor activity.
[85] *United Mine Workers of America* v. *Coronado Coal Co.*, 259 U.S. 344 (1922).
[86] *Levering and Garrigues Corp.* v. *Morrin*, 289 U.S. 103 (1933).
[87] *Duplex Printing Press Co.* v. *Deering*, 254 U.S. 443 (1921).

of labor activities from the limitations of the anti-trust laws. The court now has decided that an employer, as a result of injuries suffered by a strike, cannot recover triple damages under the Sherman Act, merely by showing that the concerted action was designed to restrain interstate commerce substantially. He must also demonstrate that the work stoppage directly restricted the market for the goods he produced and thereby reduced competition. The decisions of the court do not indicate what constitutes a restriction of the market. This definition of a restraint of trade is much narrower than the one previously used by the court.[88] In the light of this decision, it is now difficult for an employer to recover damages from a union on the ground that an injury resulted from a restraint of trade instituted by it.

Moreover, it is practically impossible at present to enjoin a strike, even though it constitutes a violation of the Sherman Act. In 1932 by the Norris-LaGuardia Act, Congress prohibited federal courts from issuing injunctions in labor disputes except in very limited circumstances. Concerning the powers of federal courts under this law the Supreme Court remarked:

> . . . For us to hold, in the face of this legislation, that the federal courts have jurisdiction to grant injunctions in cases growing out of labor disputes, merely because alleged violations of the Sherman Act are involved, would run counter to the plain mandate of the Act and would reverse the declared purpose of Congress. . . .[89]

Finally, the court has held that unions are practically freed from the criminal provisions of the Anti-Trust Act except where they act in concert with employers. In 1939 Thurman Arnold, then the head of the Anti-Trust Division of the Department of Justice, announced a policy of prosecuting the following types of labor activity under the anti-trust law: (1) strikes to prevent the utilization of cheaper and improved equipment; (2) practices designed to require the employment of unnecessary labor; (3) restraints on commerce for the purpose of promoting graft and corruption; (4) strikes and other concerted activities designed to maintain prices; (5) jurisdictional strikes.[90] Consequently the Anti-Trust Division instituted a series of criminal actions against trade unions. But the Supreme Court held that

[88] *Apex Hosiery Co.* v. *Leader*, 310 U.S. 469 (1940).

[89] *Milk Wagon Drivers' Union No. 753* v. *Lake Valley Farm Products, Inc.*, 311 U.S. 91 (1940).

[90] Thurman Arnold, *Bottlenecks of Business* (1940), pp. 249-50.

jurisdictional strikes[91] (even though the union against which the strike was called had been certified as representing a majority of the workers in the bargaining unit concerned),[92] to prevent the use of new equipment[93] as well as strikes to compel employment of unnecessary employees were not violations of the Sherman Act.[94] The court asserted that the Sherman Act and the Clayton Act must be read together with the Norris-LaGuardia Act; all three must be read as a whole. Section 20 of the Clayton Act of 1914 provides that striking, picketing, and boycotting are not to be enjoined. It then asserts: "nor shall any of the acts specified in this paragraph be considered or held to be violations of any law of the United States."[95]

By construing this provision in the light of the declaration of public policy contained in the Norris-LaGuardia Act previously quoted, the Supreme Court reached the conclusion: "The licit and illicit under Section 20 are not to be distinguished by any judgment regarding the wisdom or unwisdom, the rightness or wrongness, the selfishness or unselfishness, of the end of which the particular union activities are the means."[96] The court observed that so long as the union acted in its self-interest and not in collaboration with nonlabor groups, it committed no criminal act. This decision was handed down in a case that grew out of a jurisdictional strike against a manufacturer producing goods for interstate commerce. Justice Frankfurter, speaking for the court in the case, observed concerning jurisdictional disputes:

Such strife between competing unions has been an obdurate conflict in the evolution of so-called craft unionism and has undoubtedly been one of the potent forces in the modern development of industrial unions. . . .
. . . The fact that what was done was done in a competition for jobs against the Machinists rather than against, let us say, a company union, is a differentiation which Congress has not put into the federal legislation and which therefore we cannot write into it.

On the basis of the decisions concerning criminal prosecutions, injunctions, and civil damages, it is apparent that practically no strike is

---

[91] U.S. v. Hutcheson, 312 U.S. 219 (1940).
[92] U.S. v. Building and Construction Trades Council of New Orleans, 313 U.S. 539 (1941).
[93] U.S. v. International Hodcarriers and Common Laborers District Council et al., 313 U.S. 539 (1941).
[94] U.S. v. American Federation of Musicians, 318 U.S. 741 (1943).
[95] Act of Oct. 15, 1914, 38 Stat. 730, 738.
[96] U.S. v. Hutcheson, 312 U.S. 219, 232 (1940).

contrary to the Sherman Anti-Trust law if the union involved does not combine with employers.[97]

Since practically all strikes and other forms of concerted action have been removed from the limitation of the anti-trust laws, it is not unreasonable to assume that the federal government considered that the possible restrictions on the free flow of goods in interstate commerce would be insignificant compared to the public advantage resulting from the consequent increase in the bargaining power of the workers. But although the increase in bargaining power was the objective, the legalizing of jurisdictional strikes by the Hutcheson decision is not in accord with this goal, because the purpose of such strikes is to strengthen one group of workers as against another group, not to improve the bargaining position of the employees as against their employer. Although strikes undertaken to impose territorial trade barriers, to prevent the introduction of new techniques, or to require the hiring of unnecessary workers, may really improve the bargaining position of employees as against their employers, some people contend that these practices tend to reduce the nation's output and thereby limit opportunities for employment and reduce real wages. "The only labor interest served by such restrictions is the interest of a local group in taking work away from other labor groups elsewhere and in stretching out the work so that it will last as long as possible."[98] If these criticisms are correct, then the possible resulting restraints on commerce are not in the national interest, though the specific workers concerned might be benefited.

[97] For an example of such a combination see *Local 167 of the International Brotherhood of Teamsters* v. *U.S.*, 291 U.S. 293 (1934).

The other form of labor activity prosecuted under Mr. Arnold's program was the use of interstate commerce for purposes of bribery, racketeering, and extortion. This did not necessarily involve the use of strikes. A law to prevent the use of intrastate commerce for such purposes had been enacted in 1934 (48 Stat. 979). Where a union required the payment of the wages of an extra driver on a truck moving in interstate commerce, the court held that this was not a violation, because the act specifically provides that the use of violence or the threat of violence is not coercion when it involves the "payment of wages by a bona fide employer." (*U.S.* v. *Local 807 of the International Brotherhood of Teamsters*, 315 U.S. 521, 1942.) No person was actually employed in this case, but nevertheless the wages had to be paid. The court said Congress intended to exempt trade union activity. "Accepting payments even where services are refused is such an activity," it observed.

[98] Corwin Edwards of the Department of Justice, "Trade Unions and the Law," *Papers and Proceedings of the Fifty-fourth Annual Meeting of the American Economic Association*, December 1941, p. 443.

Other limitations on the
right to strike are few.

Only where the crew of a vessel of American registry engages in a work stoppage is participation in a strike a crime. When the ship is away from a safe port, the crew cannot cease to work without being guilty of mutiny.[99] The National Labor Relations Act did not change the criminal nature of such a work stoppage. When a member of a crew of a vessel engages in a strike under such circumstances, he does not continue to have the protection of the act.[100]

The War Labor Disputes Act makes the calling or the inciting of a strike a criminal act in certain circumstances. Where the government has taken over a plant producing war goods, the act makes it a crime for any person to urge or to persuade the employees to strike, or to give them assistance after a strike has commenced.[101] This legislation is effective only during the present hostilities and for six months thereafter. To October 1944 the government has secured under this section only 14 convictions involving 94 persons.[102]

This act also requires that the employees of a war contractor must notify the Secretary of Labor and other government officials of any labor dispute likely to lead to a strike. After such notice, neither party can change the terms of employment or cease operations for 30 days. On the thirtieth day the NLRB shall take a ballot of the employees to determine their desire to strike.[103] Even though a majority of the workers vote against the strike, the work stoppage will not be illegal if the election has been held. If a strike is called not in accordance with the law, the employer can sue the union for damages.

According to the so-called War Labor Conference Agreement of December 23, 1941, all strikes are supposedly improper during the present war. In addition to the criminal provision of the War Labor Disputes Act just discussed, only two types of action have been taken to implement this policy: (1) where a union strikes contrary to a decision of the National War Labor Board, the plant of the employer

---

[99] The Supreme Court has held that this provision of the Mutiny Act does not constitute a violation of the Thirteenth Amendment which prohibits involuntary servitude. *Robertson v. Baldwin*, 165 U.S. 275 (1897).

[100] *Southern Steamship Co. v. NLRB*, 316 U.S. 31 (1942).

[101] Act of June 25, 1943, 57 Stat. 163, Sec. 6.

[102] *Editorial Research Reports* (1944), Vol. 2, p. 237.

[103] Act of June 25, 1943, 57 Stat. 163, Sec. 8 (a)(2) .

may be seized by the federal government; and (2) in some cases where a union has called a strike contrary to this so-called agreement, the National War Labor Board has held that the union has demonstrated irresponsibility and consequently cannot be granted the privilege of maintenance of membership for six months thereafter.[104]

A strike for a closed shop is generally regarded as proper.[105] This is true even where its objective is to compel a working employer (who has but a few assistants) to join the union or stop working, although by the rules of the union he is not eligible to membership.[106]

The National Labor Relations Act does not limit the right to strike.

A strike designed to compel an employer to violate the National Labor Relations Act does not appear to be an improper form of concerted activity. For example, an employer has recognized and bargained with a union that represents a majority of his employees, as he is required to do by the act. Nevertheless the minority group, who belong to another union, strikes to get the employer to recognize them in violation of the law. The Board has never passed on the propriety of such a work stoppage, but in its decisions it has not indicated its disapproval of strikes of this type.[107] Of course similar activities of the minority also may be injurious to the exclusive bargaining rights of the majority union. The Supreme Court has held that this type of work stoppage does not constitute a crime.[108] The Norris-LaGuardia Act appears to prohibit both the employer and the union representing a majority of the workers from securing an injunction against a strike instituted to compel the employer to violate the National Labor Relations Act.[109] It is not consistent for the government to impose duties on an employer and at the same time to permit employees to freely

---

[104] *Monsanto Chemical Co.*, 2 WLR 479 (1942).

[105] *Lauf v. E. G. Shinner and Co.*, 303 U.S. 323 (1938). Such a strike on a railroad would not be consistent with the Railway Labor Act of 1934, for it prohibits the making of such agreements by employers subject to it.

[106] *Senn v. Tile Layers Protective Union*, 301 U.S. 468 (1937).

[107] *New York* and *Puerto Rico S. S. Co.*, 34 NLRB 1028 (1941).

[108] *U.S. v. Building and Construction Trades Council of New Orleans*, 313 U.S. 539 (1941).

[109] *Fur Workers Union Local No. 72 v. Fur Workers Union No. 21238*, 105 Fed. (2d) 1 (1938); affirmed 308 U.S. 522 (1939).

use methods of self-help to compel him to violate his legal obligations.[110]

Although a union agrees that it will not strike during the life of a contract, a work stoppage contrary to the agreement is nevertheless protected by the act.[111] It is not likely that the employer can discharge the employees who participated in the work stoppage. And here again the employer probably cannot secure injunctive relief in the federal courts. One of the major objectives of our labor policy is to encourage collective bargaining, and one of the main reasons an employer enters into a collective agreement is to free his plant from the interruption of strikes for its duration. The refusal of the Board to attempt to discourage strikes in violation of an agreement must in some measure defeat that objective. Similarly the inability to enjoin a strike in violation of a contract does not encourage the employees to make agreements.

President Roosevelt has asserted there is no right to strike on the part of government employees,[112] but actually this statement means only that employees who participate in a strike may not be granted the right to return to their work when they desire to. Since no law prohibits federal employees from striking, no criminal penalties can be applied to those participating in such a work stoppage, but under some circumstances the persons who promote a strike against the government may be guilty of committing an illegal act.[113]

The use of violence in a strike does not generally remove it from the protection of the National Labor Relations Act. The Board generally assumes that violence is an inevitable part of a strike. In some instances specific employees who engage in acts of violence might lose the protection of the act, but their misconduct does not make the whole strike illegal. The Supreme Court has held that sitdown strikers do not have the right to be reinstated in their former positions at the end of the strike.[114] Although the Supreme Court has held that a strike

---

[110] The NLRB considers a sympathetic strike to be a form of labor activity, protected by the National Labor Relations Act, *Firth Carpet Co.*, 33 NLRB 191 (1941).

[111] *United Biscuit Co.*, 38 NLRB 778 (1942); *Highland Shoe Co.*, 23 NLRB 259 (1940), as affirmed 119 Fed. (2d) 218 (1941).

[112] *Public Papers and Addresses of Franklin D. Roosevelt, 1937* (1941), p. 325.

[113] 35 Stat. 1097, 1127, Secs. 43 and 201.

[114] *NLRB* v. *Fansteel Metallurgical Corp.*, 306 U.S. 240 (1939). But the Secretary of Labor did not regard such strikes as illegal or undesirable. See letter to Representative John McCormack, *New York Times*, Mar. 27, 1937.

in violation of a contract is not a strike that has the protection of the act,[115] the Board has continued to regard such strikes as legal.[116] Even though a strike is illegal under the law of the state where it occurs, it does not therefore become improper under the act.[117] The NLRB does not look with disfavor on a strike carried on in violation of an injunction issued by a state court.[118] It has reinstated strikers (often with back pay) who have been convicted of misdemeanors committed during the course of a strike, or who have been adjudged in contempt of court for violating an injunction.[119]

The Board considers one type of strike to be outside the protection of the act; that is, a strike to compel an employer to grant a wage increase that has not previously been approved by the National War Labor Board as required by the act of October 2, 1942 and executive orders issued thereunder.[120] The Board held that although the employer's misconduct is the primary concern of the act, employee misconduct is not irrelevant. It went on to say that the act should be accommodated to the Stabilization Act of October 2, 1942.[121]

Workers can strike even where there are peaceful remedies to enforce their rights.

The existence of alternative peaceful methods of enforcing rights does not affect the legality of a strike. In order to enforce the rights granted to them by the Labor Relations Act, the employees always have a right to strike or to engage in other forms of self-help. At

[115] *NLRB* v. *Sands Mfg. Co.,* 306 U.S. 332 (1939).
[116] *United Biscuit Co.,* 38 NLRB 778 (1942); *Highland Shoe Co.,* 23 NLRB 289 (1940); affirmed 119 Fed. (2d) 318 (1941).
[117] *Reed and Prince Mfg. Corp.,* 12 NLRB 944 (1939).
[118] *Wilson and Co.,* 26 NLRB 1353 (1940); *Swift and Co.,* 10 NLRB 991 (1939).
[119] The Board has repeatedly held that violence is an inevitable concomitant of a strike. For example: "In any case the fact that during a strike, necessarily a time of heated emotions, the bounds of permissible conduct may have been overstepped by men or leaders cannot be used to deny to employees their full right of representation." *Rabhor Co.,* 1 NLRB 470, 478 (1936).
A Circuit Court of Appeals observed that it could not "conclude that rights given to employees under the National Labor Relations Act are destroyed because of violence of a type as common to labor disputes as a fist-fight upon a picket line." *NLRB* v. *Stackpole Carbon Co.,* 105 Fed. (2d) 167, 176 (1939).
[120] 56 Stat. 765.
[121] *American News Co. Inc.,* 55 NLRB 1302 (1944); but also note *Indiana Desk Co.,* 58 NLRB 48 (1944).

their own discretion, they can either turn to the Board to enforce their rights or they can strike.[122]

One of the main objectives of the act is to free interstate commerce from such impediments as strikes. The act, however, limits the possibility of attaining this objective, since it grants to workers who believe an unfair labor practice has been committed a free choice of either resorting to the NLRB or striking in order to redress the grievance. Where a strike was caused or prolonged by an unfair labor practice, the employer must reinstate the strikers with back pay, though new employees had been hired in their stead;[123] but where the strike was not caused or prolonged by an unfair labor practice, the strikers need not be reinstated if their positions had been filled by new employees. In only a very few cases has the Board granted back pay to employees for time lost in a strike not caused by an unfair labor practice.[124]

Strikers have all the rights granted to
employees by the National Labor Relations Act.

The Labor Relations Act provides that when a worker participates in a strike he does not thereby cease to be an employee.[125] Employers are prohibited from interfering with union activities; and strikes are considered to be a proper form of such activity.[126] Furthermore, the NLRB is given the authority to reinstate with back pay any person discriminated against by an employer, because he engaged in concerted action. Thus the striker has all the rights of an employee.

According to the NLRB, strikers do not cease to be employees; they become persons on strike. The Board has implied that it is not possible for an employer to discharge an employee during the course of a strike.[127] When the strike terminates, the employer does not have to restore the worker to his position if he has already filled the job with another worker and provided the strike was not caused by or prolonged by an unfair labor practice of the employer.[128] If an unfair

---

[122] *Remington-Rand Corp.* v. *NLRB*, 94 Fed. (2d) 862 (1938).

[123] *American Manufacturing Co.*, 5 NLRB 443 (1938).

[124] *Draper Corp.*, 52 NLRB 1477 (1943), Reilly dissenting at p. 1483; and *Gulf Public Service Corp.*, 18 NLRB 562 (1939).

[125] Sec. 2 (3).

[126] Sec. 8 (3).

[127] See *Third Annual Report of the National Labor Relations Board* (1938), p. 77 n.

[128] *NLRB* v. *Mackay Radio and Telegraph Co.*, 304 U.S. 333 (1938).

labor practice of the employer caused the strike or prolonged it, the workers are entitled to reinstatement in their jobs with back pay, even though this involves the discharge of some workers who were employed during the strike.[129] In one case where the Board found that a strike was caused partly by an unfair labor practice of the employer and partly by the workers, it considered that the strike was caused by the employer's actions, and the strikers must be rehired with back pay.[130] The duty of reinstatement with back pay exists, although the strike was contrary to the law of the state wherein it occurred.[131]

The Supreme Court has held that the striker who commits a criminal act does not have to be restored to his position,[132] but the Board generally considers that felonies are the only significant crimes. Misdemeanors including various acts of violence rarely are regarded as important, and employees who engage in such activities generally must be reinstated.[133] The only proof of a felony that the Board will accept is conviction or a plea of guilty.[134] This attitude of the Board toward illegal acts of strikers does not assist in discouraging the resort to violence in labor disputes.

The government makes difficult the operation of a struck plant.

The employer who attempts to operate a plant during a strike does so at great risk under the National Labor Relations Act. The employment of strike-breakers is regarded by the NLRB as an interference with the right of employees to organize,[135] and the movement of strike-breakers in interstate commerce is prohibited by another law.[136] Individual strikers cannot be urged to return to work, since that con-

---

[129] *Chicago Casket Co.*, 21 NLRB 235 (1940).

[130] *Remington Rand Co.* v. *NLRB*, 94 Fed. (2d) 862, 872; but in *Mayer Handbag Co.*, 18 NLRB 700 (1939) where both causes were present, the Board did not order reinstatement.

[131] *Reed and Prince Mfg. Co.*, 12 NLRB 944 (1939). In *NLRB* v. *Draper Corp.*, 15 LRR 211 (1944), a circuit court of appeals held that an employer did not have to re-employ participants in a wildcat strike that disrupted collective bargaining by their own union, reversing 52 NLRB 1477 (1943).

[132] *NLRB* v. *Fansteel Metallurgical Corp.*, 306 U.S. 240 (1939).

[133] *Aronsson Printing Co.*, 13 NLRB 799 (1939); *Electric Vacuum Cleaner Co.*, 18 NLRB 591 (1939).

[134] *Republic Steel Co.*, 9 NLRB 219 (1938); *Elkland Leather Co.*, 8 NLRB 519 (1938).

[135] *Remington Rand Co.*, 2 NLRB 626 (1936).

[136] Act of June 29, 1938, 52 Stat. 1242.

stitutes an attempted interference with the worker's right to organize and to bargain collectively.

By "undercutting" in this manner the authority of the Union to act as collective bargaining representative, and by bringing to bear the coercive force of its economic power upon the employees to the end that they disregard the Union and union leadership and terminate the strike, the Company interfered with, restrained and coerced the employees. . . .[137]

The employer cannot urge the strikers to return to work through advertisements or through the publicity activities of a citizens' committee.[138] Any of these acts constitutes an unfair labor practice, and the employer will be required to reinstate all the strikers with back pay from the time the unfair labor practice took place.

The inability of the employer to urge striking employees to return to work places him at a disadvantage. It generally has been difficult for him to secure new workers during a strike. But the Labor Relations Act increases his difficulties, for if he commits one unfair labor practice in his efforts to operate a struck plant, he will have to take back all the striking employees with back pay, even though this involves the discharge of newly hired workers. Obviously, it will not be easy for him to convince workers hired during the strike that their employment will continue after the work stoppage. As just pointed out, he cannot urge his striking employees to return to work. If the employer commits one small indiscretion in an attempt to operate his plant during a strike (that may not have been caused by him), great burdens can be imposed upon him, and consequently the easiest course may be for the owner to shut down the plant during the strike. In the meantime he might lose his markets; but the striking employees can go out to seek new employment. These burdens are imposed upon the employer without regard to the merits of the dispute or the methods used by the employees during the strikes.

The United States Employment Service grants assistance to striking employees. The act of June 6, 1933[139] provides that the state employment services should not refer workers to a plant in which there is a strike unless such persons are given specific notice of that strike. The original rules of the USES required that both written

---

[137] *Manville Jenckes Corp.*, 30 NLRB 382, 406 (1941).

[138] *T. W. Hepler*, 7 NLRB 255 (1938). But he can make an accurate statement to strikers on the state of negotiations with the union, *Essex Rubber Co.*, 50 NLRB 283 (1943).

[139] 48 Stat. 117, Sec. 11 (b).

and oral notice had to be given, but nevertheless few referrals were made to struck plants.[140] But at least by January 1942 the regulations were amended to prohibit absolutely the referral of any applicant to a struck plant, except where the strike was contrary to an order of the National War Labor Board.[141]

This regulation does not appear to be fully in accord with the Employment Service Act of 1933. The law says notice of the strike must be given and does not prohibit the making of such placements. The Employment Service thus gives aid to the union, whatever may be the merits of the strike. The theory appears to be that the workers are in the right whenever they strike, or even if not in the right, that they deserve assistance nevertheless. But can such a practice be followed without encouraging strikes for improper objectives or the use of illegal methods in the strike?

III. PICKETING

The United States courts have long recognized the propriety and legality of picketing in labor disputes.[142] In support of this position Chief Justice Taft in 1922 asserted that if it is desirable for labor to organize and to strike, then it is proper for the workers to attempt to secure the support of like-minded persons for their cause. Here the Court was justifying only peaceful picketing;[143] it maintained that a person had a right to have his property protected against picketing accompanied by violence. A state that prevented the issuance of injunctions to prevent disorderly picketing was held to deprive employers of their property without due process of law.[144]

Today there are practically no limits imposed on the right to picket.

By the Norris-LaGuardia Act, Congress in 1932 effectively prohibited federal courts from enjoining picketing in labor disputes,[145]

---

[140] Atkinson, Odencrantz, and Demming, *Public Employment Service in the United States* (1938), p. 346.

[141] U.S. Employment Service, *Operations Bulletin C2*, Jan. 5, 1942, and *C33*, May 6, 1942.

[142] The states generally regard picketing as legal, but several require that it can only be engaged in where a majority of the employees have voted for it.

[143] He also said that a "necessary element of intimidation" was involved in all picketing, and he permitted only one picket at each entrance, *American Steel Foundries* v. *Tri-City Central Trades Council*, 257 U.S. 184 (1921).

[144] *Truax* v. *Corrigan*, 257 U.S. 312 (1921).

[145] Act of Mar. 23, 1932, 47 Stat. 70, Sec. 4 (e).

and the courts have upheld the validity of the law. Although there is no actual labor dispute between an employer and his own employees, picketing cannot be enjoined.[146]

The Norris-LaGuardia Act makes it impossible to enjoin picketing even when carried on contrary to the objectives of the National Labor Relations Act. If an employer properly recognizes and bargains with a union representing the majority of the workers in a unit appropriate for collective bargaining purposes, his place of business can be picketed although no members of the union picketing are employed by him. It would be illegal for the employer to deal with that union, yet the courts have held that such picketing cannot be enjoined.[147] Again, if the employees in an establishment do not care to join a specific union and have so informed their employer, that union may picket the place of business, although it would be illegal for the employer to deal with it, because his employees have indicated their unwillingness to have it represent them in collective bargaining.[148]

The Supreme Court also has held that there is an absolute constitutional right to picket. The basis for this decision is the liberty guaranteed under the First and Fourteenth Amendments. Consequently the right cannot be impaired by either the federal government or the states. Mr. Justice Murphy speaking for the Court said:

. . . Freedom of discussion, if it would fulfill its historic function in this nation, must embrace all issues about which information is needed or appropriate to enable the members of society to cope with the exigencies of their period.

In the circumstances of our times the dissemination of information concerning the facts of a labor dispute must be regarded as within that area of free discussion that is guaranteed by the Constitution. . . . It is recognized now that satisfactory hours and wages and working conditions in industry and a bargaining position which makes these possible have an importance which is not less than the interests of those in the business or industry directly concerned. The health of the present generation and of those as yet unborn may depend on these matters, and the practices in a single factory may have economic repercussions upon a whole region and affect widespread systems of marketing. . . .[149]

[146] *New Negro Alliance* v. *Sanitary Grocery Co.*, 303 U.S. 552 (1938).
[147] *Fur Workers Union, Local No. 72* v. *Fur Workers Union, No. 21238*, 105 Fed. (2d) 1, 308 U.S. 522 (1939).
[148] *Lauf* v. *Shinner*, 303 U.S. 323 (1938).
[149] *Thornhill* v. *Alabama*, 310 U.S. 88, 102 (1940).

Consequently a state statute that prevents picketing in a labor dispute is unconstitutional.

A state cannot prohibit picketing though carried on by a union that sought unsuccessfully to organize a plant, and where the actual employees have no controversy with their employer. The Supreme Court said: "The interdependence of economic interest of all engaged in the same industry has become a commonplace. . . . The right of free communication cannot therefore be mutilated by denying it to workers, in a dispute with an employer, even though they are not in his employ."[150] An employer cannot enjoin picketing by a union which does not represent any of his employees, though its objective is to secure a closed-shop agreement.[151] The false nature of statements made by pickets does not constitute a basis for enjoining the use of such statements. Even where the courts have definitely found that the language used was false and damaging, the Supreme Court has held it cannot be enjoined by a state court.[152]

If the picketing involves violence, or when it is not carried on at the scene of the labor dispute, the state courts may intervene. Where force and violence are a part of a labor dispute, a state may permit its courts to enjoin picketing that contributes to such violence. Though violence has occurred as a consequence of picketing, peaceful picketing cannot be forbidden.[153]

However, a state court can prohibit picketing that occurs at a place removed from the scene of the labor dispute. Thus where nonunion labor was employed by a contractor to make repairs on one of two restaurants owned by the same person, the state courts can enjoin the carpenters' union from picketing the other restaurant located one and a half miles away from the place being repaired.[154]

The full extent of the constitutional right to picket is not clear. The picketing must be peaceful and must be carried on close to the scene of the dispute. It is not necessary that the union involved be the representative of any employees of the person being picketed. But does this right mean more? Can picketing, although peaceful, be in such force as to prevent access to the place of business involved? Some of the decisions seem to indicate that such conduct could not be en-

---

[150] A.F. of L. v. Swing, 312 U.S. 321, 326 (1941).
[151] Senn v. Tile Layers Union, 301 U.S. 468 (1937).
[152] Cafeteria Employees Union v. Angelos, 320 U.S. 293 (1943).
[153] Mills Drivers Union v. Meadowmoor Dairies Inc., 312 U.S. 287 (1941).
[154] Carpenters and Joiners Union v. Ritters Cafe, 315 U.S. 722 (1942).

joined. It has been shown that under the Norris-LaGuardia Act picketing is permitted even where its purpose is to get the employer to commit an unfair labor practice prohibited by the Labor Relations Act. Does the constitutional guarantee also prevent such picketing from being enjoined? There are no cases on this point, and it would not be entirely logical to believe that it would; but in decisions declaring the existence of the constitutional right, the definition of a labor dispute is broad enough to include such a situation. It would not appear to be equitable to permit persons to damage an employer's business by picketing in order to compel him to break the law.

IV. BOYCOTTS

The Supreme Court has defined a boycott as "a combination not merely to refrain from dealing with the complainant" (an employer) "or to advise or by peaceful means to persuade customers to refrain from dealing," but also for the purpose of exercising coercive pressure upon such customers, actual or prospective, in order to cause them to withhold or withdraw patronage through fear of loss or damage to themselves should they deal with that employer.[155] The Court has held that boycotts were illegal where they were carried on with the intent of reducing interstate commerce in an unreasonable manner. Consequently it permitted an injunction to be issued to prevent workers from refusing to transport or to set up printing presses made by nonunion labor.[156] Similar relief was granted where the boycott consisted of a refusal by union members to work on stone that had been partially prepared by nonunion workers employed by a previous processor.[157] A union which had gone on strike was enjoined from coercing third persons to refrain from buying goods produced by the employer.[158] In a similar case the court approved of a judgment for triple damages under the Anti-Trust Act.[159]

*Practically no boy-
cott is now illegal.*

It is very dubious whether the boycotts involved in these cases would be regarded as illegal today. The Norris-LaGuardia Act pro-

[155] *Duplex Printing Press Co.* v. *Deering*, 254 U.S. 443 (1921).
[156] The same.
[157] *Bedford Cut Stone Co.* v. *Journeymen Stone Cutters*, 274 U.S. 37 (1927).
[158] *Gompers* v. *Buck Stove and Range Co.*, 221 U.S. 418 (1911).
[159] *Loewe* v. *Lawlor*, 208 U.S. 274 (1908).

hibits the granting of injunctions in cases comparable to those just mentioned.[160] The House and Senate judiciary committees in their reports on this bill specifically stated that it was intended to prevent the issuance of injunctions in such cases.[161] In *New Negro Alliance* v. *Sanitary Grocery Co.*[162] the Court held that a boycott occurring in a labor dispute could not be enjoined because of this law.

The opinion of the Supreme Court in *U.S.* v. *Hutcheson*[163] would lead one to believe that the Court now considers that practically any boycott connected with a labor dispute would be legal. First, the Court said that the enactment of the Norris-LaGuardia Act constituted a direct disapproval of two of the leading boycott cases. And second, it stated that so long as the union acted in its self-interest and not in co-operation with employers, practically no concerted act was illegal under the Anti-Trust Act.

The discharge of an employee who engages in a boycott would be discriminatory under Section 8 (3) of the National Labor Relations Act. An employee cannot be discharged, though while actively employed, he attempts to persuade groups in the community that his employer has attempted to injure them.[164] In affirming this decision of the NLRB, the Circuit Court of Appeals said, "such activities may be highly detrimental to the employer; his customers may refuse to deal with him;—but the statute forbids him by a discharge to rid himself of those who lay such burdens upon him."[165]

The National Labor Relations Act offers the employer no protection against boycotts designed to compel him to violate that act. In a recent case the wagon drivers of a brewery had withdrawn from the teamsters' union and joined the brewery workers' union. The teamsters' union then boycotted the brewery to get it to bargain with that union. In order to end the boycott the brewery gave up its delivery business and contracted for it to be done by another company that had an agreement with the teamsters' union. Since it had no need for its wagon drivers, it discharged them (members of the brewery work-

---

[160] Act of Mar. 23, 1932, 47 Stat. 70, Sec. 4 (a).

[161] *To Define and Limit Jurisdiction of Courts Sitting in Equity*, S. Rept. 163, and the same, H. Rept. 669, 72 Cong. 1 sess.

[162] 303 U.S. 552 (1938).

[163] 312 U.S. 219 (1940); but also see *Apex Hosiery Co.* v. *Leader*, 310 U.S. 469 (1940).

[164] *Peter Cailler Kohler Swiss Chocolate Co.*, 33 NLRB 1170 (1941).

[165] 130 Fed. (2d) 503 (1942).

ers' union). The NLRB held that this discharge was discriminatory and ordered the drivers reinstated with back pay.[166] Although it would have been a violation of the act for the employer to have recognized the teamsters' union, nothing was done to punish that union for the boycott designed to compel a violation of law. It is doubtful if a court could have enjoined such a boycott under the Norris-LaGuardia Act.

The federal government in defining its attitude toward picketing appears to have assumed that the injury that might occur to innocent third parties and the burden on interstate commerce would be small, as compared with the public advantage resulting from any possible gains in the bargaining power of the boycotters.

V. RESPONSIBILITY AND LIABILITY FOR CONCERTED ACTION

The peculiar legal nature of trade unions has had a direct bearing on their civil responsibility and liability for wrongful acts committed by them against individuals. Unions are creatures of state law, and generally they are partnerships or unincorporated associations. Chief Justice Taft has said: "Undoubtedly at common law, an unincorporated association of persons was not recognized as having any other character than a partnership in whatever was done."[167] Under this theory each and every member would be fully responsible for every act done either by any member acting in his capacity as a member or by an employee or agent of the union acting within the scope of his authority.[168] This situation has been greatly modified by recent legislation.

*The legal responsibility and liability
of unions and their members is very limited today.*

The Norris-LaGuardia Act (Section 6) has greatly restricted the responsibility of unions in any proceeding in a federal court. Under it a member of a union is responsible only for the unlawful acts of members, agents, or officers where there is clear proof either of his participation in the act or of his authorization of it before or after its commission. This law would practically prevent an action to assess responsibility against the members of a union for an unlawful act

---

[166] Gluck Brewing Co., 47 NLRB 1079 (1940); affirmed CCA 8th Circuit, 14 LRR 791 (1944).
[167] *United Mine Workers* v. *Coronado Coal Co.*, 259 U.S. 344, 385 (1922).
[168] *Loewe* v. *Lawlor*, 208 U.S. 274 (1908).

such as a boycott. It would be necessary to prove in each case that the individual sued took part in it or specifically authorized it. Under the War Labor Disputes Act any labor organization which calls a strike in a war production plant without giving thirty days' notice is liable for damages resulting from such work stoppage.[169]

As partnerships under the common law, unions could be sued only in the name of their members, and their liability could be enforced only against each member.[170] Union assets could be attached only if each and every member of the union was directly or effectively served. Actually this requirement made such funds immune from liability.

In 1922 in a case involving damages for the violation of the Anti-Trust law, the Supreme Court held that a union could be sued in its common name and without joining all of its members.[171] It reached this conclusion for three reasons: (1) the difficulty of serving each member of a large union (in this case there were 400,000 members); (2) by law special privileges had been conferred on unions as entities (for example, the union label is protected); and (3) if the union's funds were immune from suit, it would not have a responsibility and liability commensurate with its power. Thus where responsibility is recognized, the federal courts impose a direct liability on the union funds to pay any judgment. Not all state courts have followed this decision, and some states have not adopted legislation modifying the normal common law rule concerning the attachment of partnership funds.

The NLRB has prevented an employer from demanding that a union assume a direct liability for its wrongful acts where this is not imposed by state law. Where the state makes it difficult to sue an unincorporated union, it is a violation of the employees' right of self organization for the employer to insist upon the union's incorporation.[172] In order to avoid the difficulty of attaching union funds in an action for breach of contract some employers have demanded that the union post a bond before entering into a collective agreement. The Board considers that this requirement is a refusal to bargain in violation of Section 8 (5) of the National Labor Relations Act.[173]

---

[169] Act of June 25, 1943, 57 Stat. 167, Sec. 8 (c).
[170] *United Mine Workers* v. *Coronado Coal Co.*, 259 U.S. 344 (1922).
[171] The same.
[172] *Jasper Blackburn Products*, 21 NLRB 124 (1940).
[173] *Scripto Mfg. Co.*, 36 NLRB 411 (1941).

VI. CONCLUSIONS

To increase the bargaining power of workers, the federal government protects their right to engage in concerted activities. Not only do employees have the right to organize, but the government encourages them to exercise that right. By the National Labor Relations Act as applied by the National Labor Relations Board, any act of an employer that might discourage organizational activities is prohibited. The right to strike is almost without limitation. Striking employees cannot be discharged, and in a number of ways the government makes it difficult for an employer to operate his plant when the workers are on strike. Other forms of concerted action are also protected. Workers have a constitutional right to picket, and this right has been construed broadly by the courts. Further, almost no restraints exist on the right to boycott. Finally the legal responsibility and liability of unions are limited.

Apparently the federal government considers the protection of these rights to engage in concerted activities to be of transcendent importance. Even where administrative or civil remedies are available, employees can enforce their rights through concerted action. Such self help can be used, though adequate peaceful remedies exist. The government does not discourage self help even where it has set up machinery to protect employees' rights. Workers can utilize concerted action, though in the process they commit illegal acts, and though they seek to accomplish undesirable objectives.

CHAPTER III

COLLECTIVE BARGAINING AND THE COLLECTIVE AGREEMENT

In the preceding chapter there have been frequent references to organized labor's practice of collective bargaining and the collective bargaining agreement, but without any attempt at definition or precise description. In the present chapter three aspects of the collective bargaining agreement will be discussed in detail: (1) What is the nature of the employer's obligation to bargain collectively? (2) What kind of contract is the collective agreement which embodies the terms of employment agreed upon through the collective bargaining process? and (3) What rights and obligations do the employers, employees, and unions have under such an agreement?

I. THE NATURE OF THE OBLIGATION TO BARGAIN COLLECTIVELY

One of the major objectives of labor organizations from their very inception has been to make definite collective agreements with employers fixing the terms of employment for workers. But the employers strongly resisted the unions' efforts to negotiate such contracts, and only ten years ago hardly more than a million employees were covered by such agreements.[1] Consequently labor sought the help of the government in its efforts to fix the terms of employment by contract. After a decade of government assistance, more than 14 million persons are employed under such agreements.[2] With this great increase in collective bargaining, the reader might well wonder what has been the government's attiude toward it. The provisions of the Railway Labor Act concerning collective bargaining will be considered first. Then the obligation as envisaged by the National War Labor Board will be discussed. Finally, the general obligation imposed by the National Labor Relations Act and applied by the NLRB will be examined.

A. The Railway Labor Act

The Railway Labor Act of 1934 declares: "It shall be the duty of all carriers, their officers, agents, and employees to exert every rea-

[1] National Labor Relations Board, press release, Apr. 12, 1943.
[2] *Monthly Labor Review*, Vol. 60 (1943), p. 817.

sonable effort to make and maintain agreements concerning rates of pay, rules and working conditions."[3] And Section 2, Ninth, provides that after the National Mediation Board has designated the representatives of the employees in the bargaining unit, the carrier "shall treat with" them. These provisions can be enforced only by an injunction restraining the carrier from dealing with any other group of workers. This will be issued only after the National Mediation Board has designated the representatives of the workers. A court can direct a carrier to treat with the representatives of a majority of the workers in the appropriate unit and can prohibit it from making a collective agreement with any other organization. The decree can be enforced by contempt proceedings.

The participation in the process and not the desirability of the results is the only test.

In the one case involving this question, the Supreme Court said with special reference to the obligation "to treat with" the representatives:

> . . . The statute does not undertake to compel agreement between the employer and employees, but it does command those preliminary steps without which no agreement can be reached. It at least requires the employer to meet and confer with the authorized representative of its employees, to listen to their complaints, to make reasonable effort to compose differences. . . . [4]

The employer then must meet with representatives, listen to complaints, and make "reasonable effort to compose differences." The obligation "to make reasonable effort to compose differences" is not defined further. Some courts have held that the agreements made under this section are not legally enforceable contracts.[5]

The National Mediation Board has said, concerning this obligation to bargain:

> As has frequently been pointed out the fundamental purpose of the Railway Labor Act is to facilitate the establishment of labor standards governing employment on the railroads and air lines through collective bargaining. The best test of the soundness of the act is therefore the extent to which labor agreements defining such standards have been entered into between

[3] Act of June 21, 1934, 48 Stat. 1185, Sec. 2 First.
[4] *Virginian Ry. Co.* v. *System Federation No. 40*, 300 U.S. 515, 548 (1937).
[5] *Moore* v. *Illinois Central Ry. Co.*, 112 Fed. (2d.) 959 (1940).

the various types of carriers subject to the act and the different crafts and classes of their employees.[6]

The law as applied constitutes little more than the expression of a wish that employees and employers should bargain. Nevertheless collective bargaining under it has spread with little friction.

B. The National War Labor Board

The National War Labor Board is given jurisdiction during the present hostilities to settle any dispute that interrupts or threatens to interrupt war production. It can by order prescribe the wages, hours, and all other terms of employment. It has repeatedly held that employers and employees have a legal duty to bargain together. Resort to the Board is no substitute for direct bargaining.[7] It has remanded cases to the parties for further bargaining when it felt that they were trying to pass on to the Board the task of settling their problem.[8] This practice of directing the parties to settle the dispute has not proved to be very successful, since the Board generally has got the case again.[9]

The NWLB required the employer to make collective agreements.

In the settlement of dispute cases, the Board has taken the attitude that not only is there a duty to bargain, but there is a legal duty to make collective agreements.[10] Further, the Board has insisted that the results of its decisions must be embodied in an agreement and not remain merely its judgment comparable to an award of a court. The employer cannot insist on including in such an agreement a statement that it was made under duress.[11]

The Board takes the attitude that its decisions constitute binding directives that the employer must obey. The Court of Appeals of the District of Columbia has held that its decisions are unenforceable and constitute only advice.[12] Nevertheless, as will be shown in Chapter X,

---

[6] *Third Annual Report of the National Mediation Board* (1937), p. 2.

[7] *Yellow Truck and Coach Mfg. Co.*, 5 WLR 244 (1942); *Chrysler Corp.*, 10 WLR 551 (1943).

[8] *Diamond State Telephone Co.*, 5 WLR 329 (1942); *Cranston Print Works*, 5 WLR 451 (1942).

[9] 44 Columbia Law Rev. 412, note 17 (1944).

[10] *Montgomery Ward and Co.*, 10 WLR 415, 420 (1943).

[11] *Montgomery Ward and Co.*, 5 WLR 80 (1942); note 11 LRRM 1720 (1943).

[12] *National War Labor Board v. Montgomery Ward and Co.*, 144 Fed. (2d) 528 (1944); *NWLB v. United States Gypsum Co.*, 145 Fed. (2d) 97 (1944).

if the employer fails to obey such a determination of the Board, it reports the matter to the President and he may seize the employer's plant that is involved in the dispute.

When the National War Labor Board settles a dispute that is presented, it does not simply issue a determination prescribing the terms of employment; it requires the parties to enter into a collective agreement containing specified terms. Although the contract is made under duress (for if it is not made the employer will lose his property by summary seizure), the Board will not permit the employer to incorporate in it a clause to that effect. The reason for refusing to permit the inclusion of such a statement is because a contract made under duress is voidable. The National War Labor Board advanced no foundation for its statement that there is a legal obligation to enter into collective agreements. Neither the National Labor Relations Act nor the National War Labor Disputes Act of 1943 constitute any basis for it.

C. Under the National Labor Relations Act

Collective bargaining, as envisaged under the National Labor Relations Act, is a procedure that ultimately culminates in the making of a collective agreement by the employer and the accredited representatives of his employees concerning wages, hours, and other conditions of employment. This act imposes upon employers the positive duty to bargain collectively[13] with the representatives selected for the purposes of collective bargaining by a majority of the employees in a unit appropriate for such purposes,[14] and it also prohibits the employer from negotiating collective agreements with representatives of minority groups of employees where a majority of the employees already has selected a representative.[15] This duty to bargain collectively includes an obligation to carry on discussions and to negotiate, with a sincere purpose of finding a basis of agreement concerning the issues presented[16] and, if an understanding is reached, the employer must be willing to sign a binding written agreement that contains these

[13] Sec. 8 (5).
[14] Sec. 9 (a).
[15] *NLRB* v. *Jones and Laughlin Steel Co.*, 301 U.S. 1 (1937).
[16] *Singer Manufacturing Co.*, 24 NLRB 444 (1940).

provisions.[17] But the employer is not required to enter into an agreement if an understanding cannot be reached.[18]

The employer must deal only with the representative chosen by a majority of his employees.

The employer is obligated to bargain collectively with the representative of all his workers. Foremen and other supervisory employees are included.[19] The term "employees" within the meaning of Section 8 (5) and 9 (a) includes any individual whose work has ceased as a consequence of or in connection with any strike or as a result of an unfair labor practice of the employer and who has not secured any other regular or substantially equivalent employment.[20] Hence, a worker does not cease to be an employee because he participated in a strike that is legal under the act.[21] Thus the employer's duty to bargain continues though his employees have ceased to work for him.

If a majority of the workers has chosen a representative, the employer can deal only with it. The representative selected by the majority of the employees in a unit appropriate for such purposes is the exclusive representative of all the employees in such unit for the purposes of collective bargaining. The act does not define the term "majority." The National Labor Relations Board and the courts have interpreted the phrase "majority of the employees" to mean a majority of the eligible employees voting in the election, and therefore the organization receiving a majority of the votes cast is the exclusive representative of all the employees.[22]

The term "representative" as used in the National Labor Relations Act, the Railway Labor Act, and the state labor relations acts includes any individual or labor organization.[23] Actually the employees have generally designated or selected labor organizations as representatives for the purpose of collective bargaining. Even though a state law requires that all union representatives be licensed, it is a violation of the obligation to bargain for the employer to refuse to deal with an

---

[17] *H. F. Heinz Co.* v. *NLRB*, 311 U.S. 514 (1941).
[18] *NLRB* v. *Sands Manufacturing Co.*, 96 Fed. (2d) 721 (1938).
[19] *Packard Motor Co.*, Case No. 7R1884 (1945) reversing, *Maryland Drydock Co.*, 49 NLRB 733 (1943).
[20] *Mooresville Cotton Mills* v. *NLRB*, 97 Fed. (2d) 959 (1938).
[21] *S. L. Allen and Co. Inc.*, 1 NLRB 714 (1936).
[22] *R.C.A. Manufacturing Co.*, 2 NLRB 159 (1936).
[23] 49 Stat. 449, Sec. 2 (4), 48 Stat. 1185, Sec. 1 (6).

unlicensed representative.[24] The employer cannot refuse to deal wth a specific representative because he believes that the labor organization is irresponsible.[25]

The employees need not hold an election to determine their representatives. The law requires only that they must be designated or selected by a majority of the employees in the appropriate unit.[26] Formal certification by the Board is not necessary either. Board action is required only when there is a dispute regarding the appropriate unit, when it is uncertain whether any labor organization represents a majority of the employees within an appropriate unit, or when two or more contending unions each claim to represent a majority of the employees.[27]

The representatives of a majority of the employees exclusively represent all the employees.

A labor organization that has been chosen by less than a majority of the workers bargains collectively for its members only. If, however, it is subsequently designated by a majority, it becomes the exclusive representative of all the employees in the appropriate bargaining unit.[28] It is not material that all the employees who designate the union as their agent should be members of it. Nor does the act require such employees to become members subsequently.[29] Even workers who for various reasons are not eligible to join a union may be included in the bargaining unit and may designate the union as their representative for collective bargaining.[30] But persons hired to take the place of strikers during a labor dispute caused by or prolonged by an unfair labor practice of the employer are not entitled to participate with the strikers in the selection of a bargaining representative.[31]

If a majority of the employees in a bargaining unit has designated a labor organization, that organization is the sole representative of the employees; the employer can deal with it solely as a principal

[24] *Eppinger and Russell Co.*, 56 NLRB 1258 (1944).
[25] *Inland Steel Co.*, 9 NLRB 783 (1938).
[26] *Benjamin and Marjorie Fainblatt*, 4 NLRB 596 (1937).
[27] *Stewart Die Casting Corp.*, 14 NLRB 872 (1939).
[28] *Burnside Steel Foundry Co.*, 7 NLRB 714 (1938).
[29] *Webster Mfg. Co. Inc.*, 27 NLRB 1338 (1940).
[30] *Luckenbach Steamship Co.*, 2 NLRB 181 (1936).
[31] *A. Sartorious and Co. Inc.*, 40 NLRB 107 (1942).

and not as agent. The employer can meet the requirements of the act only by showing a willingness to bargain collectively, accompanied by the recognition of the negotiator as the representative of the union, and of the union as the proper party to the negotiations as well as to the resulting agreement.[32] As the National Labor Relations Board put it, the employer has to accord the union "recognition as such."[33] This recognition includes the acknowledgment that the union is the exclusive bargaining agent, the sole authorized representative of the employees of the appropriate unit for the purpose of collective bargaining. This unconditional recognition cannot be made the subject of collective bargaining at any stage of the negotiations.[34] The employer thus must refrain from negotiating generally applicable labor contracts with representatives of minority groups.[35] Any minority of the employees who did not join in designating the representative selected by the majority is nevertheless represented by the organization chosen by that group. But in the absence of representatives selected by the majority of the employees, a minority group has the right to choose its own representatives.[36]

Collective bargaining involves face to face negotiating about the terms of employment.

Normally the procedure of collective bargaining involves personal conferences. Bargaining should be conducted on a face to face basis. Negotiations through the mails or by other indirect methods are not considered as fulfilling the statutory requirements unless both parties accept that procedure.[37] The employer must bargain at the place where

---

[32] *Hopwood Retinning Co.*, 4 NLRB 922 (1938); *NLRB* v. *Griswold Mfg. Co.*, 106 Fed. (2d) 713 (1939).

[33] *Lindeman Power and Equipment Co.*, 11 NLRB 868 (1939).

[34] *Acme Air Appliance Co. Inc.*, 10 NLRB 1385 (1939).

[35] *NLRB* v. *Jones and Laughlin Corp.*, 301 U.S. 1 (1937).

[36] *Peninsular and Occidental SS Co.*, v. *NLRB* 98 Fed. (2d) 411, 414 (1938).

However, it is not an unfair labor practice within the meaning of the act for an employer to refuse to discuss grievances with employee representatives not representing the majority of his employees (*Mooreville Cotton Mills*, 2 NLRB 952, 1937). The National War Labor Board in a case in which the employees were without a majority representative directed that the employer should recognize a minority union to the extent that the union could present grievances relative to its members in accordance with a procedure prescribed by the Board. But the term "grievance" as used in this decision does not include any matter properly the subject of collective bargaining. *Sperry Gyroscope Co.*, 1 WLR 167 (1942).

[37] *S. L. Allen and Co.*, 1 NLRB 714, 728 (1936).

the bargaining unit is located, even though this involves much travel and repeated negotiations.[38]

Almost any problem of employer-employee relations may be the subject of collective bargaining negotiations. Section 9 (a) of the National Labor Relations Act provides that collective bargaining includes the determination of "rates of pay, wages, hours of employment, or other conditions of employment." The term "conditions of employment" is very broad.[39] It includes negotiating concerning the reinstatement of discharged employees as well as determining in which plants of an employer various operations are to be performed. But problems not directly related to the conditions of employment are outside the subject matter of collective bargaining under the act. Employers are not required to bargain about legislative policies and other generalities.[40]

The employees must first in-
dicate their desire to bargain.

Although the employer is under no obligation to initiate collective bargaining, he must carry on such negotiations when the proper agents of his employees request it.[41] The request need not be made in a formal manner. It is sufficient that the employees or their representatives give to the employer some indication of their desire to bargain.[42] The Supreme Court has held that the employer is not obliged to bargain collectively unless the employees or their representatives either by word or act apprise him of their desire to negotiate. Consequently he may ignore or reject proposals for collective bargaining which come from third persons not purporting to act with the authority of his employees.[43]

The employer must honestly
seek to reach an agreement.

The obligation to bargain collectively within the meaning of the National Labor Relations Act is fulfilled only when the employer

[38] *Stehle and Co.,* 11 NLRB 1397 (1939); *P. Lorillard and Co.,* 16 NLRB 703 (1939); affirmed 314 U.S. 512 (1942).
[39] *Consumers Research,* 2 NLRB 57, 74 (1936); *Brown McLaren Mfg. Co.,* 34 NLRB 984 (1941).
[40] *Globe Cotton Mills* v. NLRB, 103 Fed. (2d) 91, 94.
[41] *NLRB* v. *Columbian Enamel and Stamping Co.,* 306 U.S. 292 (1939).
[42] The same.
[43] The same.

makes a forthright, candid effort to reach a mutually binding settlement with his employees. The employer must bargain in good faith. The Board can test the sincerity of the employer's efforts by the length of time involved in the negotiations, the frequency of meetings, and his persistence in offering opportunities for agreement.[44] The content that the Board has given to "good faith" will be considered more fully shortly.

The employer is under the obligation to bargain until an agreement is reached, or until he is justified in believing that further negotiations would be fruitless and settlement beyond the bounds of reasonable probability.[45] There are two principles that indicate the limits of this obligation. First, as the Senate Committee on Education and Labor said in its report on the National Labor Relations Act "the duty to bargain collectively does not carry with it the duty to reach an agreement."[46] Second, when an impasse has developed, the duty to bargain terminates. "Every avenue and possibility of negotiation must be exhausted before it should be admitted that an irreconcilable difference"[47] exists. When the facts show the futility of future bargaining, the employer's obligations are terminated.[48]

The National Labor Relations Board asserts that it wants a determination of the existence of an impasse to be based on objective facts, rather than on the personal ideas or feelings of the parties concerned. Before the Board will admit the existence of irreconcilable differences creating an impasse, the employer must show that every possibility of negotiation was exhausted, and that there existed no common ground upon which further bargaining could continue.[49] He must also demonstrate that the breakdown of the negotiations is due to differences over "real and substantial issues."[50] Hence, the onus of proof rests upon the employer.

The actual facts in each case are most important for determining the existence of an impasse. In the *Express Publishing Company* case

[44] *NLRB* v. *Sands Mfg. Co.*, 96 Fed. (2d) 721, 725 (1938).
[45] *Columbian Enameling and Stamping Co.*, 1 NLRB 181, 196 (1936).
[46] *National Labor Relations Board*, S. Rept. 573, 74 Cong. 1 sess., p. 12.
[47] *Sands Mfg. Co.*, 1 NLRB 546 (1936).
[48] *Republic Creosoting Co.*, 19 NLRB 267 (1940).
[49] *Trenton Garment Co.*, 4 NLRB 1186 (1938); *Essex Wire Corp.*, 19 NLRB 51, 63 (1940).
[50] *Seas Shipping Co.*, 4 NLRB 757 (1938); *Purity Biscuit Co.*, 13 NLRB 917 (1939).

the employer met with employees' representatives four times and permitted them to state their demands. He said the union's demands were "unreasonable and unacceptable" and would give no other reasons for rejecting them. He would not discuss them clause by clause, nor would he advance counter-proposals. The Board considered that this was a refusal to bargain and not an impasse, because the employer's conduct made productive negotiations impossible, since he avoided stating any positive terms on which an agreement could be reached.[51] But where the union was negotiating for a new agreement containing added concessions from the employer, and the employer was willing to extend the existing agreement, the Board found an impasse. Here the employer discussed each union demand and explained his reasons for rejecting it.[52]

The occurrence of an impasse does not free the employer completely from his duty to bargain collectively. Where subsequent events introduce new issues or present to the employer and the employees another opportunity to explore the situation, the employer upon request must again meet with the representatives of his employees to determine the possibility of an agreement which would be acceptable to both parties in the light of the then existing circumstances.[53]

*The employer's good faith is tested by both
the form and substance of the negotiations.*

As a result of the meaning given to the requirement that the employer must demonstrate good faith in bargaining, the NLRB has put itself in a position where possibly it can indirectly exercise a control over the conditions of employment. Good faith must be evident not only in the procedural aspects of negotiations but also in the substantive aspects.

The Board has made some broad statements concerning the nature of good faith in bargaining. Thus it has said "It must mean negotiation with a *bona fide* intent to reach an agreement if agreement is possible."[54] On another occasion it said "Interchange of ideas, communication of facts peculiarly within the knowledge of either party, personal persuasion and the opportunity to modify demands in accord-

---

[51] 13 NLRB 1213, 1223 (1939).
[52] *American Shoe Machinery Co.*, 23 NLRB 1315 (1940).
[53] *Kuehne Mfg. Co.*, 7 NLRB 304, 322 (1938).
[54] *Atlas Mills, Inc.*, 3 NLRB 10, 21 (1937).

ance with the total situation thus revealed at the conference is of the essence of the bargaining process."[55] It has stressed that the existence of good faith can only be determined in the light of each particular case.[56] But the Board's decisions tend to indicate that four principles have been used by it to determine the existence of good faith.[57] First there must be an actual exchange of views on the employees' proposals. The employer must be willing to discuss the suggested agreement and give his reasons why given clauses are unacceptable to him.[58]

Second, the employer must not use the bargaining process to discredit or undermine the bargaining representatives of his employees. He cannot utilize the process as a means of attempting to convince the employees that collective bargaining is futile. Thus the Board held that an employer demonstrated bad faith because during negotiations with a union he increased the hours of work and reduced the rate of pay by unilateral action.[59] An employer's unwillingness to embody the then existing terms of employment in an agreement indicated bad faith.[60] The employer cannot appeal to his individual employees over the heads of the bargaining representatives when they fail to accept the terms he desires.[61]

Third, if the employer gives false, untenable, or irrelevant reasons for refusing to bargain or for rejecting union proposals, he has demonstrated his bad faith. Thus he cannot refuse to bargain merely because the union involved changed its name.[62]

The fourth and last principle may be stated as follows; if the negotiations indicate that the collective bargaining process is only a sham and the employer has no real intention of making an agreement, he has demonstrated bad faith. If he rejects all of the proposals as unreasonable or unacceptable without further explanation,[63] or if he rejects a proposed agreement with many clauses because two of them

[55] S. L. Allen and Co. Inc., 1 NLRB 714, 728 (1936).
[56] M. H. Birge and Sons Co., 1 NLRB 731 (1936).
[57] See Ludwig Teller, Labor Disputes and Collective Bargaining (1940), Vol. 2, pp. 885-89.
[58] Express Publishing Co., 13 NLRB 1213 (1939).
[59] Windsor Mfg. Co., 20 NLRB 294, 318 (1940).
[60] Inland Lime and Stone Co., 24 NLRB 758, 771-72 (1940).
[61] Stewart Die Casting Corp., 14 NLRB 812 (1939); Shell Oil Co., 2 NLRB 835 (1937); Niles-Coleman Lumber Co., 4 NLRB 679 (1937).
[62] Continental Oil Co., 12 NLRB 789 (1939); Rabhor Co., 1 NLRB 470 (1936).
[63] Express Publishing Co., 13 NLRB 1213 (1939).

were "preposterous," bad faith is evident.[64] A failure on the part of the employer to make counterproposals is evidence of his determination to bargain without making an agreement.[65] If the employer does not advance counter proposals, he avoids presenting any positive terms on which an agreement can be reached, and under such circumstances negotiations productive of an agreement are impossible. Even where the counter proposals are not acceptable to the bargaining representatives, he must attempt to persuade them to accept the terms that he is willing to offer.[66]

The proposals rejected or submitted by the employer indicate his good faith.

In a number of cases the Board has tested the good faith of the employer by the results of the bargaining process. The desirability or undesirability from the standpoint of the Board of the proposals of the workers rejected by the employer and the counter proposals advanced by the employer is the final test of his good faith. Thus in one case the Board said:

Such clauses as the United [the union] sought are not unusual in collective agreements, and they tend to realize the purposes of the Act. . . . Moreover, whereas the clauses proposed by the United proceeded upon the recognition of the equal status, dignity, and responsibility of both the employer and the employees as contractually bound parties, the respondent, on the other hand, in effect insisted that the United accept an inferior position by agreeing to a contract which placed restrictions only upon the United. . . . Certainly, upon the record in the instant case, there was no warrant for such a position by the respondent.[67]

Here the Board asserted that the terms advanced by the union "tend to realize the purposes of the Act," while there was "no warrant" for the proposals of the employer. Hence the Board found that the employer lacked good faith and a sincere purpose, and therefore he had failed to bargain collectively.[68]

---

[64] *Farmeo Package Co.*, 6 NLRB 601 (1938).
[65] *Montgomery Ward and Co.*, 37 NLRB 100, 124 (1941).
[66] *Globe Cotton Mills v. NLRB*, 103 Fed. (2d) 91 (1939).
[67] *Singer Mfg. Co.*, 24 NLRB 444, 467 (1940).
[68] In several cases the Board tested the employer's good faith by evaluating the reasons for refusing the union's demands, and where his reasons were not satisfactory to the Board, it found that he had refused to bargain; *Highland Park Mfg. Co.*, 12 NLRB 1238 (1939); *Agwalines*, 2 NLRB 1 (1936); *NLRB v. Montgomery Ward and Co.*, 133 Fed. (2d) 676 (1943).

On a number of occasions the Board has held that an employer's refusal to grant a closed shop demonstrated his bad faith.[69] Thus it has said that his refusal to grant a closed shop did "not evidence a serious attempt upon the part of the respondent to come to an agreement with the Union."[70] On another occasion it observed: "Our experience has been that the cry of 'closed shop' is constantly being raised by employers who seek an excuse to evade their duty to bargain collectively under the act and to obstruct and deny the right of employees to do so."[71]

Where a union desires that an agreement should contain a clause providing for the arbitration of all disputes arising under it, the employer's refusal to grant this demand demonstrates his bad faith.[72] Similarly his failure to accept a union proposal to create a method of settling grievances indicates an unwillingness to bargain.[73]

In some cases certain positive demands made by the employer as against the union have been considered by the Board as evidence of bad faith. The Fair Labor Standards Act provides that an employer who guarantees his workers 1,000 hours of work in 26 weeks does not need to pay overtime unless his employees work more than 12 hours in any day or 56 hours in any week.[74] But if an employer demands the inclusion in a contract of a provision for such guaranteed employment, this is evidence of his unwillingness to bargain collectively.[75] Again, an employer demonstrates his bad faith if he desires that a contract provide that the union will not request a closed shop or a check-off during the life of the contract or during an extension of it.[76]

In some states it is difficult for an employer to recover damages from a union for a breach of contract. Nevertheless the employer is guilty of an unfair labor practice if he demands that the union post a bond guaranteeing its performance; this is true though he is willing

[69] *Columbian Enameling and Stamping Co.*, 1 NLRB 181 (1936); *Jackson Daily News*, 9 NLRB 120 (1938).

[70] The same, 128 (1938).

[71] *Second Annual Report of the National Labor Relations Board* (1937), p. 87.

[72] *Dallas Cartage Co.*, 14 NLRB 411 (1939); *Register Publishing Co.*, 44 NLRB 834 (1942).

[73] *Newark Rivet Works*, 9 NLRB 498 (1938).

[74] Act of June 25, 1938, 52 Stat. 1063, Sec. 7 (b) (1).

[75] *NLRB v. Reed and Prince Mfg. Co.*, 118 Fed. (2d) 874 (1941).

[76] The same.

to post one also. Posting a bond would place a handicap on labor, and "the act contemplates no such handicap to the employees."[77] Even in a state where an unincorporated union cannot be sued, the employer cannot demand that the union incorporate before he will make an agreement, because such a demand would interfere with the employees' freedom of organization.[78]

By saying what are and what are not the proper terms to include in a collective agreement, the Board tends to take upon itself the task of arbitrating labor disputes. It has done this only in a few instances, but if it can use a few substantive tests of good faith, it can use many. If the present Board can use tests that tend to aid organized labor, a Board with other members could use tests detrimental to labor unions.

Neither existing collective agreements nor individual employment contracts relieve the employer from bargaining.

The existence of a collective agreement does not preclude further bargaining between employer and employees,[79] but the employer cannot be compelled to give up his rights under a valid agreement.[80] Where an agreement already exists, the subjects of such negotiations may include extension, modification, termination, alleged violations, interpretation of the agreement, or adjustment of complaints, and the like.[81] The employer's obligation to bargain continues even though there are no particular problems or grievances to be considered.[82] The act contemplates collective bargaining as a continuing and developing process by which the relationship between employer and employees is to be molded and the terms and conditions of employment are to be progressively modified along lines which are mutually satisfactory to all concerned.

The Board's insistence on the employer's duty to bargain where an agreement exists does not appear to be entirely consistent with the main objective of the collective bargaining process—the fixing of the terms of employment through collective agreements. One reason

[77] *Interstate Steamship Co.*, 36 NLRB 1307 (1941); *Jasper Blackburn Products Corp.*, 21 NLRB 1240 (1940).
[78] *Scripto Mfg. Co.*, 36 NLRB 411 (1941).
[79] *Delaware-New Jersey Ferry Co.*, 2 NLRB 385 (1936).
[80] *Jeffery DeWitt Insulator Co.*, v. *NLRB*, 91 Fed. (2d) 134, 139 (1937).
[81] The same and *Schieber Millinery Co.*, 26 NLRB 937 (1940).
[82] *International Filter Co.*, 1 NLRB 489, 499 (1936).

an employer makes such an agreement is to fix the terms of employment for a more or less definite period. If at any time after an agreement is made, the employer is obligated to negotiate concerning its
modification, the value of the agreement to him will be reduced. Consequently the requirement that an employer must bargain even though
an unexpired agreement is in force is not consistent with the act's
objective of encouraging collective agreements.

Individual contracts of employment cannot prevent the formation
of a collective agreement or modify its terms. Their existence cannot
bar employees from claiming their full rights under a collective agreement.[83] Individual contracts limiting the worker's right not to seek
a union agreement are not binding on the employees, and it is an
unfair labor practice for an employer to make such agreements.[84] The
fact that an employer has individual agreements with a majority of
his employees does not excuse him from his obligation to recognize
and to bargain with a union representing a majority of his workers.
The obligation to bargain is a public one and cannot be avoided by the
making of agreements with individual employees. The purpose of
the National Labor Relations Act was to supersede individual contracts by collective agreements "which reflect the strength and bargaining power and serve the welfare of the group."[85] The employer
must refrain from negotiating with individual employees regarding
any modification in a collective agreement.[86] Where a legal bargaining
representative exists within the meaning of the act, the employer
cannot bargain individually with a majority of the employees to grant
them a wage increase, though on their own initiative they had declared
their desire to renounce the union. Although no coercion existed, and
the initiative came from the workers, nevertheless, the Board said
there was a violation of Section 8 (1) and (5) of the act.

Where a majority of the workers in a bargaining unit have been
organized into a union, little room exists for individual contracts.
Such agreements can be entered into legally only where a collective
agreement has expired and a new one has not yet been made because
of a deadlock in negotiations. Individual contracts would also be valid

[83] *New England Transportation Co.*, 1 NLRB 130 (1936).
[84] *National Licorice Co.* v. *NLRB*, 309 U.S. 350 (1939).
[85] *J. I. Case Co.* v. *NLRB*, 321 U.S. 332, 338 (1944).
[86] *Medo Photo Supply Corp.* v. *NLRB*, 321 U.S. 678 (1944).

where there is not a majority of the workers in any one union or where that majority has not been proved. Where an applicable collective agreement exists with an exclusive bargaining agent, "the only thing left to individual agreement is the act of hiring."[87] It would be very risky for an employer to make any individual contracts where there is an applicable collective agreement or where one is being negotiated.[88]

Despite misconduct of employees
the duty to bargain may continue.

There is a strong tendency on the part of the Board to consider that the employer's duty to bargain continues despite the misconduct of the employees or their representatives. According to the Supreme Court, even a violation of a collective agreement by a union does not free the employer from the obligation to bargain collectively, since the Congress did not provide "that violation of a private contract would deprive employees and the public of the benefits of the law."[89] The National Labor Relations Board likewise has said that the misconduct of the employees does not justify the employer's refusal to bargain collectively.[90] Also the Circuit Court of Appeals decided that, although a union may have been guilty of misconduct itself, the employer may not refuse to bargain because of the union's "past sins" if it offers to treat in good faith.[91] But on occasion the courts have held that the employer is not bound for an indefinite time to negotiate with an organization which has broken its contract.[92] However, the employer's duty to bargain collectively is not suspended even though his employees are on a strike.[93]

Since the employer's obligation to bargain continues despite illegal and improper activities of his employees, the Board does not seek to encourage employees to act legally by withholding the benefits of collective bargaining from those who do not act in conformity with the law. Unions that break contracts or engage in self-help (strikes)

[87] *U.S. Automatic Corp.*, 57 NLRB 124, 133 (1944).
[88] *J. I. Case and Co.* v. *NLRB*, 321 U.S. 332 (1944).
[89] *NLRB* v. *Columbian Enameling Co.*, 306 U.S. 292, 306 (1939).
[90] *Kuehne Mfg. Co.*, 7 NLRB 304 (1938).
[91] *NLRB* v. *Remington Rand Inc.*, 94 Fed. (2d) 862 (1938).
[92] *Jeffery DeWitt Insulating Co.* v. *NLRB*, 91 Fed. (2d) 134 (1937).
[93] *Harry Schwartz Yarn Co.*, 12 NLRB 1139, 1157 (1939).

rather than utilize available legal remedies (a suit for damages) do not lose their right to bargain. This raises the question whether the practices being followed facilitate the reduction of strikes and the maintenance of the safety of commerce, which are among the declared objectives of the National Labor Relations Act.

Does the collective bargaining provision involve the possibility of compulsory arbitration?

The act as interpreted and applied by the NLRB not only seeks to protect the right of the workers to bargain collectively, but it also has another objective—to encourage the making of collective agreements. The first objective requires a judicial attitude, the latter is a positive administrative process of a promotional nature.

Because of this second objective, the major test that the Board uses to determine whether collective bargaining took place, is: Did the process result in an agreement?[94] The process and the result are inseparably related in the Board's reasoning. The Supreme Court appears to be interested only in ensuring that the right to engage in the process of bargaining exists.[95]

The National Labor Relations Act asserts, "it is hereby declared to be the policy of the United States to eliminate the causes of certain substantial obstructions to the free flow of commerce . . . by encouraging the practice and procedure of collective bargaining." (Section 1) Therefore it is not surprising that the guarantee of the right to bargain and the encouragement of the making of collective bargaining agreements should be joined in the mind of the Board.[96] Consequently since the Board concluded that the real test of whether the process of bargaining has been followed can only be found in the end result of the process (a collective agreement), it is not illogical for the Board to decide that the main thing to determine is whether the employer bargained in good faith. It is not inconsistent with this attitude for the Board to decide, as it has done on occasion, that the good faith of the employer is tested by the proposals he rejected and the terms he offered in their stead. The Board puts itself in the position of passing on the desirability of the proposals of both sides. If it passes

---

[94] *Third Annual Report of the National Labor Relations Board* (1938), pp. 102-03.
[95] *Jones and Laughlin Steel Co.* v. *NLRB*, 301 U.S. 1 (1937).
[96] D. O. Bowman, *Public Control of Labor Relations* (1942), pp. 118-26.

judgment on the proposals, counter proposals, and concessions, it is thereby by implication saying what are the proper terms of settlement. Thus, as has been shown, the Board has repeatedly held that an employer does not bargain in good faith if he refuses to grant a closed shop when the employees request it. His refusal to provide for the arbitration of differences or to set up machinery for the settlement of grievances also constitutes evidence of bad faith. Again, if he makes the positive demand that the union post a bond, or if he asks it to incorporate, this is likewise evidence of the same thing. No statutes either require or prohibit the inclusion of such terms in agreements. If the Board can base the existence of the employer's good faith on his attitude toward any one of these questions, it can at its own discretion use the employer's attitude on other questions as a test of good faith. The Board thus is on the road to becoming a court of arbitration that will pass upon the proper terms of employment, and no standards are provided by law to guide the Board in the performance of such a function. "To the extent that the government directly or indirectly takes from the employer the right to say 'no,' it is forcing upon him unilateral compulsory arbitration."[97]

II. THE NATURE OF THE COLLECTIVE AGREEMENT AND THE RIGHTS UNDER IT

Both the National Labor Relations Act and the Railway Labor Act require the employer to bargain collectively with his employees. These acts look forward to, but do not directly require, the formation of collective agreements. But the legal nature of the collective agreements is not determined by federal law. The National Labor Relations Act and the Railway Labor Act assume that they are normal legal contracts. But by the Constitution the entire law of contracts is left to the states. What is and what is not a binding legal agreement is determined by the law of the individual states; and this is true even in a case coming before the federal courts where there is diversity of citizenship among the litigants.

Until recently many courts did not consider that
the collective agreements were binding contracts.

The courts did not always consider that collective agreements were

[97] W. H. Spencer, "Collective Bargaining under Section 7-a of the NIRA," *The Journal of Business of the University of Chicago*, Vol. 8 (1935), p. 32.

truly legal contracts but now most courts consider them to be enforceable contracts.[98] Three arguments were advanced against their legality; lack of consideration; lack of mutuality of remedy; and duress in their formulation.[99] The typical contract must be founded on a consideration running from each party to the other. In a collective agreement, the employer makes certain promises to the union concerning the conditions of employment, but the union does not promise to furnish any labor; consequently it has been contended that no consideration existed.[100] Gradually there evolved the idea that the union by implication had entered into certain understandings that constituted a consideration running from it to the employer. Thus, for example, it is assumed by the courts that the union had promised not to do anything to destroy the agreement.

The contention that there is a lack of mutuality of remedy is founded on the refusal of the courts to enforce an agreement where comparable remedies are not available to both parties. A court will not normally compel specific performance of a contract requiring the rendering of personal services. The employer thus cannot require specific employees to work for him under the agreement; therefore under the doctrine of mutuality of remedies some courts have refused to enforce the agreement against the employer when the union requested it.[101] Ultimately it was realized that the employer had contractual rights enforceable against the union other than those involved in an action for specific performances, as for example an undertaking by the union not to picket. Hence, at present this argument is not utilized extensively by the courts.

It has been alleged also that collective agreements were invalid because they were made under duress. It was argued such agreements were made only because labor applied duress against the employer by striking or by threatening to strike. The need for workers compelled the employer to yield to the union's demands, but no court ever held an agreement to be invalid on this ground.[102] Collective agreements in most jurisdictions are generally regarded as legally binding con-

---

[98] In England and throughout the British Empire they are not regarded as legally binding. *Young* v. *Canadian Northern Ry. Co.*, 1931, A.C. 83.
[99] Teller, *Collective Bargaining and Labor Disputes*, Sec. 158.
[100] *Wilson* v. *Airline Coal Co.*, 215 Iowa 855 (1935).
[101] *Chambers* v. *Davis*, 128 Miss. 613 (1922).
[102] Teller, *Collective Bargaining and Labor Disputes*, Sec. 161.

tracts. In justifying their enforcement, the courts have not always been too clear and logical in their reasoning.

Although the courts have not fully comprehended it, these agreements involve rights of the employer, rights of the union, and rights of the employees. Great confusion exists in the minds of the judges, both as to the legal basis of these rights and as to the conditions under which they will be enforced; but generally the courts now will enforce them. Such agreements sometimes contain promises of the union not to strike or to picket, and promises of the employers not to hire non-union employees. These different obligations generally will be enforced if the right party brings the action.[103]

*Unions, employers, and employees each have
separate rights under agreements.*

The collective agreement creates rights of the employees as well as rights and duties of the union. The two sets of rights are distinct, and the remedies for their violation are different. It has been difficult for some courts to realize that the same agreement can create at the same time two sets of rights against the employer. Thus a federal court held only thirteen years ago: "The agreement was clearly between the railway company and the brotherhood organization, and constituted no contract between any member employee and the railway company."[104] But generally the courts give tacit recognition to the fact that one agreement can confer rights upon the union as well as on the employees. Each of these groups must enforce its own rights. Thus a New York court said: "Another valid objection to this arbitration is the defective manner in which it is sought. The contract was between the union and the employer. . . . The union and not the petitioner should have made the application."[105]

The union alone and not an individual employee can enforce a provision of an agreement requiring arbitration.

*Only the union can enforce its
rights under an agreement.*

Under the agreement the union acquires rights of its own that are enforceable by it. A threatened violation of an agreement by the em-

[103] *Nederlandich* v. *Stevedores Union,* 265 Fed. 397 (1922).
[104] *Kessell* v. *Great Northern Ry. Co.,* 51 Fed. (2d) 304 (1931).
[105] *Petition of Minasian,* 14 N.Y. Supp. (2d) 818 (1939).

ployer can be enjoined by the union.[106] When a union has a valid closed-shop agreement, it can enjoin an attempt by another union to organize the establishment.[107] The discharge of union men and the employment of nonunion men in violation of a closed-shop agreement is a wrong for which relief can be secured.[108] It is unusual when a federal court holds that a strike is the only recourse a union has when the employer discharges a member in violation of a collective agreement.[109] A union can compel the employer to pay the contractual wage scale to all workers covered (whether members or not).[110]

The employer's means of enforcing an agreement are limited.

Several remedies previously were available to the employer for a breach of contract by the union.[111] The employer could recover damages from the union for a breach of contract. Many courts used to be willing to enjoin a strike called by the union in violation of the contract.[112] It cannot "be said that an injunction compels the men in the union to return to work. They individually do as they see fit. The injunction enjoins the union from calling or continuing the strike in violation of its contract obligation."[113] But under the Norris-LaGuardia Act no federal court can issue an injunction to enforce an agreement not to strike.[114] The making of collective agreements does not become more attractive to an employer, as a result of his inability to enforce a promise not to strike.

[106] Railway Employees Cooperative Association v. Atlanta Birmingham and Coast Ry. Co., U.S.D.C.M.C. Ga. No. 840 (1938).
[107] Kenloch Telephone Co. v. Local Union No. 275, 275 Fed. 241 (1921).
[108] Webber v. Nasser, 61 Cal. App. 1250 (1930).
[109] Illinois Central Ry. Co. v. Moore, 112 Fed. (2d) 959 (1940).
[110] Grand International Brotherhood of Locomotive Engineers v. Murphy, 109 Fed. (2d) 576 (1940).
[111] American-Hawaiian Steamship Co. v. Sailors Union of the Pacific, 37 Fed. Supp. 836 (1941); Busby v. Electric Utility Employees (Court of Appeals, D.C.), 15 LRR 706 (1945).
[112] Nederlandich v. Stevedores Union, 265 Fed. 397 (1920); Kenloch Telephone Co. v. Local Union No. 2, 275 Fed. 241 (1921); Barnes and Co. v. Berry, 156 Fed. 72 (1907); contra, D. L. and W. R. Co. v. Switchman's Union of North America, 158 Fed. 541 (1907).
[113] Greater City Master Plumbers Association v. Kahme, 6 N.Y. Supp. (2d) 589 (1938).
[114] Act of March 23, 1932, 47 Stat. 70, Sec. 1.

*On various grounds courts sustain an
employee's right to enforce an agreement.*

Although some courts have held that an employee acquires no rights under a collective agreement, courts generally find some basis on which to justify an employee's right to sue to enforce the rights granted to him by the agreement. The cases raising the problem usually involve a demand for the payment of the wages established in the collective agreement made by the employer and the union. The courts have advanced three theories justifying an employee's action under the agreement: usage, agency, and third-party beneficiary.

Under the usage theory, the collective agreement is not a contract; it is only evidence of a usage existing relative to employment conditions in the establishment involved. To recover damages on this basis, the existence of the usage must be proved, as well as the fact that the employee contracted with the employer on the basis of the usage.[115] Courts have differed concerning the amount of proof necessary to establish the usage evidenced by the agreement.

Under the agency theory the union only contracts for the employee as an agent. The employee is always the principal and consequently he can sue.[116]

. . . The agency theory encounters the difficulty of explaining how an employee may become party to the agreement, where he joins the union subsequent to the negotiations thereof. It might be reasoned, however, that he ratifies or at least adopts the agreement by entering into the employ of the employer who negotiated the contract with the union. . . .[117]

Concerning the third party beneficiary theory, it has long been held that a contract could be made for a third party who can enforce it himself, although not a party to the agreement. Thus the employee would be the beneficiary of the collective agreement and would be able to sue.[118] The agreement must have been made primarily for his benefit.

---

[115] *Moore v. Illinois Central Ry. Co.*, 112 Fed. (2d) 959 (1940); *U.S. Daily Publishing Corp. v. Nichols*, 32 Fed. (2d) 834 (1929); *Nazoo and M.V.R. Co. v. Webb*, 64 Fed. (2d) 902 (1933).

[116] *Barnes v. Berry*, 169 Fed. 225 (1909).

[117] Teller, *Collective Bargaining and Labor Disputes*, Sec. 167.

[118] *Rentschler v. Missouri Pacific Ry. Co.*, 253 N.W. 694 (1934).

A vital distinction between the individual employee's right to recovery under the usage theory and the third party beneficiary theory lies in the fact that the employee need not show, in order to recover according to the terms of the collective bargaining agreement, that he contracted with reference to it.

. . . .

A significant defect of the third party beneficiary theory is the lack of any ground, under this theory, of holding the individual employee liable, since our law does not recognize any obligation to rest upon a third party beneficiary.[119]

III. CONCLUSIONS

The employer's obligation to bargain collectively has been approached in different ways by different agencies. Under the Railway Labor Act the obligation to bargain is fulfilled if the employer engages in certain procedures; whether or not the application of those procedures results in an agreement is not material. The National War Labor Board asserts that employers have a duty to make collective agreements with their employees. If the employer fails to do so, the Board will prescribe the terms to be included in the agreement, and it will compel the employer to embody them in a contract. According to the National Labor Relations Board, the test of whether the employer bargained collectively is: Did the process of bargaining actually result in a collective agreement? If it did not, then the Board attempts to discover whether the employer failed to grant desirable demands of the workers or whether he demanded the inclusion of undesirable provisions in the agreement. If the employer did either of these things, he is assumed to have refused to bargain. This approach tacitly involves the possibility of compulsory arbitration, whereas the National War Labor Board frankly engages in compulsory arbitration.

If one major purpose of the labor policy of the federal government is to encourage the making of collective bargaining agreements, it would be desirable that such agreements be considered as legally enforceable contracts. If employers are certain that a union's agreement not to strike or to picket will be enforced, then there is a great incentive for them to enter into collective agreements. Where these agreements cannot be enforced, the employers will not readily see what they can gain from collective bargaining. Unions have much to gain from mak-

[119] Teller, *Collective Bargaining and Labor Disputes*, Sec. 168.

ing enforceable agreements. If an exclusive bargaining agreement fixes wages to be paid to both union and nonunion workers, and if such an agreement is a property right belonging to the union, then it can by injunction protect that right from attempts by a second union to upset it; under such conditions there will be at least one less reason why any union should seek a closed-shop agreement. The existence of binding collective agreements will tend to make industrial relations more orderly.

Although the federal government can and does require employers to bargain collectively, it has no authority over the character and enforceability of the resulting collective agreements. That is something that belongs exclusively to the jurisdiction of the states. Most states now consider such agreements to be binding and enforceable, but this is not true of all states. The legal reasoning of the courts regarding the nature and enforcement of such agreements is highly confused and inconsistent. The distinction between the rights of the union and the rights of the individual employees is not clear in the minds of many courts, and not all of them fully understand that the union's rights can be enforced by the union and the employees' rights by the employees. The legal reasons supporting the employees' right to sue on the agreements are confused. Whether or not the United States continues to require employers to engage in collective bargaining, it is desirable that the state law of collective agreements be clarified and made more uniform. There is little that the federal government can do about this, as the matter is competely within the jurisdiction of the states.

CHAPTER IV

THE GOVERNMENT'S POLICY TOWARD UNION ORGANIZATION

Intentionally or otherwise the federal government has affected the form of union organization. Primarily because several agencies have been given the power to designate the appropriate unit for collective bargaining purposes, the government has been in a position to shape the structure of labor organization. Since employers must bargain with the representatives of their employees, procedures were established for determining which group of employees constitutes an appropriate unit and who within that group represents the majority of the workers. The NLRB and the National Mediation Board have been given this task in their respective fields. An attempt will be made to show that, because of the power that these agencies have to select the bargaining unit, they are in a position to influence the growth of certain forms of union organization and retard or impede the growth of others.[1]

The impact of the government's policies on the form of union organization will be considered under three main heads. The relationship of the NRA to the division between the A.F. of L. and CIO will be taken up first. Second, the problem of the determination of the appropriate bargaining unit will be considered. Third, the attitude

[1] There have been cases where the government has favored one union at the expense of another by refusing contracts to employers who employed members of the undesirable union and by awarding contracts only to those who employed members of the favored union. Thus in 1941 the Federal Works Agency refused to award a contract to the low bidder who had a union-shop agreement with the Construction Workers Organizing Committee. *Investigation of the National Defense Program*, Hearings before a Senate Special Committee Investigating the National Defense Program, Pt. 8, 77 Cong. 1 sess., pp. 2368-70, 2492-2534, 2630-33. It was here argued that it would involve labor trouble to award a contract to an employer who did not employ A.F. of L. building trade members. Mr. Sidney Hillman, President of the Amalgamated Clothing Workers, while a director of the OPM and a member of the WPB made certain decisions concerning the letting of military clothing contracts that had the result of awarding contracts only to producers employing members of his union and denying contracts to employers who employed members of the International Ladies Garment Workers Union; see letters of Under Secretary of War Patterson, Donald Nelson of the WPB, and Sidney Hillman, also of the WPB, to Representative Albert Engel, *Congressional Record*, Vol. 80, Pt. 8, 77 Cong, 2 sess., pp. A956-58; and remarks of Representative Albert Engel, the same, Pt. 2, p. 1867.

of the National Labor Relations Act and the Railway Labor Act toward independent unions will be examined.

The very existence of any kind of government influence over the form of union organization runs contrary to cherished ideas of the American labor movement. The general assumption of labor in this country has been that the labor movement was purely voluntary in nature. Labor long insisted that the organization and structure of the labor movement were entirely apart from and beyond the control of the government. For almost fifty years the American Federation of Labor considered itself to be the origin and source of the labor movement, outside the four railroad brotherhoods. The A.F. of L. believed that it alone had the authority to shape the labor movement. Areas within which each union could organize workers were demarcated in charters granted by the A.F. of L. The charter conferred an exclusive right to organize. The choice of which union a worker of a given skill could join generally was not his; it was made by the A.F. of L. But now the government, by drawing the boundaries of the bargaining unit in a given manner, and not the workers themselves or the A.F. of L. (or the CIO), in effect determines the labor organization that will represent the workers in the unit. By asking for government assistance to increase its bargaining power, there is a strong probability that the labor movement will lose its complete freedom to develop in its own way.

I. THE NRA'S INFLUENCE ON UNION ORGANIZATION

The NIRA required that every code of fair competition for an industry must guarantee to the workers the right of self-organization.[2] This was the first general guarantee of such a right by the federal government, and it led to greatly increased organizational activity by practically all labor groups.

The NIRA resulted in a rapid increase in union membership especially among industrial unions.

There was a tremendous growth in the membership of all labor organizations, including both those within the A.F. of L. and those not so affiliated. The independent unions grew by more than a million under the NRA, but they never had any voice in the formulation, ap-

[2] Act of June 16, 1933, 48 Stat. 198, Sec. 7 (a).

proval, and administration of NRA codes. The labor advisory machinery of the NRA was all in the hands of the A.F. of L. and affiliated unions. The Labor Advisory Board of the NRA believed Section 7 (a), which guaranteed the right of self-organization, prohibited company unions. But the administrator of the NRA refused to make a statement endorsing this view.[3]

The type of government organization established for the formulation and administration of codes of fair competition tended to affect the form of labor organizations. All codes had to be approved by the administrator of the NRA and ultimately by the President. To assist in this process, the administrator had a Labor Advisory Board, as well as consumer and industrial advisory boards. The Labor Advisory Board was overwhelmingly made up of officials of the A.F. of L. and of unions affiliated with it. Generally, codes were drafted by the industry and were submitted to the administrator for his approval. In drafting them the Labor Advisory Board tried to influence their labor provisions. These codes were administered by code authorities; in some cases a labor member was on the board of the authority; in other instances one of the public members of the authority was designated by labor, and always the public member had a labor adviser. The entire machinery of labor administration was in the control of the A.F. of L.[4] This tended to favor the expansion of the A.F. of L. and to work to the disadvantage of the independent unions.

The organization of the code-making process on an industry basis facilitated the development of industrial unions. The A.F. of L. generally was organized on a craft or trade basis. Where an industry was codified on an industrial basis, it was difficult for unions organized on a craft basis to represent adequately the interests of workers, in the process of code formulation and administration. This difficulty was especially great in the case of an industry in which the workers had not been organized previously. In such a case many different craft or trade unions were involved, and they struggled among themselves for jurisdiction to organize the workers. In the process of code formulation and administration, it would appear that an industrial union would have had an easier time than craft unions.[5] Partly because of these diffi-

---

[3] Lewis L. Lorwin and A. Wubnig, *Labor Relations Boards* (1935), pp. 63, 64, 67.
[4] Leo Wolman, *Ebb and Flow in Trade Unionism* (1936), p. 47.
[5] Leverett S. Lyon and others, *The National Recovery Administration* (1935), p. 510.

culties, some of the staff of the Labor Advisory Board definitely favored the development of industrial unions.[6]

The NRA contributed to
the rise of the CIO.

The extension of the organizational activities of the A.F. of L. to previously untouched industries led to internal conflicts in the Federation. In traditional fields where unions were prevalent, the organizing work was carried on by the existing unions. In agriculture, service trades, and distribution, there were few existing unions to cause difficulties for the A.F. of L. organizers. But in the unorganized manufacturing industries, the long-standing jurisdictional claims of different existing unions had to be considered. Here the A.F. of L. did most of the organizing itself; it did not leave the task to the constituent international unions. It was done through "local trade and federal labor unions" newly created by the A.F. of L. Council.[7] The theory was that when a plant or company was well organized on this basis, the membership of the federal local thus formed would be split up among the regularly established craft or trade unions. The organizers of these federal locals did not look with favor upon the ultimate break-up of the new unions, but the older unions were not anxious to see new national unions rise within the A.F. of L., for that would tend to reduce their power within the Federation.

The attempts of the A.F. of L. to handle this situation met with failure. In 1934 the convention of the A.F. of L. adopted a resolution favoring vertically integrated national unions for the new industrial areas and provided that the Council should charter industrial unions in aluminum, automobile, and cement production; but the resolution stated that the jurisdiction of the craft unions was not to be disturbed.[8] However, the charters actually issued by the Council in the automobile and rubber industries overlapped the jurisdiction of the old craft unions. In 1935 the convention of the Federation adopted a resolution generally endorsing craft unions. Several industrial unions disapproved of this action, and without withdrawing from the A.F. of L. they formed the Committee for Industrial Organization to promote industrial unionism. The next year the A.F. of L. expelled the unions

[6] Lorwin and Wubnig, *Labor Relations Boards*, pp. 75-76.
[7] Lyon and others, *The National Recovery Administration*, p. 513.
[8] *The Report of the Council of the American Federation of Labor, 1934*, pp. 16-17.

that formed the Committee because they were promoting rival labor organizations.[9]

II. THE DETERMINATION OF THE APPROPRIATE BARGAINING UNIT

In this section the policy of two government agencies toward the selection of the bargaining unit will be examined. The National Labor Relations Board and the National Mediation Board will be considered.

A. Under the National Labor Relations Act

Several provisions of the National Labor Relations Act make it necessary that some public agency be given the authority to determine the appropriate bargaining unit. Section 8 (5) of the act provides that it is an unfair labor practice for an employer to refuse to bargain with the representatives chosen by a majority of his employees in an appropriate unit. Further, the representatives chosen by a majority of the employees in an appropriate unit are the exclusive bargaining representatives of all the employees in the unit.[10] In addition, an employer can make a closed-shop agreement only with a labor organization that represents a majority of the employees in the bargaining unit.[11] Consequently it was necessary that the Board be given the power to "decide in each case whether, in order to insure to employees the full benefit of their right to self-organization and to collective bargaining, and otherwise to effectuate the policies of this Act, the unit appropriate for the purpose of collective bargaining shall be the employer unit, craft unit, plant unit, or subdivision thereof."[12]

The determination of the appropriate bargaining unit is significant to the workers.

Minority groups of workers in any bargaining unit have no voice in the bargaining process. The act specifically provides that in collective bargaining the representative of the majority shall be the exclusive representative of all of the employees. No room is left for any form of proportional representation in the bargaining process. The

[9] J. Raymond Walsh, *CIO Industrial Unionism in Action* (1937), pp. 39-47.
[10] Sec. 9 (a).
[11] Sec. 8 (3).
[12] Sec. 9 (b). The Supreme Court has refused to review the Board's decisions on this subject. *AFL* v. *NLRB*, 308 U.S. 401 (1940).

Senate Committee on Education and Labor justified this in its report on the bill:

The object of collective bargaining is the making of agreements that will stabilize business conditions and fix fair standards of working conditions. Since it is well-nigh universally recognized that it is practically impossible to apply two or more sets of agreements to one unit of workers at the same time, or to apply the terms of one agreement to only a portion of the workers in a single unit, the making of agreements is impracticable in the absence of majority rule. And by long experience, majority rule has been discovered best for employers as well as employees. Workers have found it impossible to approach their employers in a friendly spirit if they remained divided among themselves. Employers likewise, where majority rule has been given a trial of reasonable duration, have found it more conducive to harmonious labor relations to negotiate with representatives chosen by the majority than with numerous warring factions.[13]

Consequently workers with special interests have a direct voice in the bargaining process only if they constitute a majority in a separate unit.

Thus it has been observed that in designating the bargaining unit "the Board must establish the electoral district for employee elections, which obviously may very well be the deciding factor in the outcome of the election."[14] Generally unions indicate plainly their awareness of this and attempt to get the Board to select a unit in which their members will constitute a majority of the employees.[15] Under such conditions any agency that designates bargaining units, which are in effect election districts, is going to be criticized. A former member of the Board summed up this problem by saying,

The people that do not like any particular unit that is fixed by the Board would say that it is gerrymandering. That is what it looks like when you have to decide how many people you are going to put in that particular voting district. This whole problem is a voting district, and when you com-

---

[13] *National Labor Relations Board,* S. Rept. 573, 74 Cong. 1 sess., pp. 13-14.
[14] E. B. McNatt, "The 'Appropriate Bargaining Unit' Problem," *Quarterly Journal of Economics,* Vol. 56 (1941), p. 96.
[15] An illustration of this is *Pacific Gas and Electric Co.,* 3 NLRB 835 (1937). Here a CIO union desired a bargaining unit embracing only the outside employees of the company, since it thought a majority of these would designate it. It opposed the inclusion of the office workers. If the office workers were included in the unit the union would not have a majority. The main reason it advanced for its desire to exclude them was "the tradition to divergence in their social outlook and in their attitude toward labor organizations." This is an indirect way of saying—exclude them because they might not designate us. Partly on the basis of this reason, the request of the union was granted.

bine two or separate two, or separate one, the people who object to it say that it is just gerrymandering.[16]

It should be emphasized that the Board designates only bargaining units; it does not designate bargaining representatives or unions. The employees in the bargaining unit established by the Board designate the bargaining representative. But the composition of the bargaining unit does have something to do with the bargaining representative that might be designated by a majority of the workers in it. For example, if in a plant only a few carpenters are employed and they belong to a union that does not admit to membership most of the other employees, and there is another union that will admit all of the employees and to which a majority of them belong, the bargaining unit designated by the Board will be a significant factor in determining what representative may be selected as the bargaining representative for the carpenters. If the Board determines that the carpenters constitute a separate unit, probably the carpenter's union will be designated as their representative. But if the Board decides that the carpenters are to bargain with the other employees, they will be represented by the union designated by a majority of all the employees. This bargaining representative is likely to be the union to which a majority of them belong, and not the carpenter's union which will not admit to membership most of the employees. Consequently although the Board designates only bargaining units, and the employees in the unit thus established select the bargaining representative themselves, the unit selected by the Board may be a most significant factor in determining which union will represent a given group of employees.

Despite its own desires, the Board inadvertently has become an arbitrator of conflicting claims of jurisdiction between rival unions. When it was first established, the Board refused to consider any representation case that involved a jurisdictional dispute between two unions; but the development of a division in the labor movement forced it to abandon this policy. It rested its decision not to consider jurisdictional disputes on the ground that it was best for it to stay out of such controversies.[17] But within a year after this decision, the split between the A.F. of L.

[16] Mr. W. M. Leiserson in *National Labor Relations Act*, Hearings before the House Special Committee to Investigate the National Labor Relations Board, Vol. 1, 76 Cong. 2 sess., p. 138.

[17] *Aluminum Co. of America*, 1 NLRB 530 (1936).

and CIO became so significant that the Board was forced to decide representation cases involving jurisdictional disputes.[18]

The National Labor Relations Act contains only broad standards to guide the Board in designating the unit.

Only two standards are provided in the statute to govern the Board in fixing the unit. In making this determination the objectives of the Board are "to insure to employees the full benefit of their right of self-organization and to collective bargaining, and otherwise to effectuate the policies of this act."[19] One of "the policies of this act" is to remove inequalities in bargaining power.[20] Thus in selecting the appropriate bargaining unit, one objective of the Board is to determine the desire of the employees, and another goal is to increase the bargaining power of the workers. In a given case these two objectives might run counter to each other. In making the choice among "the employer unit, the craft unit, plant unit, or subdivision thereof," the Board has utilized the two standards in different ways in different decisions. The act contains no other guides to the Board in the exercise of its discretion in this matter. Only in its decisions can one find the basic principles on which it has made its determination concerning the proper unit.

The Board itself refuses to state with any precision the standards that are likely to apply in any specific case. Whether one or another principle announced by the Board will be applied in a case is not always clearly evident in advance.

Only when the workers cannot agree on the unit does the Board have to select one.

If no dispute exists among the employees, the Board generally will designate any unit desired by the workers. Under such circumstances no matter whether it is an industrial, plant, craft, or employer unit the Board will approve it. Of course the Board will disregard the wishes of an employer-dominated or assisted union.[21]

Where the workers are not agreed on the appropriate unit, the really difficult problem is presented. Concerning the principles the Board uses when the employees are not agreed, it has said:

[18] *Interlake Iron Corp.*, 2 NLRB 1036 (1937).
[19] Sec. 9 (b).
[20] Sec. 1.
[21] *Pure Oil Co.*, 8 NLRB 207 (1938); *Citizens News Co.*, 8 NLRB 997 (1938).

In attempting to ascertain the groups among which there is that mutual interest in the objects of collective bargaining which must exist in an appropriate unit if bargaining is to be effective, the Board considers and weighs a number of factors. Among the most important are the following: the history, extent, and type of organization of employees; the history of their collective bargaining; the history, extent, and type of organization of employees in other plants of the same employer, or of other employers in the same industry; the skill, wages, work, and working conditions of the employees; the desires of the employees; the eligibility of the employees for membership in the union or unions involved; the relationship between the unit or units proposed and the employer's organization, management, and operation of the plant; and whether an association of employers is in existence exercising employer functions, and with a history of collective bargaining on a multi-employer basis.[22]

The history, extent, and type of organization of employees presented in each case are important factors in the determination of the bargaining unit. The Board asserts that as far as possible it has tried to fit the bargaining unit to the existing collective bargaining practices. Thus it believes that it seeks to maintain the historical unit.[23]

. . . Self-organization which has resulted in successful bargaining in the past can be relied on as a guide for future collective bargaining. . . . The Board utilizes the experienced judgment of the workers themselves as to the existence of the mutual interest in working conditions which must exist among the members of an appropriate unit.[24]

Where the workers previously have been organized on a broad basis, extensive units often have been found to be appropriate.[25] But where the employees have not been organized on a broad basis, small units sometimes have been considered suitable.[26]

Generally the Board attempts to pick as large a unit as feasible,[27] in order to bring the benefits of collective bargaining to as many workers as possible and to increase their bargaining power. Thus it has justified including several plants in the same unit, so the employer could not

---

[22] *Seventh Annual Report of the National Labor Relations Board* (1942), p. 59.
[23] *Mosinee Paper Mills Co.*, 1 NLRB 393 (1936); *Belmont Iron Works*, 9 NLRB 1202 (1938); *Southern California Gas Co.*, 10 NLRB 1123 (1939).
[24] *Third Annual Report of the National Labor Relations Board* (1938), p. 160.
[25] *RCA Communications Inc.*, 2 NLRB 1109 (1936); *Bendix Products Co.*, 15 NLRB 965.
[26] *Gulf Oil Corp.*, 4 NLRB 133 (1937); *Southern California Gas Co.*, 10 NLRB 1023 (1938), and *Lillybrook Coal Co.*, Case No. 9B 1497 (1945). But the bargaining history is not conclusive, *RKO Radio Pictures*, 59 NLRB 132 (1944).
[27] *New York Evening Journal*, 10 NLRB 197 (1938).

play the workers in one plant against those in another,[28] and it has included competing employers in the same unit, so as to prevent competition between different groups of employees in fixing the terms of employment.[29] Since one objective of the law is to increase the bargaining power of employees, it was rational for the Board to arrive at this principle.

Another principle used by the Board is the community of interest among the workers. This relates primarily to the functional cohesion of the workers.[30] Generally, production and maintenance employees in one plant will be included in the same unit.[31] Where work is passed on from one plant to another, and thus the production of the second plant is influenced by the quality of the work done in the first, both plants will be included in the same unit.[32] The Board also attempts to make collective bargaining an immediate reality. Thus if there is a choice between a unit where a majority of the employees are already organized and one where they are not yet organized, generally it will select the unit that is already organized.[33]

In some instances the Board seeks to discover what unit the employees prefer.

The Board has encountered its greatest difficulty in deciding those cases involving conflicts between craft and industrial unions. It has attempted to solve some of them by transferring the task of making the decision from the Board to the employees. This is the so-called Globe doctrine. The Board states that when it concludes that the equities are equally balanced between a craft unit and an industrial unit, it will allow craft workers within the larger unit to determine by an election whether they desire to bargain separtely from the rest of the workers or to be included as a part of the larger unit. As thus stated, the doctrine[34] worked to the advantage of the minority groups, that is, the craft groups. But in order to be permitted to make the choice, the craft workers must demonstrate that they had normally been considered as a separate craft, and at the time of the determina-

[28] *Inland Steel Co.*, 9 NLRB 783 (1938).
[29] *Admiar Rubber Co.*, 9 NLRB 407 (1938).
[30] *Second Annual Report of the National Labor Relations Board* (1937), p. 138.
[31] *Richardson Co.*, 4 NLRB 835 (1937).
[32] *Waggener Refining Co.*, 6 NLRB 731 (1938); and *First Annual Report of the National Labor Relations Board* (1936), p. 115.
[33] *Western Union Telegraph Co.*, 17 NLRB 683 (1939).
[34] *Globe Machine and Stamping Co.*, 3 NLRB 294 (1937).

tion members of the craft must actually be employed.[35] The request for an election will not be granted where only one person would be in the unit.[36] In the latter part of 1939 the Board added a further condition to the application of the so-called Globe doctrine. Where a collective agreement actually existed covering the wider unit, the Board will not permit a craft unit to be carved out of it.[37] Thus where an industrial unit has already bargained as such, the Board will not permit the craft workers to vote on whether they desire to separate from it.[38] This modification in the doctrine facilitates the designation of units that are likely to be represented by an industrial union.

It is not entirely certain that the act authorizes the use of elections actually to determine the appropriate unit which may be desirable from the standpoint of public policy. Section 9 (b) states "the Board shall decide in each case whether . . . the unit appropriate for . . . collective bargaining shall be the employer unit, craft unit, ..." Thus the law provides that "the Board shall decide." It is open to question whether the Board is deciding the case however, if it delegates to the workers the power to decide upon the bargaining unit through an election.

Since one object of section 9 is "to insure to employees . . . their right to self organization" the Globe doctrine might appear to be justified. But in order to ensure the attainment of this objective the act imposes on the Board the duty of deciding upon the appropriate unit. It would appear that the Board might use an election as part of its procedure in determining what should constitute the appropriate unit, but the results can only constitute evidence to inform the judgment of the Board. The determination of the unit is the obligation of the Board, and it cannot delegate the task.[39]

---

[35] *Bendix Products Corp.*, 15 NLRB 965 (1939); *General Electric Co.*, 58 NLRB 57 (1944).
[36] *Joseph Finch Co. Inc.*, 10 NLRB 896 (1938). It is asserted that it is logically impossible for a single person to bargain collectively. Thus one carpenter or one electrician in a plant must be merged with the production employees.
[37] *Milton Bradley Co.*, 15 NLRB 938 (1939).
[38] Ludwig Teller, *Labor Disputes and Collective Bargaining* (1940), Sec. 355.
[39] *Marshall Field and Co.* v. *NLRB*, 135 Fed. (2d) 391 (1943). In its Annual Report following this decision the Board said that in an election under the Globe doctrine it does not delegate the selection of the unit to the employees; it merely seeks their advice and then makes its own determination; *Eighth Annual Report of the National Labor Relations Board* (1943), pp. 54-55. This is not incompatible with the decision of the Circuit Court of Appeals in the Marshall Field case.

Whether several plants belonging to the same employer are to be included in the same unit is not always certain. Generally the Board has granted the multiple-plant unit where it was desired by the employees in all the plants. It has granted it especially where there was a common personnel policy for the several units, and where the plants were interdependent.[40] The multiple-plant unit is favored because it tends to increase the bargaining power of the workers.[41] The Board said that one reason it adopted this policy was to prevent the employer from playing employees in one plant against those in another.[42] Often since 1939 the Board has included in multiple-plant units only those plants where the union requesting the larger unit has actually a majority of the workers, or it has permitted the employees in each plant to vote on their inclusion in the larger unit.[43] But no uniformity exists in its decisions. In some cases where the request was opposed by another union, the Board nevertheless granted a multiple-plant unit without an election.[44]

The Board assists in the maintenance of multiple-employer units.

Where the employees of several different employers desire to bargain as a single unit, the Board aids in the maintenance of a multiple-employer unit if collective bargaining actually has been practiced on that basis. Carried to its fullest extent a multiple-employer unit would include the larger part of the employers in an industry or in a competitive area in an industry; this is generally known as industry-wide collective bargaining. Concerning bargaining on such a basis the Board commented:

> We think it clear . . . that there are many situations in which collective bargaining on a multiple employer basis has overwhelming advantages. . . .

Recent studies of labor relations in Great Britian and Sweden have shown there are many advantages to be gained from collective bargaining on a

[40] *American Woolen Co.*, 5 NLRB 144 (1938).
[41] *C. A. Lund Co.*, 6 NLRB 423 (1938).
[42] *Fourth Annual Report of the National Labor Relations Board* (1939), pp. 90-91.
[43] Emily Clark Brown, "The Employer Unit for Collective Bargaining," *Journal of Political Economy*, Vol. 50 (1942), pp. 321, 331; *Chrysler Corp.*, 13 NLRB 1303 (1939); *Briggs Mfg. Co.*, 13 NLRB 1326 (1939).
[44] *Malone Bronze Powder Works*, 19 NLRB 449 (1940); *National Distillers Corp.*, 20 NLRB 467 (1940).

scale broader than the single employer. We do not think that experimentation along these lines should be discouraged or foreclosed in this country.[45]

To increase the bargaining power of the workers is the major reason the Board approves multiple-employer units. In the Pacific longshoremen's case the Board asserted that the inability of the men to improve their working conditions by bargaining on a single-port basis was evidence that they needed to have greater bargaining power, and that could be attained only through a coast-wide unit.[46] Of course here also the employers were organized on a broad basis, and the designation of a coast-wide unit tended to put the employees on a basis comparable with that of the employers. The Board has also favored such units because it considers the establishment of uniform wages among competing plants to be desirable.[47]

The Board has only limited opportunities to establish or assist in maintaining multiple-employer units.[48] Before the Board can establish such a unit, there must already exist an association of employers with authority to bargain; the association must be in existence previous to the Board's decision.[49] This requirement is inherent in the definitions of employer in the National Labor Relations Act. Section 2 provides: "The term 'employer' includes any person acting in the interest of an employer" and the term person "includes one or more individuals, partnerships, associations, corporations, legal representatives," and the like.[50] These definitions were purposely framed in this manner, because some of the drafters of the act were anxious to ensure that the Board

---

[45] *National Labor Relations Act and Proposed Amendments*, Hearings before the Senate Committee on Education and Labor, Pt. 3, 76 Cong. 1 sess., p. 539.

[46] *Shipowners Association of the Pacific Coast*, 7 NLRB 1002 (1938).

[47] *Admiar Rubber Co.*, 9 NLRB 407 (1938); *Alston Coal Co.*, 13 NLRB 689.

[48] The OPM and WPB in war industries exercised a more aggressive role; for example, in shipbuilding see *To Investigate the National Defense Program*, Hearings before the Senate Committee to Investigate the National Defense Program, 77 Cong. 1 sess., pp. 1131-39; in construction, the same, p. 2503; and in airplanes, 10 LRR 674. The National War Labor Board also can do more to build up such practices; note, *Basic Steel Industry, Bethlehem Steel Co.*, 1 WLR 325 (1942); *Carnegie Illinois Steel Co.*, 1 WLR 325 (1942); *Big Four Rubber Cos.*, 8 WLR 537 (1943); *Boeing Aircraft Co., et al*, 6 WLR 581 (1943); *Non-Ferrous Metal Mining Cos.*, 4 WLR 147 (1942); *Joint Wage Board of the Lumber Industry*, 2 WLR 487 (1942); *Fifty-nine Cotton Textile Mills*, 2 WLR 345 (1942).

[49] Chairman Madden, *The National Labor Relations Act*, Hearings before the House Committee to Investigate the National Labor Relations Board, 76 Cong. 3 sess., p. 3174.

[50] Sec. 2 (1).

could not impose industry-wide bargaining where the practice did not already exist.[51]

Only where there has been actual bargaining on a multiple-employer basis will the Board approve such a unit.

Not only must there be an existing practice of collective bargaining in the unit, but the employers' association must have the authority to really bargain for and bind its members.[52] What is meant by such authority is not clear. It would seem that it could not have the authority to bind its members not to operate their plants if the association could not secure the desired terms, as that would involve a violation of both the Sherman Anti-Trust Act[53] and the National Labor Relations Act.[54] Thus the employer association probably would not have as great bargaining power as the union, which can strike. Nevertheless if the association of employers exists, if collective bargaining is being practiced, and if the employees in the unit are united in desiring it, the Board generally establishes the multiple-employer unit.[55] But in many cases the situation has been complicated by conflicting claims of competing unions. If the Board refuses to grant a large unit where a union conflict exists, it generally has done so because of a lack of bargaining history or a lack of an employers' association with the power to contract.[56]

[51] Chairman Madden, *National Labor Relations Act*, Hearings before the House Special Committee to Investigate the National Labor Relations Board, p. 3173. One member of the Board has said that an employer can withdraw from the association at will and thus leave the multiple unit. The same, p. 3174.

[52] No practice of bargaining, *F. F. Booth and Co.*, 10 NLRB 1491 (1939); no association with authority to bind members, *Metro-Goldwyn Mayer*, 7 NLRB 662 (1938); *Mobile Steamship Association*, 8 NLRB 1297 (1938); *M. and J. Tracey Co.*, 12 NLRB 936 (1939).

[53] The mere bargaining for conditions of employment for a large segment of an industry would not be illegal; *Apex Hosiery Co.* v. *Leader*, 310 U.S 469, 503-04 (1940); see also *National Association of Window Glass Manufacturers* v. *United States*, 263 U.S. 403 (1923). But an agreement designed to influence manufacturers not to operate if the right terms of employment are not secured probably would violate the Sherman Act; *American Column and Lumber Co.* v. *United States*, 257 U.S. 377 (1921).

[54] A lock-out would be a violation of Section 8 (3); *Triplett Electrical Instrument Co.*, 5 NLRB 835 (1938); *Washington Mfg. Co.*, 4 NLRB 970 (1937); *National Motor Bearing Co.*, 5 NLRB 409 (1938).

[55] *Associated Banning Co., and Waterfront Employers Association*, 19 NLRB 140 (1940); *National Dress Manufacturers Association, Inc.*, 28 NLRB 386 (1940).

[56] *Pacific American Fisheries*, 28 NLRB 244 (1940) lack of bargaining history; *Sebastion Stuart Fishing Co.*, 17 NLRB 352 (1939) association did not have the power to contract.

The Board generally favors the continuation of an existing multiple-employer unit when the workers in one establishment desire to leave the larger unit and to bargain separately. Where collective bargaining actually has been practiced on the basis of the large unit, the employees in one plant will not be permitted to withdraw.[57] The Board opposes the break-up of such units because of the consequent reduction in the bargaining power of the employees. Thus where the miners in one bituminous coal mine desired to withdraw from the United Mine Workers of America (which bargained on an industry-wide basis) and to be represented by the Progressive Miners of America in order to bargain as a separate unit, the Board would not designate that mine as a separate unit. "Bargaining and making contracts on such a basis had helped to stabilize the coal-mining industry and place the mines on a fair competitive basis, a condition which would be very difficult of achievement if separate contracts were negotiated with each operator."[58]

In anthracite coal mining, the Board also upheld industry-wide bargaining against attempts by some workers to bargain on an employer basis:

We are convinced that the full benefit of their right to self-organization and to collective bargaining cannot be insured to the employees by breaking up the collective bargaining unit which has been established by a long history of contractual relations between the operators and miners of the anthracite region. . . .[59]

Thus the Board seemed to consider that the maintenance of bargaining power was more important than the workers' freedom of organization. But where a multiple-employer unit has been recognized by the Board and the employees in some parts of it still bargained separately, the Board permitted them to decide whether they desired to withdraw from the larger unit and to set up one of their own.[60]

Most of the standards utilized by the Board in designating bargaining units give the advantage to large units and prevent specialized

[57] *New Bedford Cotton Manufacturers Association*, 47 NLRB 1145 (1943); *John Kausel*, 28 NLRB 906 (1941). *Hyman Michaels Co.*, 11 NLRB 96 (1939); and *Admiar Corp.*, 9 NLRB 407 (1939).
[58] *Alston Coal Co.*, 13 NLRB 683, 689 (1940).
[59] *Stevens Coal Co.*, 19 NLRB 98, 110 (1940).
[60] *Shipowners Association of the Pacific*, 32 NLRB 668 (1941); see also *Gulf Refining Co.*, 21 ULRB 1033 (1940).

groups of workers from engaging in collective bargaining on an independent basis. Its principle of community of interest, its objective of maximizing collective bargaining, its opposition to a bargaining unit consisting of one individual worker, and its support of multiple-plant and employer units, all tend toward the formulation of decisions supporting the more inclusive unit. The Globe doctrine with its corollaries that prevent the carving up of a large unit where it has actually engaged in bargaining and that require that the craft unit must already be at least partially organized before it can be permitted to express a choice also works in the same direction.

By establishing vague and partially inconsistent standards, Congress gave the Board wide discretion in selecting the bargaining unit.

The only guides Congress provided for the Board in selecting the appropriate unit are two partly inconsistent goals. One of these objectives is the increase in the bargaining power of workers, which would tend to favor the development of large bargaining units. The other goal is the guarantee of the workers' right to freedom of organization. The smaller the unit the greater is the self-determination allowed to separate groups of workers with diverse interests who would be minorities if included in a larger unit. Of course generally speaking the smaller the unit the less is its bargaining power. So the guarantee of self-determination and the goal of increasing bargaining power clash in some cases. When the two objectives are in conflict, the Board favors increasing bargaining power though as a result some workers become minority groups.[61]

These various principles used by the Board for determining the bargaining unit leave it with wide discretion. They overlap and they are not formulated with such exactness as to permit one to predict the Board's decision in a given case. Thus where an employer has several plants, the Board can determine whether it will set up a unit embracing only those plants that have been organized or one that includes all of his plants. In the first instance it would be making collective bargaining an immediate reality; in the second instance it would be following the principle of interdependence. The Board has done nothing that

[61] *Final Report of the Special Committee to Investigate the National Labor Relations Board*, H. Rept. 3109, 76 Cong. 3 sess., pp. 70-71.

restricts its freedom of choice in determining the bargaining unit in any situation.

B. The National Mediation Board

Under the Railway Labor Act of 1934, the National Mediation Board is given the task of determining the true representatives of the employees of rail carriers. Concerning this function of the Board, the act provides:

Employees shall have the right to organize and bargain collectively through representatives of their own choosing. The majority of any craft or class of employees shall have the right to determine who shall be the representative of the craft or class for the purposes of this Act. . . .[62]

If any dispute shall arise among a carrier's employees as to who are the representatives of such employees designated and authorized in accordance with the requirements of this Act, it shall be the duty of the Mediation Board upon request of either party to the dispute, to investigate such dispute and to certify to both parties, in writing, within thirty days after the receipt of the invocation of its services, the name or names of the indivduals or organizations that have been designated and authorized to represent the employees involved in the dispute, and certify the same to the carrier. . . .[63]

The task of the National Mediation Board under these sections of the law differs somewhat from that of the National Labor Relations Board in designating a bargaining unit under Section 9 (b) of the National Labor Relations Act. The National Mediation Board has only the task of certifying who represents a majority of the employees in any "craft or class." It does not have the discretion that the NLRB has, for that organization must designate bargaining units, and it can do so on a craft, plant, or employer basis. The National Mediation Board must determine the representative majority of the employees in a given craft or class. Where the employees are not agreed as to what is the composition of the craft or class wherein the representatives are to be chosen, the Board must define the limits of the group that is going to make the selection. Despite the fact that the Board felt that "the Railway Labor Act does not give the Board any authority to define the crafts according to which railway employees may be organized,"[64] it shortly discovered that it could not avoid determining

[62] Sec. 2 (fourth).
[63] Sec. 2 (ninth).
[64] *First Annual Report of the National Mediation Board* (1935), p. 18.

what constitutes a craft or class.[65] When it is engaged in drawing the boundaries of a craft or class, its function approximates that of the NLRB in designating a bargaining unit under Section 9 (b) of the National Labor Relations Act.

Despite the Board's dislike of handling representation disputes, it has the full responsibility for deciding all such cases. The National Mediation Board does not like to settle disputes between conflicting unions concerning what constitutes a craft or class in a given instance. It prefers that the unions settle all such controversies among themselves. Thus a former chairman of the Board has said, "I think the main responsibility is on the labor organizations themselves to settle their own disputes. We scare them a little bit. Whenever these disputes come up, we do not pretend that we like to decide them."[66] Nor will the courts decide whether a given group of workers is covered by a collective agreement. The courts refuse to review the Board's determinations in representation cases.[67] That would be determining a bargaining unit, and that function is in the hands of the Board.[68]

The Board has developed definite principles for determining a craft or class of employees.

Congress provided no more precise standard for the Board's guidance than it did for the National Labor Relations Board. But under the Railway Labor Act, the bargaining representatives are to be selected on a craft or class basis. The National Mediation Board does not believe that this provision makes its task easier than that of the NLRB, which must choose between craft, plant, and employer units.[69] In the section of the Railway Labor Act, that deals with the creation of the National Railroad Adjustment Board, Congress specifically named twenty-nine different types of railway workers.[70] This listing might be some guide to the Board in determining what constitutes a

[65] *Second Annual Report of the National Mediation Board* (1936), pp. 11-12.
[66] W. M. Leiserson, *National Labor Relations Act and Proposed Amendments*, Hearings before the Senate Committee on Education and Labor, Pt. 6, p. 1005.
[67] *Switchman's Union of North America* v. *National Mediation Board*, 320 U.S. 297 (1943).
[68] *Brotherhood of Locomotive Engineers* v. *Southern Pacific*, 320 U.S. 338 (1943).
[69] Mr. W. M. Leiserson, *National Labor Relations Act and Proposed Amendments*, Hearings before the Senate Committee on Education and Labor, Pt. 6, p. 993.
[70] Sec. 3, First (h).

separate craft or class. The Board has differentiated between these two terms:

Analyzing the phrase "craft or class" (which the law fixes as the unit for collective bargaining), it is to be noted that there are two types of organization in the railroad industry, one being the craft as ordinarily known to trade unionism where definite provision is made in the rules and working agreements for the education and development of apprentices and helpers. This type is found more particularly in the shops engaged in maintenance of equipment. All other railroad labor has been in the past recognized and dealt with by management in reasonably well defined classes. For example; the organization of Maintenance of Way employees has been made and recognized for many years as consisting of section foreman, track laborers, bridge and building foremen, bridge and building mechanics and helpers.[71]

Thus the "crafts" include all the ordinary craft unions, while the "classes" embrace all other types of employees.

The Board has enumerated three main principles used in determining what constitutes a craft or class:

When it became necessary for the Board to determine those eligible to participate in the selection of representative by the majority of the craft or class, the Board has been guided by these general principles:

(a) To follow, so far as practicable, the past practice in grouping of employees for representation purposes;

(b) To consider the nature of the employment, supervision, practicable lines of promotion and demotion, with accompanying seniority, to develop on the one hand protection of the employees from arbitrary action of management and a definite line of development of employees with a view to efficient operations;

(c) The public interest in preventing interruptions of commerce.[72]

All the employees of one carrier cannot constitute a single craft or class. The law says the employer must bargain with classes or crafts. This provision clearly precludes treating the entire working force of a carrier as constituting a single craft or class:

The employees of a steam railroad taken generally could not be considered as a single craft or class even if such employees including all the occupations on the railroad were joined in a single agreement. The words "craft or class" certainly imply something specific as distinguished from a general collection of employees related to each other only as employees of a single carrier. It must be considered that Congress employed the phrase

[71] *Delaware, Lackawanna and Western R. R. Co.*, Cases M-199 and R-358 (1937).
[72] The same.

"craft or class" in the usual and ordinary sense and meaning of the words, as distinguishing a group of employees who perform a certain type of work from another group or groups who perform other types of work.[73]

A bargaining unit can consist only of employees engaged in one type of transportation; the inclusion of workers for other types of carriers would tend to make more difficult the maintenance of uninterrupted transportation service.

. . . If railroad labor were grouped with the craft or class of other industry for representation purposes, it might very well be that disputes growing out of the different conditions prevailing at the steamship and other piers would justify the calling of a strike, whereas the condition did not affect the railroad operation. The result in such instances might be disastrous to the community dependent upon the railroads for food and certainly would tend to drive the traffic to the one line of railroad which has land facilities for handling such freight. . . .[74]

All the employees of a carrier in a single class or craft must act as a single unit in selecting a representative. The workers of a class or craft in a given locality cannot be set up as a separate entity for selecting a representative. Section 2 (9) seems to definitely imply that all the carrier's employees of a given class or craft wherever employed must act together for this purpose.[75]

The Board has opposed breaking into subdivisions the existing crafts or classes as such action would complicate its task. For example, it would oppose separating cooks from other dining car employees if this whole group of workers ever had been considered to constitute a single class.

. . . the Board views with some concern the tendency to divide established and well recognized crafts or classes. Typical of such instances are applications to represent only a few selected occupations of an established craft or class or applications for representation of the employees of a craft or class at only one terminal or on only one division of a carrier whose lines may extend over hundreds of miles. To permit such divisions would give rise to more divisions and subdivisions. Once the bars are down, there is no logical stopping place and such a course would ultimately defeat real collective bargaining as contemplated by the law. On the other hand, stabilization of well recognized crafts or classes as they have been generally established on

---

[73] *Chicago, Aurora, and Elgin Railroad Co.*, Case R-865 (1942).
[74] *Delaware, Lackawanna and Western R. R. Co.*, Cases M-199 and R-358 (1937).
[75] *New York, Chicago and St. Louis Railroad, Switchmen* (Buffalo and Cleveland Yards), Case R-74 (1935).

carriers under the act by the employees and managements after long years of negotiations, will also tend to stabilize collective bargaining relationships.[76]

Generally the Board has favored a wide definition of a craft or class based on existing bargaining practices, and it has insisted that the unit embrace all the employees of one class or craft of a single carrier. Thus nothing comparable to industrial units, plant-wide units, or multi-employer units is possible under the Railway Labor Act.

Although the act does not actually permit the designation of a bargaining unit that includes more than one carrier or that embraces employees of more than a single class or craft, the National Mediation Board looks with favor upon collective bargaining of an industry-wide character embracing all carriers and all workers of whatever type. It said, "the consummation of such nation-wide understandings is . . . deserving of all possible encouragement and commendation."[77]

III. UNAFFILIATED UNIONS

In the past ten years the number of workers in unions not affiliated with national organizations has declined from approximately 3,000,000 to about 1,000,000,[78] while at the same time the total membership of all unions has increased from 5,700,000 to 13,000,000.[79] Consequently it is pertinent to inquire into the attitude of the federal government toward unaffiliated unions. The relationship of the National Labor Relations Board and Railway Labor Act to the problem will be considered.

A. The National Labor Relations Board

When the National Labor Relations Act was passed in 1935, almost 3,000,000 workers belonged to unaffiliated unions. This was almost twice the number of workers that were in such unions three years earlier.[80] Many of these unaffiliated organizations were controlled by

---

[76] *Eighth Annual Report of the National Mediation Board* (1942), p. 6.

[77] *Third Annual Report of the National Mediation Board* (1937), p. 3. Most of the major changes in railroad wages in recent years have been on an industry-wide basis; the reduction of 1932 and its termination in 1935; *Public Papers and Addresses of Franklin D. Roosevelt*, 1934 (1938), pp. 97-98, 187, 201; the attempted reduction of 1938, *Report of Emergency Board, Santa Fe Railroad, et al.* (1938); the increase of 1941; *Report of Emergency Board*, Nov. 5, 1941, and again 1943, *Report of Emergency Board*, May 24, 1943.

[78] Lyon and others, *The National Recovery Administration*, p. 524, and Harry A. Millis and others, *How Collective Bargaining Works* (1942), p. 13.

[79] Memorandum of National Labor Relations Board, printed in 12 LRR 204.

[80] Lyon and others, *The National Recovery Administration*, p. 524.

the employer. In order to prevent such an interference with the worker's right of self-organization, Congress made it an unfair labor practice for an employer "to dominate or interfere with the formation and administration of any labor organization or contribute financial or other support to it."[81] Since the application of this provision to employer's activities has been examined already,[82] only its implications for unaffiliated labor organizations will be considered here.

The charge of employer domination is not used in cases involving nationally affiliated unions.

Although Section 8 (2) would appear to prohibit the domination of or interference with any labor organization, it is primarily used where the organization involved is not affiliated with the A.F. of L. or CIO.[83] Where the union concerned is affiliated with one of these major national organizations, and where the facts are such as to warrant a finding of domination under Section 8 (2), the Board prosecutes and decides the case as a violation of Section 8 (1), which is a general prohibition against employer interference.

The different consequences of a finding under these two provisions may affect the Board's choice of which one it will use in a given case. When a union is found to be dominated by the employer, it is disestablished,[84] but when an employer is found to have interfered with a union, nothing happens to the labor organization. The result of an order of disestablishment is that the union cannot act as the bargaining representative of a majority of workers. The Board will not certify an employer-dominated union as a representative, but it will certify a union that had been interfered with in violation of Section 8 (1). Thus if a union is found to be employer dominated, its name cannot even appear on the ballot in a representation election. The employees cannot express a choice for the independent union involved; they can select another union or refuse to be represented. But the affiliated union that has been interfered with can be put on the ballot.[85] This works to

---

[81] Sec. 8 (2).

[82] Chap. 2.

[83] G. O. Pratt, Chief Trial Examiner, NLRB, *National Labor Relations Act*, Hearings before the House Special Committee to Investigate the National Labor Relations Board, Pt. 9, p. 1909.

[84] *NLRB* v. *Folk Co.*, 308 U.S. 453 (1940).

[85] G. O. Pratt, *National Labor Relations Act*, Hearings before the House Special Committee to Investigate the National Labor Relations Board, Vol. 10, pp. 2050-51, 2060.

the disadvantage of the non-affiliated union. In justifying the disestablishment of the union involved in a violation of Section 8 (2), the representative of the Board said "that interference" had "so penetrated into the whole structure of the independent union that we have found that in no case" would it be possible that "you could simply by ceasing those acts relieve that organization from that domination and control by the company."[86]

As a further explanation of the Board's attitude, it is significant that the Secretary of the Board instructed a regional director: "We feel that the 8 (2) allegations should be saved for situations in which there are actually company unions." "By bringing an 8 (1) charge in this instance you save yourself the embarrassment of trying to prove the A.F. of L. is a company union."[87] A Board spokesman has said the reason the Board never brings a proceeding under Section 8 (2) against a local of the A.F. of L. or CIO is because no employer can dominate the A.F. of L. or CIO.[88] It is possible that an employer could not dominate the A.F. of L. or CIO, but that does not prove that it is impossible for him to dominate a local union that is affiliated with a national union that is a member of the A.F. of L. or CIO.

Certain acts of employers are considered to indicate domination.

Because of the great economic power of the employer, some of his activities normally "innocuous" of themselves are considered to constitute evidence of domination. Thus the Board has said:

In considering the effect of the employer's conduct upon the self-organization of employees, there must be borne in mind the control wielded by the employer over his employees—a control which results from the employees' complete dependence upon their jobs, generally their only means of livelihood and economic existence. As the natural result of the employer's economic power, employees are alertly responsive to the slightest suggestion of the employer. Activities, innocuous and without significance, as between two individuals economically independent of each other or of equal economic strength, assume enormous significance and heighten to proportions of coercion when engaged in by the employer in his relationship with his employees. For this reason the Board has been guided by the disparity in eco-

---

[86] The same, pp. 2052-53.
[87] The same, Pt. 11, p. 2242.
[88] The same, Pt. 9, pp. 1867, 1908.

nomic power between employer and employee in evaluating the significance of an employer's conduct as an unfair labor practice under Section 8 (2).[89]

If an employer is in a position to dominate an unaffiliated union, domination is usually assumed. It is not necessary to prove that the employer attempted to use his power but failed to dominate the labor organization. The mere existence of the potentiality of domination is sufficient.

In determining whether an employer controls both sides of the bargaining table because of his power to control the organization of his employees, it is immaterial whether the record reveals any situations showing that he *exercised* his power of control. The more effective his control is, because of possessing this power, the less occasion there will be for him to exercise it in order to bend the organization to his will. In fact the mere existence of such control over a labor organization necessarily precludes the possibility of the controlled organization acting as a free and independent agency for the representation of employees for the purposes of collective bargaining, such as is contemplated by the Act.[90]

Consequently it is immaterial that all the members joined the unaffiliated union of their own free choice despite the employer's activities.[91] Nothing in the act itself makes the mere existence of the power to dominate, an unfair labor practice. Finally, if domination existed at any time, it is generally assumed to continue as long as the union exists.[92]

The rapid recognition of an unaffiliated union has been considered to constitute evidence of domination.[93] Of course if the employer is slow in recognizing a union entitled to recognition, he is guilty of violating Section 8 (1). If at the time an unaffiliated union is recognized, an affiliated union is seeking to bargain, there is a presumption that the unaffiliated organization is dominated.[94]

The existence of a collective agreement with an unaffiliated union that contains provisions not unfavorable to the employer tends to raise a presumption of domination. [95] The fact that the labor organization

---

[89] *Third Annual Report of the National Labor Relations Board* (1938), p. 125.
[90] *Phelps Dodge Corp.*, 15 NLRB 732 (1939).
[91] *Hicks Body Co.*, 33 NLRB 858, 877 (1941).
[92] *Bethlehem Shipbuilding Co. Ltd.*, 11 NLRB 105 (1939); *Grace Co.*, 7 NLRB 766 (1938).
[93] *Swift and Co.*, 15 NLRB 992 (1939).
[94] *National Linen Service Corp.*, 48 NLRB 171 (1943).
[95] *Ed. Friedrich Inc.*, 17 NLRB 397 (1939).

agrees not to strike for the duration of the agreement has been considered evidence of domination. The Board considers the strike "labor's most powerful economic weapon," and consequently its surrender tends to indicate domination.[96] This idea is surprising, since one of the main reasons for encouraging collective bargaining is to promote industrial peace.

The grant to an unaffiliated union of a closed shop or the checkoff is of significance in indicating domination. The Board implied that by granting the closed or union shop to an unaffiliated union, the employer prevented the hiring of workers desiring to join a national organization.[97] A grant of the right to check off union dues is also evidence of a violation of Section 8 (2).[98] By the very act of permitting the checkoff the employer gives prestige and assistance to the organization.[99] If an unaffiliated union with a checkoff is found to be dominated, the employer must repay to the workers the dues deducted from their pay.[100] If a nationally affiliated union with a checkoff is found to be assisted by the employer in violation of Section 8 (1), the employer need not repay the dues to the employees. As a result employers will hesitate to grant the checkoff to non-affiliated unions.

Some employee activities are considered
to indicate domination.

In several cases the Board has held that an unaffiliated union that limits membership to the employees of a single employer was company dominated. It was argued that the employer can affect the membership of the union by discharging employees.[101] Since the act guarantees the right of self-organization, it would be logical to assume that the workers can determine the qualifications for membership. The Board has repeatedly implied that it does not object to a union refusing to admit to membership colored employees in a bargaining

---

[96] *Metal Mouldings Corp.*, 39 NLRB 107, 119 (1942).

[97] *Williams Coal Co.*, 11 NLRB 579, 611-12 (1939); *Hicks Body Co.*, 33 NLRB 858, 876 (1941). But see *Aeolian-American Corp.*, 8 NLRB 1043 (1938) where an unaffiliated union with a closed shop agreement was found to be free from domination.

[98] *Red Diamond Mining Co.*, 44 NLRB 1234 (1942), reversed 135 Fed. (2d) 13.

[99] *Clinton Cotton Mills*, 1 NLRB 97 (1935); *Blossom Products Corp.*, 20 NLRB 335, 348 (1940).

[100] *Heller Bros.*, 7 NLRB 646 (1938).

[101] *Vail-Ballou Press*, 15 NLRB 378, 397 (1939): "It is manifest that an organization is neither free nor independent unless it is competent to determine its own membership without employer interference."

unit, consequently it is not consistent for it to object to a union limiting its membership to employees in the unit it desires to represent. The restriction of membership to the employees of a single employer is very prevalent among unaffiliated unions. Does the Board imply that all unaffiliated unions are dominated if they have such a requirement?

In a recent case the Supreme Court sustained the Board in holding that an unaffiliated union with a closed-shop contract was employer dominated, because it refused to admit to membership leaders of a former CIO union.[102] A strike had been called by the CIO union to secure recognition. Finally at the suggestion of the CIO local the employer, the independent union, and the CIO affiliate agreed to a consent election by the NLRB and the winning union was to get a closed-shop contract. With the knowledge of this agreement, the Board held an election and certified the unaffiliated union. Upon this union's demand the employer made a closed-shop agreement with it. This labor organization then refused to admit to membership the leaders in the old CIO local. It demanded that the employer discharge these men under the closed-shop agreement; after protesting against this request, the employer finally acquiesced and discharged the men not admitted to the unaffiliated union. The Board held that the closed-shop agreement was illegal because the unaffiliated union, despite its certification by the Board, was employer dominated (Section 8 [2]). The main evidence of domination was the union's refusal to admit to membership the leaders in the old CIO union. The Board ordered the disestablishment of the non-affiliated local.

If the union requires that bargaining representatives and officers be members and employees, this requirement is also evidence of domination. The Board argues that it gives the employer control over the representative of the workers.[103] The act gives the worker the right to name as a representative a person who is not an employee, but it does not require that representatives be non-employees. It is not consistent with the idea of self-organization to assert that employees cannot require their representatives to be members and employees.

Under some circumstances the Board considers an unaffiliated union

[102] *Wallace Co.* v. *NLRB*, 323 U.S. 248 (1944); enforcing *Wallace Corp.*, 50 NLRB 138 (1943).
[103] *El Paso Electric Co.*, 13 NLRB 213 (1939).

to be dominated when it succeeds either a disestablished employer-dominated organization or an employee representation scheme.[104] A similarity between the constitutions and by-laws of the two organizations is evidence of domination.[105] Any similarity of officers and of members active in organizational work constitutes material evidence.[106] The Board summed up its attitude toward successor unions as follows:

> When an employee-representation plan or company union has been dissolved, and succeeded by an ostensibly independent union, the Board must decide on the basis of the entire record whether the new union is a genuinely different and unassisted labor organization. Identity of officers and leaders of both organizations, similarity in structure, bylaws and constitution, transfer of assets from the old to the new organization, and favoritism by the employer to the new organization as against a rival union, have all been found in various cases to indicate continued company domination.[107]

As applied Section 8 (2) appears to work to
the disadvantage of unaffiliated unions.

The difference in treatment of affiliated and non-affiliated organizations in comparable situations gives an advantage to the former. The affiliated organization is not disestablished where there has been interference, while in a similar situation the independent organization is disestablished. Thus the unaffiliated organization that is found to be dominated cannot be certified as a representative, while the local of the national union that had been dominated can be certified.

Many normally innocuous acts of the employer and even of employees are assumed to constitute evidence of domination. The mere power to dominate, even though not exercised, is construed to constitute actual domination. Rapid recognition, the making of a collective agreement not disadvantageous to the employer, and the grant of the closed shop and the checkoff are all of evidential value. An unaffiliated union succeeding a dominated organization must overcome an assump-

---

[104] *NLRB v. Southern Bell Telephone Co.*, 319 U.S. 50 (1943).
[105] See Chap. 2.
[106] For an example of a successor not dominated, see *Providence Gas Co.*, 41 NLRB 1121 (1942).
[107] *Seventh Annual Report of the National Labor Relations Board* (1942), p. 46. The Supreme Court has held that such a rebuttable presumption is not improper, *NLRB v. Southern Bell Telephone Co.*, 319 U.S. 50 (1943). Previous to 1939 an allegedly employer-dominated union received no notice of a proceeding involving its disestablishment. Since January 1939 it receives notice of the complaint, and generally it can become a party to the case; D. O. Bowman, *Public Control of Labor Relations* (1942), pp. 243-46.

tion of impropriety. The House Committee investigating the Board said: "In regard to independent unions, the National Labor Relations Board has consistently pursued a policy aimed at the extermination of these nationally unaffiliated organizations."[108]

B. The Railway Labor Act

The National Railroad Adjustment Board was established to arbitrate disputes between the carriers and their employees concerning the interpretation of collective agreements. Half the members of the Board are selected by the carriers and half by the workers. Only national labor organizations can participate in the selection of the employee members. Thus members of unaffiliated unions have no voice in the selection of the members of this agency. Mr. Joseph Eastman, the Federal Coordinator of Transportation, drew up the bill. He testified that this provision was designed to work against independent organizations. He said independent unions could have a voice in selecting members of the Board only by joining an existing national organization or by forming their own federation on a national basis.[109]

By the Railway Labor Act closed-shop agreements are prohibited because unaffiliated unions had found them advantageous. Before 1934 the closed-shop contract was used to assist in the formation of local unions by freezing out the national organization. In order to prevent the carriers from encouraging local unions by this device, the national unions sought the prohibition of such agreements. Consequently the Railway Labor Act actually prohibits the use of closed-shop agreements. As will be seen in another place,[110] the railroad brotherhoods generally do not desire closed-shop agreements for themselves because of peculiarities of organization. But they desired an absolute prohibition of such agreements in order to prevent un-

---

[108] H. Rept. 3109, Pt. I, p. 85. Not all of the decline in the membership of non-affiliated organizations is due to the Board's attitude; some independent unions voluntarily affiliated with the A. F. of L. and CIO before the Board really became effective. But the policies of the Board did not encourage the existence of independent unions. The Board of course has not found that all independent unions are employer dominated, not for example, *Solvay Process Co.*, 5 NLRB 330 (1938); *Aeolian American Corp.*, 8 NLRB 1043 (1938); and *Uxbridge Worsted Co. Inc.*, 11 NLRB 333 (1939). The act does not and cannot require membership in affiliated unions, *De Bardeliben* v. *NLRB* 135 Fed. (2d) 13 (1943).

[109] *To Amend the Railway Labor Act*, Hearings before the Senate Committee on Interstate Commerce, 73 Cong. 2 sess., p 156.

[110] Chap. 6.

affiliated unions from entrenching themselves and freezing out the national organization through such agreements.[111]

This act also forbids the checkoff. Here again this prohibition was aimed at the unaffiliated unions. These groups desired the checkoff and the national organizations,[112] feeling that they did not need it, opposed it because of its use by independent unions.[113] Here also Mr. Eastman indicated that the prohibition was included to weaken the independent unions.[114]

IV. CONCLUSIONS

Both the A.F. of L. and the railroad brotherhoods long had taken the attitude that the determining of what union a worker was to join was not up to him. The A.F. of L. had assumed that it was the sole source of the jurisdiction of legitimate labor unions. Of course as regards unions affiliated with the A.F. of L. this attitude was logical, but that organization tended to regard all non-affiliated unions as improper and illegitimate. Under its assumption that the unions chartered by it had exclusive jurisdiction over the fields covered by their charters, the workers had no right to determine to which A.F. of L. union they might wish to belong. Now this situation has greatly changed; the shape and form of labor organizations are to a large degree in the hands of government agencies, and to some extent they are in the hands of the workers actually on the job.

The government has definitely influenced the organization of the American labor movement.

The federal government, through several agencies, now has a definite influence on the form of labor organizations. Generally it has favored the development of large bargaining units, and it has encouraged unions that are affiliated with the A.F. of L. and CIO, while discouraging independent organizations. These attitudes were first evident under the NRA; only since the establishment of the NLRB

---

[111] *To Amend the Railway Labor Act*, Hearings before the Senate Committee on Interstate Commerce, pp. 150, 157.

[112] Mr. W. M. Leiserson, *National Labor Relations Act and Proposed Amendments*, Hearings before the Senate Committee on Education and Labor, Pt. 6, p. 997.

[113] *To Amend the Railway Labor Act*, Hearings before the Senate Committee on Interstate Commerce, p. 118.

[114] The same, p. 23.

have they been fully developed. Under the Railway Labor Act as applied by the National Mediation Board these tendencies have been less marked. Since the National Mediation Board has assumed a much less active role than the NLRB in shaping the development of the labor movement, most of the observations that follow are directed toward the problems arising from the decisions of the NLRB.

Because the National Labor Relations Act makes it an unfair labor practice for an employer to refuse to bargain with the true representatives of his workers, it was necessary to empower the NLRB to select appropriate bargaining units. If one did not believe in the desirability of imposing upon the employer an obligation to bargain collectively, this task would not have to be performed.

Further, it should be remembered that a closed-shop agreement can be made only with a labor organization representing a majority of the employees in the bargaining unit. This requirement also makes it necessary that the NLRB be vested with the authority to designate appropriate bargaining units. If one did not believe it desirable to legalize the closed shop and to require the employer to bargain collectively, then it would not be necessary to vest an agency with the power to designate bargaining units.

Any agency designating bargaining units is bound to have some influence on the organization of the labor movement. Even though one believes that the unit should be the free choice of the workers expressed by ballot, the agency administering such elections will inevitably affect their outcome, because it must draw the boundaries of the alternative units between which the workers must choose.

The National Labor Relations Act does not contain any standards to guide the Board in choosing between craft, industrial, employer, or plant units. The two objectives of the act—the protection of the right of the workers to self-organization and the increase of bargaining power—may or may not be in harmony, depending on the facts of each specific case. In any event they do not constitute a very definite guide to the Board in exercising its discretion in selecting the appropriate unit.

Congress has left the Board discretion to determine the relative weight to be given to these two objectives. The Board generally gives more consideration to the increase of bargaining power than to the protection of the workers' right of self-organization. This is true not only when the Board is deciding on the size and composition of the bargaining unit, but also when it is considering whether independent unions or organizations affiliated with the A.F. of L. or CIO are the best representatives of the majority in a unit.

CHAPTER V

THE GOVERNMENT AND THE LABOR MARKET

Some government activities have been undertaken to bring about an adjustment between the demand for and the supply of labor. These attempts to influence the labor market have been of three main types. Frequently the government has sought to influence the demand for labor through monetary devices, extension of credit, public works, or other measures designed to stimulate employment. The problem has also been approached from the standpoint of the supply of labor, some efforts being made to restrict the supply, while others have been designed to increase the number of available workers. A third line of activity has been directed toward bringing together employers with job openings and workers who desire employment. The government has sought to improve the functioning of the labor market by establishing a federal employment service.

This chapter will be confined to a consideration of government activities affecting the supply of labor and of federal efforts to produce a market place for labor. Consideration of broad efforts to increase the general demand for labor would take us too far afield. In examining the government's policy toward the supply of labor, we will consider first its actions designed to increase the supply of available workers and then those which tend to restrict the supply of labor. In the final section of the chapter the United States Employment Service and the War Manpower Commission will be discussed.

I. INCREASING THE SUPPLY OF LABOR

Most activities that increase the supply of labor are of an educational nature. Vocational education, vocational rehabilitation, and apprentice training will be considered. The work of the Committee on Fair Employment Practice will be surveyed.

Largely because the states had neglected vocational education, the federal government began to encourage it in 1917. The proponents of the original program believed that if grants-in-aid were made to the states, the total expenditures for vocational education would be greatly increased since the federal grants would have to be matched by state and local funds.[1] The program includes training in agriculture, home economics, industry, and marketing. Only the last two types of training are of concern here. On various bases the federal government distributes more than $8,000,000 annually for these different programs.[2] Practically all of this money must be matched dollar for dollar by state or local funds. All of the states participate in the programs, but probably only 15 per cent of the demand for trained workers is being met by this type of training.[3]

The vocational training offered is not exclusively determined by the requirements of the labor market.

Instruction can be given in full-time, part-time, and evening classes. Whatever the means of instruction, the work must be of less than college grade. "The controlling purpose of such education shall be to fit for useful employment . . . and shall be designed to meet the needs of persons over fourteen years of age who are preparing for a trade or industrial pursuit or who have entered upon" such work.[4] In day school classes for persons who have not begun to work, at least half of the instruction must consist of practical work "on a useful or productive basis." Part of the money must be used for part-time day schools. Evening schools can be maintained for persons above sixteen years of age and they "shall confine instruction to that which is supplemental to the daily employment."[5]

In the full-time classes there has been little effort to train people in skills for which there is a potential demand. Training is offered to prepare young people to be electricians, automobile mechanics, plumbers, carpenters, pattern-makers, and so forth. There is evidence that instructors are desirous of securing large enrollments and consequently many youths are lured into these classes, though they might profit little from the instruction. It appears that not much effort has been made to steer persons into occupations where there is likely to exist a potential demand for labor. The staff of the Advisory Committee on Education observed: "Representatives both of organized labor and of

[1] Advisory Committee on Education, *Vocational Education* (1938), pp. 14-19.
[2] *Department of Labor—Federal Security Agency Appropriation Bill for 1944,* Hearings before the Subcommittee of the House Committee on Appropriations, Pt. 2, 78 Cong. 1 sess., p. 157.
[3] Advisory Committee on Education, *Vocational Education,* p. 114; and TNEC *Hearings,* Pt. 30, pp. 17, 148.
[4] Act of Feb. 23, 1917, 39 Stat. 929, Sec. 11.
[5] The same.

industrial management are critical of the inadequate preparation for skilled trades that is given in some of the all-day schools."[6] "It operates without definition of responsibility either to industry or to adult labor already engaged in the trades. Within its own vacuum it produces a legion of graduates, unrelated in numbers to any competent standard of employment needs."[7]

Many people are of the opinion that the part-time and evening classes give better results than the day classes.[8] The part-time classes are mainly designed for the instruction of apprentices. The evening classes are for persons over 16 and can offer only instruction that is supplemental to the daily employment of the students. This requirement has some undesirable consequences. As interpreted, it prevents a person from receiving instruction in a skill or trade that he is not actually following. This restriction is disadvantageous to persons who are employed in a trade that is declining, and who therefore are desirous of learning a new trade that has greater possibilities.

Vocational training normally has been approached almost exclusively from the standpoint of education. Little concern has been shown for the potential demand for the skills in which training is offered. The federal government entered the field primarily because the states did not carry on such activities, and the grants-in-aid were designed to encourage the states to assume the function. But many states still make available only the minimum amount of money necessary to secure the maximum aid available from the federal government.

Vocational rehabilitation has been undertaken
as a welfare and educational measure.

Mainly as a result of interest aroused by the rehabilitation of veterans disabled in World War I, the federal government undertook to encourage the states to adopt programs of general vocational rehabilitation for persons injured in any manner. It developed a program of grants-in-aid to the states to assist them in vocational rehabilitation. The states must at least match the federal funds.[9] Actual execution of the program is in the hands of the states, but they are subject to the supervision of the Office of Vocational Rehabilitation, a part of the

[6] Advisory Committee on Education, *Vocational Education*, p. 153.
[7] The same, p. 260.
[8] The same, pp. 153, 159; and TNEC *Hearings*, Pt. 30, pp. 17, 155.
[9] Act of June 2, 1920, 41 Stat. 735; as amended by act of July 6, 1943, 57 Stat. 374.

Federal Security Agency. Originally the program was undertaken largely for humanitarian reasons, but operations have been expanded to increase the supply of labor because of wartime needs.[10]

The program now involves both physical rehabilitation (including treatment and the purchase of necessary equipment) and training. But most of the available funds are utilized for training rather than rehabilitation.[11] The type of training is generally determined on an individual basis, and it may be in school or on a job.

In 1941 about 19,747 persons were rehabilitated, and in 1944 (fiscal year) 53,000, according to estimates. The average cost per case is $179.[12] The federal government spent $2,281,941 in 1941 and $2,900,000 in 1943. It has been estimated that the program meets the needs of about 20 per cent of those who could benefit from it.[13]

Where an individual has a remedial handicap, it is the aim of the rehabilitation program to provide for his physical restoration rather than for his "training around a disability." The removal of the physical defect and the restoration of capacity of the disabled person are considered a more efficient type of service than the preparation for a new occupation without such measures. Surgical and medical rehabilitation are now also permitted.[14] As a result of physical rehabilitation, in some cases the economic rehabilitation follows without further steps.

The program is primarily one of education and rehabilitation undertaken for humanitarian reasons. Its effect on the total labor supply is very small. Since it was carried on during a period of great unemployment, it appears that its primary objective has not been to increase the labor supply.

*Limited encouragement for the training
of apprentices is offered.*

Because of a number of circumstances, the federal government undertook to encourage the training of apprentices. Since apprenticeship

[10] *Department of Labor—Federal Security Agency Appropriation Bill for 1944,* Hearings before the Subcommittee of the House Committee on Appropriations, Pt. 2, pp. 127-36.

[11] *Vocational Rehabilitation, Education and Training,* Hearings before House Committee on Education, 78 Cong. 1 sess., p. 34.

[12] *Department of Labor—Federal Security Agency Appropriation Bill for 1945,* Hearings before the Subcommittee of the House Committee on Appropriations, Pt. 2, 78 Cong. 2 sess., pp. 413, 427.

[13] Advisory Committee on Education, *Vocational Rehabilitation of the Physically Disabled* (1938), p. 75.

[14] See act of July 6, 1943, Sec. 3 (a), (3) A.

had been declining for a considerable period of years, there was a need for some agency to bring about such action. In 1920 there were 140,400 apprentices in the United States; in 1930, 92,642;[15] and in 1935-36 the number reached a low of 37,890.[16] The decline in apprenticeship was a result of several factors: (1) the reductions in immigration; (2) the specialization of work; (3) the increased mobility of journeymen caused many employers to be unwilling to undertake training; (4) the belief that increased use of machines reduced the need for skilled men. Of course, the depression also was a contributing influence.[17] Many of the original NRA codes made in 1933 contained no provisions permitting employers to pay to apprentices wages below the minimum fixed by the codes. Consequently apprenticeship declined still further.

Primarily because of the impact of the NRA on apprenticeship, the federal government first became interested in it. In March 1934 the NRA created a committee to consider the position of apprentices under the codes.[18] Later that year the President, by an executive order, permitted employers to pay apprentices wages below the minimum, and he also directed the Secretary of Labor to set up a special committee on apprentice training.[19] In the summer of 1935 this committee was transferred to the NYA; ultimately it became a part of the Department of Labor.

In 1937 Congress enacted legislation authorizing the Department of Labor to encourage apprenticeship. The House Committee on Labor in reporting this legislation said that there was a need for a federal agency to bring employers and employees together to develop apprenticeship standards.[20] The law that was passed authorized the Secretary of Labor to formulate standards of apprentice training and to encourage their inclusion in contracts of apprenticeship, and directed the Secretary to appoint an advisory committee on the subject.[21] A section on apprenticeship was set up in the Division of Labor Standards to carry on these promotional activities. It was transferred to the War Manpower Commission in 1942.[22]

---

[15] *Editorial Research Reports* (1940), Vol. 2, p. 439.
[16] *To Safeguard the Welfare of Apprentices*, Hearings before the House Committee on Labor, 75 Cong. 1 sess., p. 39.
[17] Statement of Clara M. Beyer, the same, pp. 2-7.
[18] The same, p. 3.
[19] Executive Order No. 6750 C, June 27, 1934.
[20] *Safeguard Welfare of Apprentices*, H. Rept. 945, 75 Cong. 1 sess., p. 2.
[21] Act of Aug. 16, 1937, 50 Stat. 664.
[22] Executive Order No. 9279, Dec. 5, 1942.

The federal program is entirely voluntary. The section on apprenticeship encourages the states to adopt apprenticeship laws, and it also seeks to educate employers concerning the need for establishing apprentice training programs. At least 20 states have enacted laws providing for the supervision of apprentice training. An apprenticeship program to meet the standards formulated by this section must be based on a written agreement. It has to provide for at least 2,000 hours of reasonably sustained employment a year, and it must involve a progressive program of training including at least 144 hours of class-room instruction annually. It must also establish a system of wage increases.

The number of apprentices has increased since the program was set up. In 1935-36 the number reached a low of 37,890; by March 1941 it had increased to about 125,000, of whom 51,000 were being trained under federally approved programs.[23]

Apprenticeship training is encouraged by certain provisions of the Fair Labor Standards Act. Apprentices are exempt from its minimum wage provisions[24] if they are being trained under an approved program. The standards used in determining what constitutes an approved program are essentially those developed by the Division of Labor Standards. Since practically all apprentices receive more than the minimum wage provided in the act,[25] this provision is not very important from the standpoint of their basic wage rates. But in determining when it is necessary to pay overtime rates to apprentices, the existence of an approved scheme is important for the employer. Time-and-a-half must be paid for all hours worked beyond 40 per week, and for regular workers in computing time worked, the attendance at required classes is considered as time worked. But under an approved apprentice training program the time spent in classes is not considered as time worked.[26] It will be remembered that an approved apprentice program requires at least 144 hours of instruction.

The decline in apprenticeship was resulting in a reduction in the

---

[23] *Department of Labor—Federal Security Agency Appropriation Bill for 1942,* Hearings before the Subcommittee of the House Committee on Appropriations, Pt. 1, 77 Cong. 1 sess., pp. 93-95.

[24] Act of June 25, 1938, 52 Stat. 1068, Sec. 14.

[25] Paul T. David, *Barriers to Youth Employment* (American Council on Education, 1942), p. 77.

[26] Wages and Hours Division, *Interpretative Bulletin,* No. 13, Pt. 3 (1940).

supply of skilled workers. Little was being done to meet this problem until the federal government undertook to encourage apprentice training. Since the federal government has become interested in the problem, the number of apprentices has increased.

*The Committee on Fair Employment Practice seeks
to eliminate discrimination in employment.*

With the man-power shortage that developed in World War II, maximum utilization of the available labor supply was imperative. Because of prejudices of both employers and employees, some persons with needed skills were not used at all, or were employed in work that did not fully utilize their capacity. These prejudices were directed against social, racial, national, and religious groups.

By executive order, President Roosevelt, attempted to end such discrimination during the war. The President found that the war demanded maximum employment regardless of race, religion, or nationality, and he observed that all available workers were not being used. Consequently he asserted: "I do hereby reaffirm the policy of the United States that there shall be no discrimination in the employment of any person in war industries or in government by reason of race, creed, color, or national origin."[27]

The order provided that in all contracts negotiated by the government there shall be no discrimination in employment.[28] The Comptroller General held that this prohibition of discrimination did not authorize the rejection of the lowest bid because the contractor would not include such a clause in the agreement.[29] Subsequently the President wrote the Attorney General that in all government contracts the inclusion of such a clause was mandatory.[30] The executive order went on to declare that there shall be no discrimination in government training programs.[31]

A Committee on Fair Employment Practice was created consisting of a full-time chairman and six other members. The order says "the

---

[27] Executive Order No. 9346, May 27, 1943, *Federal Register*, Vol. 8, p. 7183. This modified Executive Order No. 8802, June 26, 1941, *Federal Register*, Vol. 6, p. 3109.

[28] The same, Sec. 1.

[29] 23 Decisions of Comptroller General 362 (1943).

[30] Nov. 5, 1943; *Manpower Reports*, 70:125.

[31] Sec. 2.

Committee shall formulate policies to achieve the purposes of this Order."[32] It "shall receive and investigate complaints of discrimination forbidden by this order." It can hold hearings, make findings of fact, and take "appropriate steps to obtain elimination of such discrimination."[33]

The jurisdiction, types of discrimination handled, and the powers of the committee will be considered. This agency asserts a general jurisdiction over discrimination in defense industries, and in locally essential services.[34] Section 5 of the order provides that it shall investigate complaints of discrimination forbidden by the order. But only discrimination in employment in war industries and in government training facilities is forbidden. To justify its position, the committee looks to the statement of policy against discrimination in the preamble and the grant of authority to formulate policies to achieve the purpose of the order.[35] Of course its power to investigate is derived exclusively from Section 5 where its use is limited to alleged violations forbidden by the order. On one occasion the chairman said his jurisdiction was not entirely derived from the order.[36] The House Committee on Appropriations believes that the executive order specifically limits the jurisdiction of the FEPC.[37] The FEPC has taken jurisdiction of cases involving railroads, local transportation, and newspapers.[38] If its order prohibiting discrimination on the railroads should be obeyed, the supply of labor available to the southern carriers would be greatly increased. Because of the prevalence of racial discrimination in this field, many competent Negroes were not being utilized.

The committee generally takes jurisdiction only when a complaint is made by an individual or the government. But on the basis of its own survey of employment advertisements, it has taken jurisdiction in some cases on its own initiative.[39] It generally tries to settle cases

---

[32] Sec. 4.

[33] Sec. 5.

[34] Opinion of Council of War Manpower Committee to FEPC, Sept. 28, 1942, *Manpower Reports* 70:45.

[35] Chairman Ross, *To Investigate Executive Agencies*, Hearings before the Special House Committee to Investigate Executive Agencies, Pt. 2, 78 Cong. 2 sess., pp. 1897-98.

[36] The same, p. 1893.

[37] H. Rept. 1511, 78 Cong. 2 sess., p. 13.

[38] It ultimately backed down in the case of newspapers. *National War Agencies Appropriation Bill, 1945*, Hearings before the Senate Committee on Appropriations, 78 Cong. 2 sess., p. 179.

[39] The same, p. 167.

without resorting to hearings, because it has no power to subpoena witnesses.

It has taken jurisdiction over all types of cases involving discrimination. Most complaints are against private employers (68 per cent), but the government is involved in 25 per cent, and the other complaints allege discrimination by unions.[40] Most cases involve racial discrimination mainly against Negroes (80 per cent), religion is involved in 9 per cent, nationality in about 6 per cent, and alien status in 5 per cent.[41]

The FEPC believes it can issue an order to end any form of discrimination. It has ordered employers to desist from discriminating against Negroes in hiring workers.[42] Collective agreements with unions have been ordered terminated when they required discrimination.[43] Unions have been directed to cease discrimination in the admission of new members.[44]

The committee has no direct authority to enforce any of its orders. On three occasions it referred to the President cases where its orders had not been obeyed.[45] In such cases of noncompliance government contracts could be cancelled, but such action was not considered desirable, as it would hinder production.[46] The President has never taken over any plant solely because of discrimination. Congress now has effectively barred the committee from appealing to the President to take over plants for failure to comply with its orders. It has also provided that the government should not have a right to appeal that is not open equally to the accused.[47] Only after the enactment of this law did the President seize a property because of discrimination. But here the employer attempted to carry out the order of the committee, the employees struck in opposition, and the property was seized because of the strike.[48]

[40] Chairman Ross, *To Prohibit Discrimination in Employment*, Hearings before the House Committee on Labor, 78 Cong. 2 sess., p. 152.
[41] FEPC, How It Operates (1944) by Division of Review and Analysis, FEPC, *Manpower Reports* 70:144.
[42] Douglas Aircraft Co. (1941), *Manpower Reports* 70:1.
[43] Southwestern Carriers Conference (1943), the same, 70:59.
[44] International Union of Boilermakers and Kaiser Co. (1943); the same, 70:69.
[45] Chairman Ross, *To Prohibit Discrimination in Employment*, Hearings before the House Committee on Labor, p. 158.
[46] *National War Agencies Appropriation Bill for 1945*, Hearings before House Committee on Appropriations, Pt. 2, p. 559.
[47] Public Law No. 372, Title 1, June 28, 1944.
[48] 14 LRR 721.

Although the FEPC was established to increase the labor supply by reducing discrimination in employment practices, one gets the impression from studying the committee's decisions that it considers the elimination of discrimination as an end in itself.

II. LIMITING THE SUPPLY OF LABOR

The regulation of prison work is one method of restricting the available supply of labor. The sale in the open market of goods made by convicts is strongly opposed by organized labor because of the low wages paid to convicts. The amount of prison-made goods has not been large partly because of restrictive legislation. Goods produced in prisons in 1932 were worth $75,369,000 and only $29,949,000 entered into direct competition with free labor.[49] In 1940 their total value had declined to $56,731,000, and of this amount only $9,000,000 was sold in the open market.[50] But in the case of some specific products the amount thus produced constituted such a large proportion of the total production that its sale in the open market might have had some effect on wage rates. For example, in 1931 over one third of the national output of wide duck was produced in the federal penitentiary at Atlanta.[51] The restriction of production by prison labor offers a difficult problem because the employment of convicts in useful work is generally considered to be a desirable correctional measure.

The competition of prison
labor has been limited.

In 1930 Congress prohibited the sale to the public of goods produced in federal prisons, but at the same time it directed the Attorney General to provide employment for all physically fit convicts in federal institutions.[52] Such employment must be "in such diversified forms as will reduce to a minimum competition with private industry and free labor."[53] In the same year Congress also prohibited the importation of goods made by prison labor.[54] The control of production in fed-

---

[49] *Monthly Labor Review,* Vol. 50 (1940), p. 1422.
[50] Bureau of Labor Statistics, *Prison Labor in the United States in 1940,* Bulletin 698, pp. 2, 27.
[51] *Prison Industries Board,* H. Rept. 235, 73 Cong. 1 sess., p. 3.
[52] Act of May 27, 1930, 46 Stat. 391.
[53] The same, Sec. 1.
[54] Act of June 17, 1930, 46 Stat. 689, Sec. 307.

eral penal institutions and the prohibition of the importation of prison-made goods was only a partial solution of the problem.

Most prison-made goods offered for sale in the United States are produced in state penal institutions. But Congress has no direct authority over work done in such institutions. Consequently indirect means have been utilized to restrict the public sale of these products. In 1929 Congress provided that goods made by prison labor when shipped in interstate commerce become subject to the laws of the state of their destination immediately upon arrival.[55] Without such a federal law, a state could not effectively prohibit the importation of such products made in another state, because a state does not have jurisdiction over goods moving in interstate commerce as long as they remain either in their original package or in the hands of the original recipient. The act of 1929 thus facilitated the enforcement of state laws that prohibited the sale of prison-made goods. In order to permit the states to reorganize their prison industries the law did not become applicable until 1934. The Supreme Court upheld the constitutionality of this legislation, saying:

All such legislation, state and federal, proceeds upon the view that free labor, properly compensated, cannot compete successfully with the enforced and unpaid or underpaid convict labor of the prison. A state basing its legislation upon that conception, has the right and power so far as the federal Constitution is concerned, by non-discriminating legislation, to preserve its policy from impairment or defeat, by any means appropriate to the end and not inconsistent with that instrument. . . .[56]

This law was strengthened one year after it became applicable. In 1935 Congress made it illegal to transport in interstate commerce goods made by prison labor when the state of destination prohibited their resale.[57] The Supreme Court also held this act constitutional in 1937.[58]

By 1940 only ten states did not prohibit the sale of prison-made goods, and the value of such products moving in interstate commerce declined to $2,291,000.[59] Congress could restrict the market for such goods in these ten remaining states only by absolutely prohibiting their

[55] Act of June 19, 1929, 45 Stat. 1084.
[56] *Whitefield v. Ohio*, 297 U.S. 431, 439-40 (1936).
[57] Act of July 24, 1935, 49 Stat. 494.
[58] *Kentucky Whip and Collar Co.* v. *Illinois Central R. R. Co.* 299 U.S. 334 (1937).
[59] Bureau of Labor Statistics, Bulletin 698, p. 27.

shipment in interstate commerce. Consequently, it did exactly that in 1940.[60]

*The restriction of immigration is one of the most
important devices for limiting the supply of labor.*

With the passage of the Immigration Act of 1924, the restriction of immigration became a permanent national policy.[61] One of the major reasons for the enactment of this law was the desire of organized labor to restrict the supply of low-wage immigrant workers.[62] When the depression began in 1930, even the limited immigration permitted under this law was considered to be undesirable. Consequently, use was made of the provision of the Immigration Law of February 5, 1917 that prohibited the entry of aliens who were likely to become public charges.[63] The Department of Labor in October 1930 adopted the policy of enforcing this prohibition very vigorously by refusing visas to immigrants who did not have a definite means of support.[64] The Secretary of Labor said: "Nearly all immigrants are potential wage-earners. We have long realized that the unlimited immigration of the past is in a large measure responsible for the over-supply of some classes of labor. . . . Only one immigrant is admitted now where five were admitted a year ago."[65] As a result of this policy, emigration exceeded immigration in a number of years in the period from 1930 to the outbreak of World War II.[66]

*The Fair Labor Standards Act through its child labor, wage,
and hour provisions tends to restrict the supply of labor.*

By the child labor provisions of the Fair Labor Standards Act, Congress sought to keep young people out of the labor market. The act prohibits all labor by children under 14 years of age when they are employed in interstate commerce or in the production of goods intended to move in such commerce, and persons under 16 cannot be employed in mining and manufacturing.[67] One reason for these pro-

[60] Act of Oct. 14, 1940, 54 Stat. 1134. This law became effective the next year.
[61] Act of May 26, 1924, 43 Stat. 153.
[62] *Restriction of Immigration*, H. Rept. 176, 68 Cong. 1 sess., pp. 17-20.
[63] Act of Feb. 5, 1917, 39 Stat. 874, Secs. 6 and 19.
[64] *Annual Report of the Secretary of Labor* (1931), p. 53.
[65] The same, p. 4.
[66] The same (1937), p. 83.
[67] Act of June 25, 1938, 52 Stat. 1060, Sec. 3 (b).

visions was a purely humanitarian desire to protect children. Another objective was the protection of the labor market from the competition of children. It was argued that because of the poor bargaining position of children, their employment tended to depress the wages of all workers.[68]

The minimum wage provisions tend to limit the employment of handicapped workers. The act provides for a minimum wage of 30 cents an hour, and under certain conditions this can be increased to 40 cents.[69] Exemptions for handicapped persons, learners, and apprentices can be granted by the administrator of the Wage and Hour Division. Although handicapped persons can secure exemptions, employers have manifested an increasing unwillingness to employ such persons, because of the need for securing in advance certificates permitting their employment.

The employment of learners is also restricted by the wage provisions. Under the regulations issued by the administrator of the Wage and Hour Division, employers seeking to hire learners at less than the minimum wage must show that their employment is necessary in order to prevent a curtailment of production. The employer must first demonstrate that he "has made diligent efforts to secure experienced workers and is unable to obtain them. No certificate will be issued if it is found that experienced workers are available."[70] Not more than 5 or 10 per cent of the workers for any one employer can be learners receiving less than the minimum wage.[71] At least one investigator has concluded that these regulations restrict the training and employment of learners.[72] The minimum wage provisions have little effect on the employment of apprentices since most of them are generally paid more than the minimum rate provided by the law.[73]

The provisions regulating the hours of work also restrict the supply of trained workers. The law requires the payment of time-and-a-half for all work done in excess of 40 hours per week. Many workers undergoing training attend classes in addition to working regular

---

[68] *Fair Labor Standards Act of 1937*, Hearings before the House Committee on Labor, 75 Cong. 1 sess., pp. 382-83.

[69] Sec. 14.

[70] Wage and Hour Division, Learners' Regulations Explained, Oct. 10, 1939, Bureau of National Affairs, Inc., *Wage and Hour Manual* (1942), p. 587.

[71] David, *Barriers to Youth Employment*, p. 78.

[72] The same, p. 80.

[73] The same, p. 77.

hours. The administrator of the Wage and Hour Division generally has considered that the time thus spent must be considered as time worked for the purpose of computing wages.[74] As a consequence many industrial establishments curtailed their training programs. But because of the need for war production, the administrator found it desirable to modify his attitude toward training activities that increase the skills actually being used by the workers.[75] Thus it appears that a number of sections of the Wage and Hour Act directly or indirectly tend to reduce the supply of labor.

III. THE UNITED STATES EMPLOYMENT SERVICE AND THE WAR MANPOWER COMMISSION

In a large country containing several hundred separate labor markets, there is a real problem of securing a proper supply of labor at the right time in each of the markets. One means of bringing the available workers into touch with the existing employment opportunities in the different areas is through an employment service. It can assist in bringing about a proper flow of labor to areas where there is a demand, and it can reduce the flow of potential workers to areas where a surplus of job-seekers exists. Independent privately operated exchanges, or unco-ordinated state services, could not perform this function as effectively as a service with nationwide coverage and with information available on both the supply of and the demand for labor in all areas.

The first federal employment agency was set up in 1907 as an adjunct to the Bureau of Immigration. A number of states had already set up employment agencies, Ohio having pioneered in this field with the establishment of such an organization in 1890. It was designed to distribute immigrants more evenly throughout the country.[76] In World War I a federal employment service developed as a separate organization in the Department of Labor. It operated side by side with state and municipal services.[77] After the end of that war, available federal funds were greatly reduced and the United States Employment Service became only a central information organization. For a field service it utilized local offices that were financed almost entirely by states and cities.[78] In 1920 there were 269 offices in 41 states, but

---

[74] Wage and Hour Division, *Wage and Hour Manual*, Information Bulletin No. 13 (1942), p. 127.

[75] The same; Letter by the administrator to Sidney Hillman of the OPM. No one of these conditions is applied to training classes for apprentices. The same, p. 127.

[76] John Lombardi, *Labor's Voice in the Cabinet* (1942), pp. 144-45.

[77] Darrell H. Smith, *United States Employment Service* (1923), pp. 13-24.

[78] Ruth B. Kellogg, *The United States Employment Service* (1933), Chap. 1.

by the end of 1930 the number of offices had declined to 151 in 24 states. In 1931, largely because of pressure from veterans' organizations, the Employment Service set up some field offices of its own; but they were discontinued in April 1933.[79]

To establish "a national system of employment offices," Congress enacted the National Employment Service Act on June 6, 1933.[80] This provided for the creation of a co-operative employment service financed on a grant-in-aid basis. To aid in the maintenance of state employment services, the act authorized an annual appropriation of $3,000,000 to be allocated among the states on the basis of population. A state has to meet certain conditions to receive federal funds. It must make available a sum equal to the federal grant and it must accept the provisions of the act. Originally the United States Employment Service was a part of the Department of Labor, but in 1939 the agency was transferred to the Social Security Board, where it was merged with the Bureau of Unemployment Compensation to form a Bureau of Employment Security.[81] Late in December 1941 the state employment services were taken over completely by the federal government,[82] and in September 1942 the United States Employment Service was transferred to the War Manpower Commission.[83]

Section 3 of the Employment Service Act of June 6, 1933 provides:

> . . . The bureau [U. S. Employment Service] shall also assist in coordinating the public employment offices throughout the country and in increasing their usefulness by developing and prescribing minimum standards of efficiency, assisting them in meeting problems peculiar to their localities, promoting uniformity in their administrative and statistical procedure, furnishing and publishing information as to opportunities for employment and other information of value in the operation of the system, and maintaining a system for clearing labor between the several States.

The objective was to create a national system operating uniformly throughout the nation.

In order to develop this national system of employment services, the USES prescribed detailed records, statistics, procedures, and clearance practices for all the employment services. The states had to agree

---

[79] Raymond C. Atkinson, Louise C. Odencrantz, and Ben Deming, *Public Employment Service in the United States* (1938), pp. 2-3.

[80] 48 Stat. 113.

[81] *Reorganization Plan No. 1*, 53 Stat. 1425, Sec. 203. The reason for this was its intimate relationship to unemployment compensation administration.

[82] Executive Order No. 8990, Dec. 24, 1941. *Federal Register*, Vol. 6, p. 6727.

[83] Executive Order No. 9247, Sept. 14, 1942. *Federal Register*, Vol. 7, p. 7379.

to follow these procedures. Thus detailed placement machinery was set up. When a request for a worker is received, supposedly the skills of all applicants are considered, and the best available applicants are recommended. But recently the head of one state unemployment compensation organization said many services do not make such a careful survey of applicants to find the best one for the opening. He asserted that often they are run on what he called a "cafeteria basis." The vacancy is only brought to the attention of the applicants who happen to visit the office, and no careful search of the files is made.[84]

Problems of relief and unemployment compensation administration made difficult the development of a national employment service.

The close tie-up of the Employment Service with the administration of unemployment compensation has had undesirable results. For a state system of unemployment compensation to receive assistance from the federal government, it must provide for the payment of unemployment benefits through public employment offices.[85] Consequently all states accepted the Employment Service Act, before they began to pay unemployment benefits. From money appropriated for the administration of unemployment compensation, additional federal funds that do not have to be matched are made available to the state services.

An agency responsible for the administration of an insurance program attempts to minimize the drain on its funds resulting from the payment of benefits. The state employment services as a part of the machinery administering unemployment insurance have done exactly this. It has been only natural for them to give preference to an unemployed insured person for any job opening. Therefore it is not surprising that the head of the Employment Service testified in 1941 that the organization was not much interested in placing employed persons. He said the application of an employed person would be accepted, but such an applicant probably would never be referred to a job.[86] At that

---

[84] *Department of Labor—Federal Security Agency Appropriation Bill for 1944,* Hearings before the Subcommittee of the House Committee on Appropriations, Pt. 3, pp. 560; the same for 1945, Pt. 3, p. 142.

[85] Act of Aug. 14, 1935, 49 Stat. 626, Sec. 303 (a) (2).

[86] *Department of Labor—Federal Security Agency Appropriation Bill for 1942,* Hearings before the Subcommittee of the House Committee on Appropriations, Pt. 2, p. 843.

time less than 5 per cent of the persons registered at the employment offices were employed.[87] The Select Committee of the House of Representatives Investigating National Defense Migration found that because of this attitude the Employment Service was not doing the job that was expected of it. It said:

This committee believes that because State employment services have traditionally served as referral agencies for persons who are unemployed for longer or shorter periods of time they are today ill-fitted for dealing with labor scarcity, especially under wartime conditions. Their offices have characteristically worked closely with relief agencies. Operating under conditions of labor surplus, they have not been primarily concerned with the labor production problems of employers.[88]

It is not the objective to argue that it is undesirable to require recipients of unemployment insurance to register with public employment offices. It is absolutely necessary that they do so in order to enforce the desirable requirement that a recipient of benefits must be willing to work. But it may well be argued that for the good of the Employment Service, it should be independent of the agency responsible for the administration of unemployment insurance.

The present Employment Service was organized in a period when most openings were in relief work or public construction. Even in the fiscal year 1940 over a quarter of all regular placements made by it were on relief projects and public works. As a result of its role in the relief program and because of its relationship to the administration of unemployment compensation, only 5 per cent of its registrants were actually employed. About one fifth of all placements made were in skilled and semiskilled occupations, about one third were in the service trades, and only one tenth were in positions requiring white-collar workers.[89] Thus most of the work of the Service consisted of placing unskilled workers and persons in the service trades. An official of the War Manpower Commission has testified: "The U.S.E.S., to me, as a manufacturer, five or six years ago, was a relief agency. . . . It was handling a type of labor I was not interested in."[90]

[87] *Sixth Annual Report of the Social Security Board* (1941), p. 86.
[88] *National Defense Migration*, H. Rept. 2396, 77 Cong. 2 sess., p. 25.
[89] *Fifth Annual Report of the Social Security Board* (1940), p. 69.
[90] L. A. Appley, *Department of Labor—Federal Security Agency Appropriation Bill for 1945*, Hearings before the Subcommittee of the House Committee on Appropriations, Pt. 3, p. 159.

The usefulness of the Service has been limited
by the attitudes of a number of groups.

Many of the state organizations were unwilling to exchange information concerning unfilled job openings and unplaced workers. One of the main reasons for establishing the USES was to develop a national employment service. An important device for accomplishing that objective is a system of interstate clearance of information concerning employment opportunities and available employees, so the proper amount of labor can be moved from areas of underemployment to areas where there is a demand for work.[91] The act says: "The bureau shall also assist in . . . maintaining a system for clearing labor between the several States."[92] A manual of instructions for clearance was developed, and in 1936 the Service filled by this means 207,152 jobs on relief projects or public works, as well as 19,925 in private employment.[93] But even in the last half of 1941 only about 2 per cent of all openings were filled through interstate clearance.[94]

In 1941 the Chairman of the Social Security Board testified that many states refused to inform other states about either available openings or surplus workers available for work in other states.

> . . . There are still some States and localities—in fact, I think a considerable number—which may prefer, or feel it is their obligation to their community and State to comb their own territory for applicants, even though it means going two or three hundred miles, rather than to go across the State line, which may be only five miles, to get men to fill the job openings.
> The reverse is also true: When they have a surplus of skilled workers that they think they will need some time in the future, they are reluctant many times to fill requests coming from other States or other communities in the State for that type of worker. . . .[95]

And the House Select Committee on National Defense Migration found that the interstate "clearance is a negligible factor in the labor market." "Jealousies between states, reflected on occasion by the

[91] Atkinson, Odencrantz, and Deming, *Public Employment Service in the United States*, p. 356.
[92] Sec. 3 (a).
[93] A. W. Motley, "Clearance, Its Development and Future," *Employment Security Review*, Vol. 7, December 1940, p. 5.
[94] *Department of Labor—Federal Security Agency Appropriation Bill for 1943*, Hearings before the Subcommittee of the House Committee on Appropriations, Pt. 2, 77 Cong. 2 sess., pp. 697-98.
[95] *National Defense Migration*, Hearings before the House Select Committee Investigating National Defense Migration, Pt. 17, 77 Cong. 1 sess., p. 6783.

refusal to clear workers, hinder the establishment of a unified labor market policy."[96]

The need for the development of a system of interstate clearance is one of the major reasons for creating a national service. As long as the Service was administered by the states on a grant-in-aid basis, it never developed an effective clearance system. All the reasons for its failure to develop an effective system of interstate clearance are not evident. But state jealousies did impede it. Some believe that the problem can only be solved through the nationalization of the Employment Service.

At least two policies of the national service restrict the utility of the system, because they tend to lessen employer confidence in the organization. These policies are its unwillingness to fill positions that involve substandard terms of employment and its refusal to fill jobs in a struck plant. Relative to filling positions with substandard terms of employment its instructions to state services provide:

> Although it is not the prerogative of the employment service to dictate standards for employment, there is an obligation to the community not to participate directly or indirectly in the exploitation of workers. It should, therefore, be a matter of policy for local offices not to refer workers to employment which, because of wages, hours, working, or sanitary conditions, is clearly below the standard accepted by the community for the class of work involved. . . .[97]

Openings with substandard conditions can be listed, but an attempt should be made to get the employer to offer better terms.[98] Applicants are not to be called in to fill substandard positions; they can only be brought to the attention of workers who come to the office.[99] By its unwillingness to fill such positions the Service is indirectly attempting to raise wages and reduce hours.[100]

Its refusal to fill jobs at a struck plant is based on the provision of the organic act of the Service which requires that the Director shall "provide for the giving of notice of strikes or lockouts to applicants

[96] *National Defense Migration*, H. Rept. 1286, 77 Cong. 1 sess., pp. 30, 32.
[97] *Employment Service Handbook of Information*, State Operations Bulletin, No. 10, Pt. 4, Sec. 1040.
[98] The same, Sec. 1043.
[99] *USES Manual* (1942), Pt. 2, Sec. 3242.
[100] The regulations contain no standards for the determination of what constitutes substandard wages or other conditions of employment. *Employment Service Handbook of Information*, Pt. 4, Sec. 1042.

before they are referred to employment."[101] The inclusion of lockouts is probably intended to demonstrate impartiality. Under the rules first adopted by the Service, an office could refer an applicant to a position where a strike existed, only after it had given him both oral and written notice, acknowledged in writing, of the dispute. And even with such notice, referrals to struck plants were not generally made.[102] When the Service was transferred to the Social Security Board, the rules were amended to preclude such a referral, even where notice of the strike is given.[103] Although the workers strike illegally or in violation of a contract, the Employment Service will not assist the employer in securing new employees. Thus in a strike the Service aids the employees, irrespective of the merits of the dispute.

The opposition of some of the craft unions tends to limit the utilization of the Service by employees. In many instances these labor organizations are very desirous of maintaining the seniority of their members, and consequently they do not look favorably on any placements made through the Service.[104]

Pressure from competing private agencies has limited the field of operations. About twelve states with federal funds allocated for the financing of employment offices had set up teacher placement services

[101] Sec. 11 (b).

[102] Atkinson, Odencrantz, and Deming, *Public Employment Service in the United States,* p. 345.

[103] *USES Manual* (1942), Pt. 2, Sec. 3244. In giving a job order to the Service, an employer cannot indicate a preference for nonunion workers, but he can indicate that he desires only union workers. The same.

[104] Atkinson, Odencrantz, and Deming, *Public Employment Service in the United States,* p. 345; and Emily Huntington, *Doors to Jobs* (1942), p. 108.
The Employment Service co-operates with unions in a number of ways. Spokesmen for the Employment Service have admitted that in some fields a nonunion man has no chance of being placed through the Service. (*National Defense Migration,* Hearings before the House Select Committee Investigating National Defense Migration, Pt. 23, 77 Cong. 2 sess., p. 8898.) Local officers are instructed in all cases where a closed-shop contract exists, and the employer asks for workers to be referred by the Employment Service, the office shall notify the union before filling the order (9 LRR 534). Thus it becomes an agency to enforce compliance with closed-shop contracts. In at least one instance an office of the USES has become little more than a union hiring hall. In New York City one office handles all placements in the women's garment industry. All persons, union and nonunion, are referred to jobs on the basis of the rules of the ILCU governing rotation and priorities. (Helen Whipple and V. K. Kiefer, "Serving the Garment Center of the World," *Employment Security Review,* Vol. 8, April 1941, p. 6; "The Dress Industry's Placement Unit," *Employment Review,* January 1941.) Nonunion employees and employers who do not have closed-shop agreements are made subject to the rules of the union if they use the Employment Service.

in competition with private agencies operating in that field.[105] The private teacher placement agencies objected to this.[106] As a consequence the House Committee on Appropriations demanded the termination of this type of work because the function was adequately performed by private agencies.[107] Ultimately the Employment Service gave up this activity.[108]

According to the USES one of its major problems has been to secure co-operation from employers,[109] who asserted that they did not have confidence in it.[110] Although the National Defense Advisory Commission and the Office of Production Management directed war contractors to do their hiring through the Employment Service,[111] many large war contractors with rapidly increasing personnel requirements testified in 1941 that they never utilized it and had no intention of doing so.[112]

*The employer confidence necessary for
successful operation has been lacking.*

For a number of reasons the United States Employment Service has not had the full confidence of employers. It does not appear to have always performed its placement function adequately. Frequently it merely has served as a referral agency rather than as a placement agency.[113] Instead of attempting to find the best available per-

[105] N. S. Pedraza, "Employment Service to Teachers," *Employment Security Review*, Vol. 8 October 1940, p. 3.

[106] *Department of Labor—Federal Security Agency Appropriation Bill for 1942*, Hearings before the Subcommittee of the House Committee on Appropriations, Pt. 2, p. 839.

[107] The same, H. Rept. 668, 77 Cong. 1 sess., p. 34.

[108] *Department of Labor—Federal Security Agency Appropriation Bill for 1945*, Hearings before the Subcommittee of the House Committee on Appropriations, Pt. 3, p. 224.

[109] *Department of Labor—Federal Security Agency Appropriation Bill for 1941*, Hearings before the Subcommittee of the House Committee on Appropriations, Vol. 2, 76 Cong. 3 sess., p. 686. It has stated that even in 1940 only 15 to 20 per cent of all vacancies were filled through it. A. J. Altmeyer in *National Defense Migration*, Hearings before the House Select Committee Investigating National Defense Migration, Pt. 17, p. 6781.

[110] Huntington, *Doors to Jobs*, p. 421.

[111] *Sixth Annual Report of the Social Security Board* (1941), pp. 83-84.

[112] *National Defense Migration*, Hearings before the House Select Committee Investigating National Defense Migration, Pt. 14, p. 5712; Pt. 15, p. 6011, Pt. 22, p. 8411.

[113] L. A. Appley, *Department of Labor—Federal Security Agency Appropriation*

son,[114] it has often referred applicants who had only the minimum qualifications. It has been more interested in finding work for the unemployed than in locating the best person for the opening. This attitude is a result of two factors. During the period before 1940 much of the work of the Service consisted of referring persons to relief projects and public works.[115] The mental attitudes developed in this work carried over in the performance of other functions. Second, the responsibility of the state services for the administration of unemployment compensation would tend to encourage them to give special attention to the placement of unemployed persons drawing compensation.

Employers in some instances have the feeling that the Employment Service is pro-labor.[116] Irrespective of the actual existence of such a bias on the part of the Service, a number of things might contribute to this opinion among employers. The refusal of the Service to refer workers to a struck plant, its refusal to permit an employer to express a preference for nonunion workers, and its refusal to refer applicants to substandard openings, all contribute to that state of mind on the part of employers.

As a result of the increase in the armed forces in World War II and the great expansion in war production, there has been a greatly increased demand for man power. In fact, it soon became apparent that a man-power shortage would develop. Some agency had to determine what types of work were most necessary for the war effort. After such a determination had been made, an agency was needed to guide employees into the more essential types of work. With civilian production declining in some areas and war production expanding in areas where small reserves of workers existed, there was a demand for some organization to facilitate the flow of workers from areas of potential unemployment to areas of expanding production.

When these problems began to develop early in 1942, no federal agency existed with power to allocate man power in order to secure the maximum utilization of the available labor supply. There was no central organization even with the authority to formulate plans on how man power was to be apportioned as between the armed forces,

---

Bill for 1945, Hearings before the Subcommittee of the House Committee on Appropriations, Pt. 3, p. 159.
[114] Huntington, *Doors to Jobs*, p. 121.
[115] The same, p. 158.
[116] The same, pp. 128-29, 153-58.

war production, and essential civilian needs. The Selective Service System established a system for draft deferment for essential workers, but the actual determination of what constituted an essential worker was in the hands of local draft boards.

In an attempt to meet these problems, the War Manpower Commission was established by executive order in April 1942. Representatives of the War, Navy, Agriculture, and Labor Departments, WPB, and the War Shipping Administration became members of the Commission. Mr. Paul V. McNutt was made Chairman and was vested with all the power conferred upon the Commission. A number of agencies were placed under its control.[117] In September 1942 the Employment Service and the National Youth Administration were transferred to it.[118] The transfer of the Employment Service was significant, because it logically constituted the operating division of any agency engaged in allocating man power. On December 5, 1942, the Selective Service System was transferred to the Commission, but the latter agency was given no authority to determine the allocation of man power as between the armed forces, war production, and essential civilian functions.[119] The functions of the Commission were purely advisory. Since it was not authorized by an act of Congress, it had no legal sanctions to compel individuals to obey its orders.

Only by voluntary means has man power
been allocated during the war.

By executive order and not by statute the Commission has been authorized to attempt to control the allocation of civilian man power. The Chairman was directed to take all lawful steps to see to it that all hiring is done through the USES.[120] He was also directed to take "all lawful and appropriate steps to assure that . . . no employer shall retain in his employ any worker whose services are more urgently needed in any establishment, plant, facility, occupation, or area designated as more essential."[121] No positive steps were taken to carry out this provision of the executive order, but only by directly trans-

[117] Executive Order No. 9139, Apr. 18, 1942, *Federal Register*, Vol. 7, p. 2919.
[118] Executive Order No. 9247, Sept. 17, 1942, *Federal Register*, Vol. 7, p. 10177.
[119] Executive Order No. 9279, Dec. 5, 1942. Congress subsequently removed the Selective Service System from the War Manpower Commission. Act of Dec. 5, 1943, 57 Stat. 598, Sec. 2(b).
[120] The same.
[121] The same, Sec. 3.

ferring employees from one employer to another could it be made effective.

The Commission attempted to exercise these powers in labor shortage areas by means of employment stabilization plans. The plans were designed to prevent labor turnover and the unnecessary migration of workers, and to bring about the maximum utilization of the labor force. They supposedly were formulated by representatives of labor and industry chosen by the War Manpower Commission and were put into force by the order of the regional director of the Commission. In more than 200 areas such programs were in force. Minimum standards for the controls to be included in such plans were fixed by the Commission.

A plan had to provide at least that an employer in an essential industry could not hire a person who had worked in an essential industry locally during the past 60 days unless such person had a certificate of availability from his last employer. Even with a certificate of availability, a worker previously employed in an essential industry could be employed only in such an industry, unless referred to a position by the USES.[122] Of course he could get around this restriction by remaining unemployed for 60 days. In some instances a new employee could not be hired on the presentation of a certificate of availability alone, but he must have been referred to the employer by the Employment Service. Where the employee had not worked or lived in the district for 30 days, he must have been referred by the USES. This requirement was designed to reduce migration. But it did not prohibit the movement of workers, because a person from outside the area could live in the area for 30 days and then seek employment in an essential industry without a certificate. A person who had been employed in or who sought employment in a critical industry also had to be referred by USES. The same was true of agricultural employees who sought nonagricultural employment. It should be remembered that these were the minimum standards for the controls to be included in the plan—the regulations could be more extensive. Thus under the employment stabilization plan for Washington, D.C., private hiring had to be done through the Employment Service.[123]

[122] WMC Regulation No. 4 (Feb. 5, 1943, amended Aug. 16, 1943), Sec. 907 4a.
[123] *Manpower Reports*, 65:226.

On July 1, 1944 in all labor shortage areas the Commission established priority referral and employment ceiling programs.[124] Under the priority referral program, employers could hire only male workers through the Employment Offices. Referrals to employers were made on a priority basis: the employers in the most essential types of work got first call on the job applicants. Employment ceilings were set for all major employers in each area. Employers could hire workers only if their employment was below the ceiling, and as long as the number of employees was above the ceiling, vacancies were not supposed to be filled.

Supposedly acting under the wage control provisions of the act of October 2, 1942[125] the President conferred upon the commission additional authority to control employment:

> The Chairman of the War Manpower Commission is authorized to forbid the employment by any employer of any new employee or the acceptance of employment by any new employee except as authorized in accordance with regulations which may be issued by the Chairman of the War Manpower Commission . . . for the purpose of preventing such employment at a wage or salary higher than that received by such new employee in his last employment unless the change of employment would aid in the effective prosecution of the war.[126]

Under this grant of authority the Chairman of the WMC declared that in an area where a stabilization plan existed, no person could accept a job and no employer could hire a person at a salary higher than he previously was paid unless the employment was authorized by the stabilization plan.[127] This requirement meant that a person to be hired in such an area in any job at an increase in pay had to have a certificate of availability, or had to have been referred by the USES to the position, or he had to have remained without work for 60 days before taking the new position.

The War Manpower Commission had no authority to enforce any provision of a stabilization agreement. Mr. McNutt, the Chairman of the Commission, said that the entire program was voluntary in nature. No employer or employee who violated the agreement would be

---

[124] *Manpower Reports,* 127:25, and directive of the Office of War Mobilization, Aug. 4, 1944, the same, 127:41.

[125] 56 Stat. 766, Sec. 4.

[126] Executive Order No. 9328, Sec. 3, Apr. 8, 1943. *Federal Register*, Vol. 8, p. 4681.

[127] WMC Regulation No. 4, Sec. 904.1, Apr. 18, 1943, as amended Oct. 20, 1944.

prosecuted.[128] If an employer violated it, the possibility existed that the USES might not help him to secure new employees. The WMC contended that the stabilization plans were agreements made between labor, management, and the government, and consequently all parties desired the terms of the program.[129] Of course the so-called representatives of labor and management on the committees that formulated the plans were chosen by the WMC itself and not by any organization authorized to speak for these groups. The Chairman admitted that persuasion and public opinion were mainly used to secure employer compliance,[130] and that a clever persevering employee could generally succeed in getting permission to take almost any position he desired.[131]

IV. CONCLUSIONS

There has not been a consistent policy toward the labor market. To accomplish diverse objectives, the government has done a number of things that have influenced the labor supply. But during both periods of employment and unemployment the same policies have been pursued, and inconsistent policies have been applied to meet a given problem. Among the activities tending to increase the number of workers, assistance in vocational education is considered primarily as an educational problem. The approach to vocational rehabilitation has been from the standpoint of social welfare. The encouragement of apprentice training was undertaken mainly to counteract other government activities that tended to discourage apprenticeship. All these programs were carried on during periods of unemployment as well as during a man-power shortage. The Fair Employment Practice Committee is designed to increase the labor supply during the war by reducing discrimination. If it is to be continued after the close of hostilities, a new justification must be advanced for discouraging discrimination.

Many of the activities that reduce the number of workers available were undertaken largely for that express purpose. The control of

---

[128] *Department of Labor—Federal Security Agency Appropriation Bill for 1945,* Hearings before the Subcommittee of the House Committee on Appropriations, Pt. 3, pp. 3, 9.

[129] The same, p. 17.

[130] *Department of Labor—Federal Security Agency Appropriation Bill for 1946,* Hearings before the Subcommittee of the House Committee on Appropriations, 79 Cong. 1 sess., Pt. 3, p. 12.

[131] The same, p. 8.

child labor, the limitation of immigration, and the regulation of prison industries had that primary objective. Each was adopted as a result of specific pressures and not as a part of a consistent program. The control of learners and the overtime provisions in the Fair Labor Standards Act were not designed to limit the available supply of workers, but they have had that result. These several laws are applied even when a labor shortage exists.

A nationwide public employment service fills a very useful role in a large country like the United States that contains many separate labor markets. It can minimize migration to areas where few employment opportunities exist, and it can influence the flow of labor from areas of labor surplus to places where a need exists. It is also a necessary adjunct to a system of unemployment compensation; by requiring unemployed insured persons to register at an employment exchange, their unwillingness to work can be tested, and it minimizes the possibility that they will remain unemployed through a lack of knowledge of employment opportunities.

Although the Employment Service was organized because of the need for such an agency operating on a national basis, it had not fully attained this objective before World War II. Because of its early preoccupation with problems of relief and unemployment insurance, it was mainly concerned with the placement of the unemployed. Consequently the better workers did not use it extensively. Employers did not have much confidence in it. It never developed an effective system of interstate clearance. With its new role in the wartime control of employment, it may be able to overcome these difficulties.

CHAPTER VI

CONDITIONS OF EMPLOYMENT: UNION PREFERENCE

Labor organizations long have sought to compel employers to give special preference to their members when workers are being hired or discharged. The objective of such preferential treatment is to increase the union's bargaining power and membership. The closed shop provides the greatest special advantage for union members.[1] Under a closed-shop contract the employer agrees to hire only persons who are already members of the contracting union. The union shop is a modification of this; it requires that all employees must join the union within a specified time after they begin to work, provided the union will admit them. If the union will not admit an employee, or if it subsequently expels him, the employer must discharge him. Under a preferential hiring agreement, the employer must first offer positions to union members. Only if he cannot find sufficient union members who are willing to work for him, can he employ nonmembers. Unions not strong enough to secure one of these forms of preference generally enter into agreements that grant to them the exclusive right to bargain for all employees, whether or not they belong to the organization.

From 1939 to 1945 the number of workers employed under agreements requiring union preference has more than doubled. In 1939 about 3,000,000 persons were employed under closed-shop or union-shop agreements.[2] This was about 30 per cent of the total union membership. At the beginning of 1945 about 6,500,000 workers were employed under such contracts, or close to 50 per cent of all workers who belonged to unions.[3]

With this increase in the use of union preference clauses, one may well ask: What is the attitude of the federal government toward the inclusion of such provisions in collective agreements? Its position

[1] The classification of the types of union preference here used is that presented by the Bureau of Labor Statistics, *Monthly Labor Review*, Vol. 58 (1944), pp. 700 ff.; see also H. A. Millis and R. E. Montgomery, *Organized Labor* (1945), pp. 477-78; J. L. Toner, *The Closed Shop* (1942), pp. 28-49, and Twentieth Century Fund, *How Collective Bargaining Works* (1942), pp. 24-25.

[2] *Monthly Labor Review*, Vol. 49 (1939), p. 830.

[3] The same, Vol. 60 (1945), p. 818.

toward the following types of union preference will be considered: closed shop, union shop, preferential hiring, maintenance of membership, and exclusive bargaining rights. Then the policy of the government toward the check-off of union dues will be discussed. With the increase in employment under closed-shop and union-shop agreements, the right of admission to the union and right of the union to expel members becomes increasingly important to workers. Consequently the attitude of the various federal agencies toward these problems will be examined.

I. THE CLOSED SHOP

Under a closed-shop agreement all employees must be union members when hired, and they must remain members while employed.[4] Not all states consider the closed shop to be desirable. The courts of many states once held closed-shop contracts illegal, but the trend of judicial decisions is now generally favorable to them.[5]

Most of the courts which still declare specific closed shop contracts illegal base their views on the tendency of the contracts to create an unlawful monopoly in which a non-union worker can find no employment in the industry or in the city involved. There is some difference of opinion as to how many shops in an industry or a city may be covered before the agreement establishes a monopoly.[6]

Although not all states have taken action on the question, more than twice as many states have now ruled upholding the closed shop than have ruled forbidding it.[7]

A strike to secure a closed shop is made illegal by statute in some states, although not all of these states consider a closed-shop clause in an agreement to be illegal.

In some instances the federal government has discouraged the closed shop, in others it has permitted and possibly encouraged it, and in still others it has actually insisted that such a provision be included in a collective agreement.

---

[4] The parties may also agree that all employees must be hired through the union. While over 30 per cent of all workers covered by agreements were employed in closed shops in January 1944 about 95 per cent of such workers covered by agreements in the construction trades were in closed shops, 23 per cent in manufacturing, and 25 per cent in transportation.

[5] *Gassway* v. *Borderland Coal Corp.*, 278 Fed. 56 (1921).

[6] David Ziskind, *The Law Behind Union Agreements* (1942), p. 13.

[7] Carl R. Schedler, "Union Security," *Seventh Annual Economics Conference at Rollins College* (1942), p. 5.

Only the Railway Labor Act
forbids the closed shop.

The Railway Labor Act provided that representatives selected for collective bargaining purposes should be designated without interference, influence, or coercion exercised by either party over the other.[8] The 1934 amendment to the act specifically declares that carriers may not require a person seeking employment to sign any contract promising to join (or not to join) a labor organization.[9]

This provision was directed primarily against closed-shop agreements between unaffiliated unions and carriers rather than against closed-shop contracts in general. Since the closed- or union-shop contract with an unaffiliated union was one of the most effective means by which employers could keep out national labor organizations, the railroad brotherhoods desired a prohibition against the use of such agreements to help them in their struggle against independent unions. Here the closed shop was being used by management against a national union, instead of being used by the labor organization for the purpose of spreading unionization. The hearings before the Senate and House committees that considered this bill show that the national railroad labor organizations wanted primarily to prohibit closed-shop contracts when made with company or nonaffiliated unions. They did not ask that the closed shop be completely banned. They pleaded, on the contrary, that it be legalized for organizations that were not company unions.

However, Mr. Joseph Eastman, the Federal Co-ordinator of Transportation, strongly opposed making such a distinction between the independent unions and other national or international labor organizations. "If genuine freedom of choice is to be the basis of labor relations under the Railway Labor Act, as it should be," he said, "then the yellow dog contract and its corollary, the closed shop, and the so-called 'percentage contract' have no place in the picture."[10] Congress followed his advice and completely prohibited the closed-shop contract. For several reasons the national labor organizations were not sufficiently

[8] Act of May 20, 1926, 44 Stat. 578, Sec. 2, Third.
[9] Act of June 21, 1934, 48 Stat. 1188, Sec. 2, Fifth.
[10] *To amend the Railway Labor Act*, Hearings before the Senate Committee on Interstate Commerce, 73 Cong. 2 sess., p. 157. As passed by the House, it prohibited the closed shop only with company unions, but the Senate insisted on a general prohibition: *Congressional Record*, Vol. 78, Pt. 11, 73 Cong. 2 sess., p. 12,402.

interested in the closed shop to press hard for its legalization for them-selves.[11] The long stabilization of labor relations in the industry, the general acceptance of unionization by the carriers, and overlapping claims of jurisdiction between several major unions tended to reduce the importance of the closed shop to them. Their fight against the company unions seemed more important to them than the legalization of the closed or union shop for themselves; consequently they were willing to accept a general prohibition of the closed shop, in order to prevent the independent unions from using it against them.

The Bankruptcy Act of 1933 prohibits a trustee in bankruptcy from entering into a closed-shop agreement with a union[12] covering employ-ment in any enterprise for which he is acting as trustee.

The Norris-La Guardia Act in its general statement of policy de-clares that employees shall have full freedom of association and self-organization, and the right to designate representatives of their own choosing, free from interference, restraint, or coercion of their employers.[13] In *Lauf* v. *Shinner* the Supreme Court held that this language does not make illegal the use of concerted action to compel an employer to make a closed-shop agreement. Here a union de-manded a closed shop from an employer, although none of his em-ployees belonged to it. Since none of his employees were members of the union, it would have been a violation of the National Labor Relations Act for the employer to have entered into such an agree-ment. When the union picketed his place of business to compel him to yield, he sought an injunction in the District Court. The Circuit Court of Appeals considered the issuance of an injunction was proper in this case, because the employer could not grant a closed shop with-out violating the declared policy of the act concerning the right of self-organization.[14] But the Supreme Court nevertheless refused to enjoin the picketing.[15]

President Roosevelt expressed opposition to the use of force by the federal government to compel an employer to enter into a closed-shop agreement. On November 14, 1941 he asserted: "the Government of the United States will not order, nor will Congress pass legislation

---

[11] Toner, *The Closed Shop*, pp. 100-01.
[12] Act of Mar. 3, 1933, 47 Stat. 1481, Sec. 77 (p), (q).
[13] Act of Mar. 23, 1932, 47 Stat. 70, Sec. 2.
[14] 82 Fed (2d), 68, 72 (1936).
[15] 303 U.S. 323 (1938).

ordering, a so-called closed shop. . . . "That would be too much like the Hitler methods toward labor."[16] Here the President did not oppose the closed shop, nor even government encouragement of it; he opposed only the use of government sanctions to compel an employer to enter into a closed-shop agreement.

Under certain conditions the National Labor Relations Act
explicitly legalizes closed-shop contracts.

The National Labor Relations Act provides that an employer is permitted to make a closed-shop contract only with a labor organization that represents the majority of employees in an appropriate collective bargaining unit[17] and that is not dominated by or assisted by the employer.[18]

If the act did not thus specifically authorize closed shop agreements, it would be an unfair labor practice for an employer to refuse to employ or to discharge a person because he was not a member of a designated union. But it narrows the formerly existing federal law, since before the enactment of the act there was no general federal law placing any limit on closed-shop agreements. It does not affect state laws prohibiting such agreements.[19] Consequently the same case may be determined differently under the federal and state law. A contract may be legal within the purview of the National Labor Relations Act and illegal under the law of the state concerned.

Since an objective of many unions is to secure closed-shop agreements, and since the National Labor Relations Act gives assistance to unions in organizing and bargaining, the act actually helps to spread the closed shop.[20] Although the act appears only to make closed-shop agreements permissible, the Board has taken a different view. In some cases it has held that an employer failed to bargain collectively where he refused to grant a closed shop when the union requested it.[21]

Where a valid closed-shop agreement exists, the employer can re-

[16] Statement to mine union and steel company leaders, *New York Times*, Nov. 15, 1941. Despite the wording of the President's letter the issue here was the union shop and not the closed shop.
[17] Sec. 8 (3).
[18] *International Association of Machinists* v. *NLRB*, 311 U.S. 72 (1940).
[19] *National Labor Relations Board*, S. Rept. 573, 73 Cong. 1 sess., p. 11.
[20] D. O. Bowman, *Public Control of Labor Relations* (1942), pp. 113-14.
[21] *International Filter Co.*, 1 NLRB 489 (1936); *Uhlich and Co.*, 26 NLRB 679 (1939).

fuse to hire a worker, because he is not a member of the proper union, or because he ceased to be a member of it.[22] But before an employer can legally discharge an employee under a valid closed-shop agreement, he must give him notice of the provisions of the agreement. Only by such notice can the employee distinguish between a discriminatory discharge that is required by a closed-shop provision and discrimination that is contrary to the law.[23]

Since a closed-shop contract can be made only with a union that represents a majority of the workers, a difficult problem is presented by a newly established or a rapidly expanding plant. If the agreement is made when only a few workers are employed, all additional workers must be members at the time they are hired; consequently when full employment is attained, most of the workers will probably support the union.[24] But if the agreement is not made until the establishment is in full production, it is not as likely that a majority will designate the union, because it would have been illegal for the employer to select his employees on the basis of their union membership. In newly developed war industries the NLRB encountered this problem of determining the time when a closed-shop agreement can be made. In 1942 members of the Board said that, even though only a minority of the total number of workers were as yet employed, a closed-shop agreement could be made with a union that represented a majority of those on the pay roll at the time provided the union was not being assisted by the employer.[25] But in 1943 the Board changed its mind and said such an agreement could not be made until a majority of the total number of prospective employees had been hired.[26] A bare majority of the employees in a factory only half manned would of course be a minority of the workers at peak employment.

In 1943 Congress greatly limited the Board's authority to declare invalid a closed-shop agreement made before most of the workers were employed. The Board had brought a complaint against the Oregon

<hr>

[22] *Rosedale Knitting Co.*, 20 NLRB 326 (1940).

[23] *Electric Vacuum Cleaner Co.*, 8 NLRB 112 (1938).

[24] Such an agreement cannot be made before any employees have been hired, *Merry Shoe Co.*, 10 NLRB 457 (1938).

[25] *Department of Labor-Federal Security Agency Appropriation Bill for 1943*, Hearings before the House Committee on Appropriations, 77 Cong. 2 sess., Pt. 1, pp. 496-500.

[26] *The same*, 1944, 78 Cong. 1 sess., Pt. 1, p. 324.

Shipbuilding Company, charging that it had entered into a closed-shop agreement with the Metal Trades Department of the A. F. of L. when it had only several hundred workers on the pay roll and ultimately employment increased to 90,000. Consequently the Board claimed that Section 8 (3) was violated by the discharge of employees who did not belong to the unions represented by the Metal Trades Department. The complaint also alleged that the employer violated Section 8 (1) of the National Labor Relations Act by aiding and assisting the A. F. of L. unions for several months before this agreement was made.[27] By the Labor-Federal Security Appropriation Act for 1944, Congress prohibited the Board from using any of its funds for prosecuting a complaint case against an employer because of an agreement that had been in force for three months and that had been made public.[28] This prohibited the Board from bringing an action against an employer because he had made a closed-shop agreement before he had hired most of his employees.[29] It even prohibited such a proceeding where the agreement was with a union that had been assisted or dominated by the employer in violation of Section 8 (1) and (2) of the National Labor Relations Act. As a result, the 1945 appropriation act was amended to permit the prosecution of a proceeding if the agreement was made with a union dominated by the employer in violation of Section 8 (2).[30] This does not permit a proceeding where it is charged that the contracting union was assisted or aided in violation of Section 8 (1).

What happens to a closed shop when a majority of employees switch unions?

Difficulties arise when a majority of the members of a union with a closed-shop agreement change their union affiliation. Owing to the rivalry of the A. F. of L. and the CIO and similar inter-union competition, employee majorities frequently change their allegiance after their unions have made valid closed-shop contracts with their employers. Nothing in the National Labor Relations Act precludes a

[27] The charges and complaints are printed in *Labor-Federal Security Agency Appropriation bill for 1944*, Hearings before the Senate Committee on Appropriations, 78 Cong. 1 sess., pp. 392-418.
[28] Act of July 12, 1943, 57 Stat. 515, Title 4.
[29] The same.
[30] The same.

change in union membership. The Supreme Court has held that although an employee designates a union as a bargaining representative for a fixed time, he can switch his union affiliation at will.[31]

When a majority of the workers switch their allegiance, is the employer compelled by the closed-shop contract to discharge the employees who thus change their affiliation and to hire new employees who are members of the contracting union, or must he retain his old employees under the assumption that they continue to have the rights of the contract despite their new affiliation? A similar problem arises when the contracting union itself changes its affiliation. So far this problem of the change in union affiliation has not been solved unequivocally by the Board or the courts. The NLRB in 1938 appeared to believe that the employees maintained the rights under the existing contract, although all employees changed their union membership from the A. F. of L. to the CIO.[32] But the courts have leaned toward the view that the rights belonged to the contracting union and not to the workers.[33] Under such a view the workers who changed their designation would have to be discharged and be replaced by members of the original union. In 1939 the Board reversed its decision of the previous year and held that, although a majority of the employees withdrew from the contracting union and joined another organization, this action did not affect the validity of an existing closed-shop contract.[34] The employer was not guilty of discrimination in discharging the employees who joined the new union.

The Board did not clarify its attitude when the problem was presented to it in 1942 in a little different form. In the *Rutland Court Owners* case[35] a closed-shop agreement was about to expire. Some of the employees negotiated to switch their membership to a new union. When the original union began negotiations for a renewal of the agreement, it told the employer that the employees who were negotiating with the new organization were not in good standing and should be discharged. The employer complied, members of the old union were hired in their stead, and the closed-shop agreement was renewed.

[31] *NLRB* v. *Electric Vacuum Cleaner Co.*, 315 U.S. 685 (1942).

[32] *M. and M. Woodworking Co.*, 6 NLRB 372 (1938).

[33] See, for example, *M. and M. Woodworking Co.* v. *NLRB.*, 101 Fed. (2d) 938 (1939).

[34] *Ansley Radio Co.*, 18 NLRB 128 (1939).

[35] 44 NLRB 587, 594, 596, 597 (1942).

The Board held it was discrimination to discharge the employees who joined the new union, and said:

. . . The employees' right to select representatives to be meaningful must necessarily include the right at some appropriate time to change representatives. . . . Effectuation of the basic policies of the Act requires, as the life of the collective contract draws to a close, that the employees be able to advocate a change in their affiliation without fear of discharge by an employer for so doing.

. . . .

. . . The mere fact that all closed shops are not unlawful, by virtue of the proviso, is no reason for holding that closed shops may be made perpetual because validly initiated pursuant to the proviso.

. . . .

. . . To insist that employees can never transfer their affiliation from one union to another, or to prevent employees toward the close of one contract period from changing their representatives for the purpose of negotiating and administering a new contract for the succeeding term is to impair rather than protect self-organization, to thwart rather than encourage collective bargaining by representatives of the employees' genuine choice, and accordingly to produce contracts which will not tend to stabilize mutually satisfactory labor relations or safeguard industrial peace. The stability intended by the Act is not that involved in perennial suppression of the employees' will.

Mr. Leiserson, in his dissenting opinion, observed:

There is no contention in this proceeding that the closed-shop contract of 1939 is invalid. The discharges were made pursuant to the terms of that contract and are therefore within the terms of the proviso to Section 8 (3) of the Act. To reach a contrary result, the majority has in effect assumed authority to suspend enforcement of the provisions of a valid collective bargaining agreement although this Board has previously held that it was not permitted to do so. If valid closed shop contracts, which are expressly permitted by the Act, have undesirable effects, it is for the Congress, and not for the Board, to make the modifications. I would dismiss the complaint.

The Board appears to be torn between a desire to protect the workers' right of self-organization and a desire to sustain a closed-shop agreement that was valid when made. If during a closed-shop agreement a majority of the workers in the bargaining unit change their union affiliation, do the rights granted by the agreement belong to the new organization or do they remain in the old organization? The NLRB has not been willing to answer the question directly.

Section 8 (3) provides that the agreement must be made with a "labor organization," and under the contract only members of the contracting organization can be employed. Since under the act the agreement is with the "labor organization," it would be logical for the Board to hold that the employer would have to discharge employees who changed their affiliation and employ persons who were members of the contracting organization. Such a solution would be completely contrary to the employees' right of freedom of organization. But to hold that an employer does not have to discharge these employees would mean the destruction of a collective agreement that was valid when made. These opinions show very clearly that the rise of a dual labor movement and the intensification of inter-union competition present difficulties which cannot be overcome easily by the application of judicial principles, established while a unified labor movement existed.

*Rarely has the government
imposed the closed shop.*

The National Defense Mediation Board recommended the closed shop in one case.[36] Apparently this was done despite strong employer opposition, although the employer did indicate that it would accept the recommendation. The company stated that it would prefer a recommendation from the Board to a voluntary grant of the clause, because such a concession on the part of the company might serve as a precedent in its plants in other parts of the country. In the other cases in which the closed or union shop was demanded, the Board refused to grant it.

The National War Labor Board generally requires the continuation of an existing closed- or union-shop agreement. It argues that existing employee-employer relations would be made unstable if it did not require the renewal of such agreements.[37] In one instance the Board came very close to imposing a closed shop where none existed previously. It required the renewal of an existing preferential hiring agreement, and in addition it demanded that the agreement contain a clause requiring the maintenance of union membership for all union members employed.[38]

[36] No. 37, Bethlehem Steel Company, Shipbuilding Division.
[37] *Harvill Aircraft Die Casting Corp.*, 6 WLR 334 (1943).
[38] *Shell Oil Co.*, 6 WLR 45 (1943).

The Conciliation Service and the Department of Labor now contend that in mediation proceedings they do not encourage the closed shop.[39] But soon after the Department of Labor was created, the Secretary of Labor asserted that it was the policy of the Department to encourage the closed shop in conciliation proceedings.[40] After the National Defense Mediation Board refused a union shop in the captive coal mine case in 1941, the dispute was submitted to arbitration at the request of the President. The head of the Conciliation Service was the neutral member of the three-man panel. He sided with the labor member and granted the union shop.[41]

II. THE UNION SHOP

Under the union-shop agreement all persons employed must become and thereafter remain union members within a specified time after being hired. When a union shop is first imposed, the agreement usually provides that employees who are not members of the union must join it within a stated period, such as 30 or 60 days. As contrasted with the closed shop, the employer is not restricted concerning the employees he chooses to hire provided the union will admit them. He may hire union or nonunion men, but all must become union members within the stated period. Otherwise the employer must discharge them. About 2,500,000 persons are employed under union-shop agreements; this is almost 20 per cent of the total number of employees under collective agreements.[42]

The government treats the union
shop the same as the closed shop.

Generally, the government treats the union shop in the same manner as the closed shop. A union-shop agreement would be discriminatory and in violation of Section 8 (3) of the National Labor Relations Act if the labor organization concerned does not represent a majority of the employees at the time the agreement is made and

[39] *Department of Labor—Federal Security Agency Appropriation Bill for 1943,* Hearings before the House Committee on Appropriations, Pt. 1, p. 197.
[40] *Industrial Relations,* S. Doc. 415, Vol. 11, 64 Cong. 1 sess., p. 10,833; *Investigation of the National Defense Program,* Hearings before the Senate Select Committee to Investigate the National Defense Program, 78 Cong. 1 sess., pp. 7352-53; 7583-86.
[41] *New York Times,* Dec. 8, 1941.
[42] *Monthly Labor Review,* Vol. 60 (1945), p. 819.

if it is assisted by the employer.[43] The policy of the National War Labor Board toward the union shop is comparable to its policy toward the closed shop. As a rule it will require the union shop only where it had existed previously.[44]

In the captive mines case[45] the National Defense Mediation Board refused to grant the union's demand for the union shop. In the bituminous coal industry as a whole, the UMWA represented an overwhelming proportion of the employees, and it had secured union-shop agreements with nearly all the commercial mine operators; but few of the captive mines were operated under union-shop agreements. Some of the Board members were influenced by the fact that the extension of the union shop to the captive mines would mean a union monopoly of all existing jobs in the industry. Furthermore, in the opinion of the Board the mine workers did not show the need for the union shop as a measure of protection, because they had not renounced their right to strike as a contribution to national defense. The final report on the Board's activities justified its refusal to recommend the union shop or the closed shop with the argument that it was not necessary in the absence of a demonstrated need, and in the absence of any government policy requiring a union or closed shop.[46] The demand of the UMWA for the union shop was subsequently granted by arbitration arranged by the President.

III. PREFERENTIAL HIRING

Under a preferential hiring agreement, union members are given preference when the working force is decreased or increased, or when any other changes in personnel are made. Such agreements vary in the extent to which preference must be given. Frequently the employer agrees to give the union members preference as to employment, shifts, seniority, vacations, and lay-offs. About 3 per cent of all persons covered by agreements are employed under preferential hiring contracts. While agreements containing such provisions exist in most industries, they are most common in maritime shipping, including longshoremen.[47]

[43] *National Electric Corp.*, 3 NLRB 475 (1937).
[44] *Harvill Aircraft Die Casting Corp.*, 6 WLR 334 (1943).
[45] No. 22-B.
[46] *Report on the Work of the National Defense Mediation Board, March 19, 1941-January 12, 1942*, Bureau of Labor Statistics Bulletin No. 714 (1942), p. 24.
[47] *Monthly Labor Review*, Vol. 60 (1945), p. 819.

Preferential hiring agreements are permitted.

According to a ruling of the general counsel of the National Labor Relations Board, the limitations of the closed-shop clause of Section 8 (3) are applicable to preferential hiring agreements.[48] Both the Board and the courts have upheld the validity of preferential contracts.[49] An employer may enter into a preferential agreement with a labor organization not established, maintained, or assisted by the employer.[50] But as in the case of closed-shop contracts, difficulties may arise when the employees transfer their union affiliation to a union other than the one that made the agreement. The rights that exist in such a situation are not clear in the Board's decisions.[51]

The National Defense Mediation Board recommended some form of preferential hiring in three cases. One such clause that was recommended provided that: "The employer give first consideration to local unemployed members of the union, provided that they were qualified and readily available; when satisfactory men can't be obtained in the above manner, the hiring of others shall not be deemed a breach of this agreement."[52] On occasion the National War Labor Board has required the inclusion of a preferential hiring clause in an agreement.[53]

IV. MAINTENANCE OF MEMBERSHIP

Under a maintenance-of-membership agreement, all employees who are union members at the time the contract is made or who thereafter become members must maintain their membership for the duration of the agreement. More than 3,000,000 workers (20 per cent of all employees working under union agreements) are now covered by maintenance-of-membership clauses. The large majority of the workers thus covered are in the basic iron and steel, electrical equipment, shipbuilding, aircraft, rubber products, farm equipment, and paper industries. Although such clauses have been included in agreements for some years, they have become much more common during the

---

[48] Released by the National Defense Mediation Board, Sept. 19, 1941.
[49] *Peninsular and Occidental Steamship Co.* v. *NLRB*, 98 Fed. (2d) 411 (1938).
[50] *Vacuum Cleaner Co.* 8 NLRB 112 (1938).
[51] *Waterman Steamship Corp.* 7 NLRB 237 (1938); 309 U.S. 206 (1940).
[52] *Columbia Basin Area Loggers and Sawmill Operators*, Case No. 34.
[53] *Hotel Employers' Association of San Francisco*, 1 WLR 91 (1942).

last three years, largely as a result of orders of the National War Labor Board.[54]

The general counsel of the National Labor Relations Board has ruled that an employer does not engage in an unfair labor practice within the meaning of Section 8 (3) of the National Labor Relations Act by including a maintenance-of-membership clause in a contract with a labor organization, provided that the union was not aided by the employer and that a majority of the employees had selected it as their representative.[55] But the Railway Labor Act prohibits maintenance-of-membership contracts by carriers that are subject to it.[56]

The Defense Mediation Board required the maintenance of union membership to avoid deciding between closed and open shops.

By requiring the maintenance of union membership, the National Defense Mediation Board, operating without any legislative statement of policy, attempted to resolve the conflict between the unions' demand for a closed shop and employers' desire for an open shop. This Board recommended a maintenance-of-membership clause seven times.[57] The recommendation in one case[58] contained an "escape clause" providing that during a fixed period after the decision any employee might withdraw from the union for legitimate reasons not related to wages, hours, or conditions of employment. In four cases,[59] the Board explicitly refused to recommend a maintenance-of-membership clause, and in a like number of cases the parties themselves agreed to such a clause.

The National War Labor Board imposes the clause if a union asks for it.

The NWLB generally requires the maintenance of union membership when the workers desire it. In fact it is now the declared policy of the Board to impose maintenance of membership if the

---

[54] Bureau of Labor Statistics, *Types of Union Recognition in Effect in December 1942* (1943), p. 6, mimeographed.

[55] Released by National Defense Mediation Board, Sept. 19, 1941.

[56] 40 Op. Att. Gen. No. 59 (1942).

[57] *Report on the Work of the National Defense Mediation Board*, pp. 64-67.

[58] *Lincoln Mills*, No. 57.

[59] *General Motors*, No. 21; *Alabama Drydock*, No. 85; *Ingalls Shipbuilding*, No. 92; and *Sloss Sheffield*, No. 94.

union requests it even though the employer objects.[60] It is questionable whether the Board has this power under the War Labor Disputes Act.[61] Section 7 (a) (2) of this law provides that all decisions of the National War Labor Board must be in conformity with the National Labor Relations Act. Section 8 (3) of the act provides that a closed shop (or any lesser form of special advantage to a union) can only be granted by an employer if a majority of the employees belong to the union and if the organization is not employer-dominated. Thus the act by implication requires that both the employer and the union must approve of such preferential treatment.[62] From the congressional debates it appears that the provision in Section 7 (a) (2) was put in the War Labor Disputes Act to prevent the Board from requiring the inclusion of union security clauses.[63] This question has not been considered by any court.

The Board set forth its policy on maintenance of membership in its decision in the *Little Steel* case.[64] Speaking through public member Frank P. Graham, it advanced these arguments in support of maintenance of membership:

> By and large, the maintenance of a stable union membership makes for the maintenance of responsible union leadership and responsible union discipline, makes for keeping faithfully the terms of the contract, and provides a stable basis for union-management cooperation for more efficient production. . . .
>
> . . . .
>
> Not only does the record show that this union is worthy of security and responsibility, but the history of unionism in the Steel Belt in general and the fears remaining from experiences in Little Steel in particular make necessary and wise more definite provisions for the freedom and security of the union.

In another case the National War Labor Board specifically advanced two arguments in support of maintenance of membership.[65]

---

[60] *Humble Oil and Refining Co.*, 15 WLR 380 (1944); *Ace Foundry Co., Ltd.*, 14 WLR 755 (1943).

[61] Act of June 23, 1943, 57 Stat. 166.

[62] See statement of Rep. Howard Smith, *Congressional Record*, Vol. 89, Pt. 4,

[63] See statement of Rep. Howard Smith, *Congressional Record*, Vol. 89, Pt. 4, 78 Cong. 1 sess., p. 5786, and Senator Warren Austin, both conferees, the same, p. 5831.

[64] 1 WLR 325, 340, 342 (1942).

[65] *Federal Shipbuilding and Drydock Corp.*, 1 WLR 140, 143 (1942).

First, "experience . . . has shown how strong, responsible union leadership can keep production rolling. . . . An unstable membership contributes to an irresponsible leadership. Too often members do not maintain their membership because they resent the discipline of a responsible leadership." Second, "the government is under a moral and equitable compulsion not to take advantage of the national nonstrike agreement which has disarmed this union of its only weapon."

Thus the Board said that the clause is designed to increase production and to compensate unions for their no-strike pledge. When the Board asserts that the clause compensates the unions for their no-strike pledge, it assumes that it is desirable to prevent the loss of union membership that might be a consequence of their decline in bargaining power resulting from an abandonment of strikes. With conditions of employment largely fixed by the government, the direct advantages of union membership will not be apparent to the workers, and therefore membership in labor organizations might decline. If strong unions are generally desirable, it is not advantageous to have them weakened as a result of their co-operation in the war effort. Further, if union membership had declined, union leaders might have become critical of the war effort in general and of the wartime labor policies of the government in particular. Maintenance-of-membership provisions tend to reduce any drift of workers away from unions, and thus the policy of the Board may help to prevent the development of a possible cause of dissatisfaction among labor leaders. If strong unions are desirable, and if the support of trade union leaders was important for the war, then maintenance of membership has been an effective means to that end. If a policy of encouraging maintenance of membership is to be followed after the war, new arguments must be found for it. It is not entirely consistent with the general policy of freedom of organization as interpreted by the decisions of the NLRB, which has held that workers can change their representatives at any time.

Before the clause becomes effective, employees are given an opportunity to leave the union.

Maintenance-of-membership clauses imposed by the Board usually provide that all employees who are union members 15 days after the Board's order must continue their membership for the duration of the agreement. Thus employees who desire to withdraw from the

union have 15 days in which to do so.[66] Before the present form of
the clause was developed, several variations were used. In one case
maintenance of membership was imposed unconditionally on all
employees who were union members at the time of the decision.[67]
In another case the Board made it apply to all members "provided
the majority of the members in good standing vote in its favor."[68]
Finally the present type of clause was evolved.[69]

Through the misuse of the so-called "escape clause" employers or
unions possibly might misapply or evade the standard maintenance-
of-membership clause.[70] In a resolution the Board has declared that
in all cases in which it grants the maintenance-of-membership provision, the Board intends that any employee may withdraw from
his union without losing his job, at any time prior to the effective
date of the maintenance-of-membership clause irrespective of any
rules, regulations, laws, or constitutional provisions of the union
which would make such withdrawal ineffective. Employers must not
attempt to influence employees to resign from the union.[71]

*Unions that strike improperly are
not granted this assistance.*

In a number of decisions the Board denied maintenance-of-membership to a union that it considered an irresponsible organization.[72]
Where the reliability of the union was questionable,[73] the Board
granted the privilege only on a probationary basis. It has threatened
to cancel the clause,[74] and has actually done so, where the union has
subsequently misbehaved.[75] Improper strikes are the only form of
misbehavior that the Board has recognized, and strikes to compel

[66] Without explanation no escape clause was provided in *Powers-Davis and Eaton
Logging Co.*, 16 WLR 492 (1944).
[67] *Federal Shipbuilding and Drydock Co.*, 1 WLR 140 (1942).
[68] *The International Harvester Co.*, 1 WLR 112 (1942).
[69] *Bethlehem Steel Co. et al.*, 1 WLR 325 (1942); and *Humble Oil Co.*, 15 WLR
380 (1944). First applied in *Marshall Field and Co.*, 1 WLR 47 (1942).
[70] The problem was evident to the Board in *S. A. Woods Machine Co.*, 2 WLR
159 (1942).
[71] Release of National War Labor Board, Nov. 28, 1942.
[72] *Monsanto Chemical Co.*, 2 WLR 479 (1942).
[73] *Yellow Truck and Coach Mfg. Co.*, 5 WLR 244 (1942).
[74] *Ohio Steel Foundry Co.*, 6 WLR 24 (1943).
[75] *East Alton Mfg. Co.*, 5 WLR 47 (1942).

the Board to decide a controversy are considered to be especially reprehensible.[76]

V. THE EXCLUSIVE BARGAINING SHOP

Under an exclusive bargaining clause, a particular union is designated as the exclusive representative of all employees, whether members of it or not; often certain groups such as supervisors, salaried employees, and the like are excepted. Approximately 25 per cent of all workers employed under collective agreements are covered by provisions which grant the union only sole bargaining rights but no other form of union security.[77]

Any union representing a majority has the exclusive right to bargain for all employees.

The National Labor Relations Act provides that the true representatives of a majority of the workers in a bargaining unit shall have the exclusive right to bargain for all the employees.[78] If a union represents a majority of the employees, it is an unfair labor practice for the employer to bargain with any other organization. This is true under the Railway Labor Act.[79] The National War Labor Board in several decisions has ordered an employer to recognize a particular union as the sole bargaining agent for all the employees. The customary form of the clause that the Board has imposed is as follows: The employer recognizes and will deal with the Union as the sole and exclusive collective bargaining agency for the employees during the life of this agreement for the purposes of collective bargaining in respect to wages, rates of pay, hours of employment, or other conditions of employment.[80]

VI. THE CHECK-OFF

Where labor organizations have won some form of preferential treatment, they frequently seek to transfer the task of dues collection to the employer. This is commonly known as the check-off. The union desires it, because it shifts the task of dues collection to the employer,

[76] *Harriman Mfg. Co.,* 17 WLR 8 (1944).
[77] *Monthly Labor Review,* Vol. 60 (1945), p. 820.
[78] Sec. 9 (a).
[79] *Steele* v. *Louisville and Nashville R. R. Co.,* 323 U. S. 192 (1944).
[80] *Marshall Field and Co.,* 1 WLR 47 (1942).

and consequently the union is assured a steady income for the duration of the agreement.

Under the check-off clause the employer must periodically deduct
the union dues from the employee's pay and turn them over to the
union. It may or may not provide that the employee must specifically
authorize such deductions. In some cases where specific authorization
is required, the employee's consent can be withdrawn before the
expiration of the union contract. About 6 million workers—or more
than 40 per cent of all employed under collective agreements—are
covered by some form of a check-off. At present about 2.5 million
workers are covered by agreements which provide for an automatic
check-off, while approximately 2 millions work under agreements which
provide for the check-off only by the individual employee's authorization.[81] The check-off prevails in the coal mining and basic iron and
steel industries, and it is fairly common in the aircraft, nonferrous
metals, hosiery, silk, rayon, and cotton textile industries.

The check-off is permitted where
a closed shop is legal.

The National Labor Relations Act imposes the same limitations
on the check-off as it does on the closed shop. The union designated
for the purposes of collective bargaining by the majority of the employees is entitled to receive the check-off,[82] provided of course that
it represents the free choice of the employees.[83] An employer commits
an unfair labor practice if he agrees to check off the dues of a union
which has not demonstrated that it represents such a majority.[84] A
check-off agreement with an employer-dominated union in unlawful.[85]
Where the Board finds that an unaffiliated union which had the
check-off was employer-dominated, it can order the employer to return
to the workers the money thus deducted from their wages.[86] The
Board has held in several instances that the grant of the check-off by

[81] *Monthly Labor Review,* Vol. 60 (1945), pp. 822.
[82] *NLRB v. Gutman and Co.,* 121 Fed. (2d) 756 (1941).
[83] *National Electric Corp.,* 3 NLRB 475 (1937).
[84] *NLRB v. Blossom Products Corp.,* 121 Fed. (2d) 260 (1941).
[85] *The Heller Bros. Co.,* 7 NLRB 646 (1938).
[86] *Virginia Electric and Power Co. v. NLRB,* 319 U.S. 533 (1943).

the employer to an unaffiliated union is evidence tending to indicate employer domination.[87]

The Railway Labor Act prohibits the check-off of union dues along with the closed shop.[88] The railway labor organizations were instrumental in getting this prohibition included in the act.[89] The national organizations desired to ban the check-off because the independent unions had been using it in the past; and the national unions desired to weaken the position of the unaffiliated unions.[90] Only a few independent employees' organizations were opposed to this prohibition.

The NWLB generally imposes the check-off when it requires maintenance of membership.

If the union requests it, the NWLB generally requires the employer to check off union dues when it imposes maintenance of membership or continues a closed shop.[91] In support of this policy the Board said that the prohibition of strikes and the limitation of wage increases made it difficult for unions to maintain their membership, without a disproportionate amount of organizing activity. Since collective bargaining was desirable for the war effort, a decline in union membership, which resulted in a decline in bargaining power, might have hindered the war effort.[92] The check-off also makes it unnecessary for the employer to discharge union members for nonpayment of dues under a maintenance of membership provision.[93] The Board generally refuses to grant the check-off and maintenance of membership to a union that engages in improper strikes.[94]

The NWLB usually requires that an employee voluntarily approve of any deduction from his pay.[95] In some cases it has permitted indi-

---

[87] *Clinton Cotton Mills,* 1 NLRB 96 (1935); *Blossom Products Corp.,* 20 NLRB 335 (1940).
[88] Sec. 2 (fourth).
[89] Mr. Leiserson, *To Amend the National Labor Relations Act,* Hearings before the Senate Committee on Education and Labor, 77 Cong. 1 sess., pp. 996-97.
[90] *To Amend the Railway Labor Act,* Hearings before the Senate Committee on Interstate Commerce, pp. 23, 118.
[91] *Little Steel Cos.,* 1 WLR 325 (1942).
[92] *Westinghouse Air-Brake Co.,* 13 WLR 221 (1943).
[93] *Little Steel Cos.,* 1 WLR 325 (1942).
[94] *Mead Corp.,* 8 WLR 471 (1943); *Commercial Solvents Co.* 12 WLR 323 (1943).
[95] *The Bower Roller Bearing Co.,* 1 WLR 61 (1942).

viduals to cancel their authorization of the check-off.[96] At least once
the Board has required that if a union member should cease to be in
good standing, the company, under certain circumstances, should
nevertheless continue to deduct and pay to the union a sum equivalent
to the employee's union dues.[97]

The policy of encouraging or tolerating the check-off rests on the
argument that trade union leaders should be relieved of the task of
collecting dues, so that they can devote more time to organizational
and bargaining activities. It is also asserted that the check-off promotes
union stability, and thereby increases bargaining power. One argument against the check-off is that the cost of dues collection is shifted
to the employer. Further, it is not entirely consistent with the workers'
right to change their bargaining representative at will. The employees'
right of self-organization would seem to include the members' right
to make the labor organization responsible. If the workers have the
right of self-organization, they would seem to have the right to
withdraw their support from an organization at any time, and one of
the most direct means of withdrawing support is to terminate financial
assistance. Under the check-off this is impossible, and thus it tends
to reduce union responsibility.

VII. THE INDIVIDUAL WORKER AND UNION MEMBERSHIP

Although the federal government permits and in some cases encourages various forms of union preference, it has done nothing to
ensure that all employees shall have the right to join and remain
members of a union, even where the union enjoys a preferential position. Practically all unions are voluntary associations created under
state law, and consequently the federal government has no control
over admission to or expulsion from such organizations.

*Unions usually can determine
their own membership.*

Unions are left free as a rule to select their own members.[98] They
can demand any initiation fee they desire, be it $500 or $3,000.[99] They

[96] *Remington Rand Co. Inc.* 1 WLR 137 (1942).
[97] *Walker Turner Co. Inc.* 1 WLR 101 (1942).
[98] See Ralph A. Newman, "The Closed Union and the Right to Work," 53 Columbia L. Rev. 42 (1943).
[99] *Cameron* v. *International Alliance*, 118 N. J. Eg. 11, 16 (1935).

can refuse membership for any reason or for no reason. A few states have made it illegal for a union to refuse membership because of race, creed, or color,[100] but such laws are exceptional.[101] More than 20 national labor organizations prohibit the admission of Negroes either through their constitutions and by-laws, or by custom.[102] Unions can enact almost any by-laws they desire governing the conduct of their own members, and they can expel members for violation of such rules. Thus the United Mine Workers of America union has prohibited its members from criticizing a decision of a union officer.[103] Generally the courts will not interfere with the dismissal of a member if the procedure established by the union's by-laws and constitution is followed.[104]

In most instances the courts will not grant an injunction or any other form of relief to a person who has been refused admittance to a union. Thus under the laws of the states, there is practically no public control over the privilege of joining a union or over the right of the union to dismiss a member.[105] If a union refuses to admit a person, he cannot secure employment where that organization has closed- or union-shop contracts. Expulsion from the union means the worker will lose his job under a closed-shop, union-shop, or main-tenance-of-membership agreement.

The government is not generally concerned
with the conditions of union membership.

In designating a bargaining unit the National Labor Relations Board will not take into consideration the fact that some of the employees in the unit established by it cannot become members of the labor organization chosen by the majority as their representative, nor will it set up a separate bargaining unit for those who might not be admitted to membership in that union. The Board included in a bargaining unit represented by a labor organization, a watchman who

[100] *New York Statutes Annotated*, McKinney, Supp. 1942, Civil Rights Law, 41, 43.
[101] Several state labor relations acts provide that a union cannot be designated as the representative of a majority of the workers in an appropriate bargaining unit if it refuses to admit a worker because of his race or color. Kansas Gen. Stat. Supp. 1943, c. 44-801; Pennsylvania, 43 Pa. *Stat. Annotated*, Sec. 211.3 (4).
[102] Herbert R. Northrop, *Organized Labor and the Negro* (1944), Chap. 1.
[103] UMWA Constitution (1938), Art. 21, Sec. 3.
[104] *Sullivan* v. *Barrows*, 303 Mass. 197 (1938).
[105] *Maguire* v. *Buckley* 301 Mass. 355 (1938).

was also a local police officer, and who consequently was forbidden by the city to join a union.[106]

The problem of including workers in a unit represented by a union that will not admit them has arisen mainly in connection with Negroes. Since Section 9 (b) of the National Labor Relations Act provides that the bargaining unit is to be set up on a plant, craft, or employer basis, and since it makes no mention of race, the Board has held that it cannot set up a separate unit[107] composed of Negro employees. In one case the union selected by a majority of the employees expressed unwillingness to represent Negroes since they could not be admitted to membership. Nevertheless Negroes were included in the bargaining unit represented by it.[108] The Board will certify a union as the representative of a majority of the employees, though that union will not admit to membership the Negroes employed in the unit it represents.[109] Of course the choice of bargaining representatives is made by a majority of the employees and not by the Board; that agency merely certifies the choice of the employees in the unit it has designated.

The National Mediation Board will designate as collective bargaining representative a union that will not admit Negroes although persons of that race are employed in the craft or class that it is to represent. The Supreme Court has sustained this decision.[110] Here again it should be recalled that the National Mediation Board only designates the craft or class; the bargaining representatives for the craft or class are not chosen by the Board but by a majority of the employees. Although a closed-shop agreement cannot be made in the railroad industry, the union designated as a collective bargaining representative has exclusive bargaining rights, and thus the excluded Negroes cannot bargain as a separate group.

Even when a union demands a closed shop, the federal courts have

[106] Luckenbach Steamship Co., 2 NLRB 181 (1936).
[107] Crescent Bed Co., 29 NLRB 34, (1941); U. S. Bedding Co., 52 NLRB 382 (1943); American Tobacco Co., 9 NLRB 579 (1938); Union Envelope Co., 10 NLRB 1147 (1939).
[108] Brashear Freight Lines, Inc., 13 NLRB 191, 201 (1939).
[109] Interstate Granite Co., 11 NLRB 1046 (1939); Sloss-Sheffield Steel and Iron Co., 14 NLRB 186 (1939).
[110] Brotherhood of Railroad and Steamship Clerks v. United Transportation Service Employees, 320 U.S. 816 (1944); National Federation of Ry. Workers v. National Mediation Board, 110 Fed. (2d) 529 (1940); 310 U.S. 628 (1940).

revealed a similar lack of desire to consider the ineligibility of some of the employees to union membership. The Supreme Court refused to enjoin a strike and picketing carried on to secure a closed-shop agreement, in an establishment wherein the union would not admit to membership all the persons who were then working.[111] Undoubtedly this decision was dictated by the Norris-LaGuardia Act.

To prevent racial and religious discrimination in war industries, the President set up a Committee on Fair Employment Practice.[112] In Chapter V it was pointed out that the Committee had directed unions to admit Negroes although their constitutions or by-laws prohibited it. Since the Committee has no power to enforce its orders, it has not always been able to end discrimination.

The Supreme Court and the NLRB have said that a majority union must represent fairly the interests of nonmembers for whom it has the exclusive right to bargain collectively. In a case arising under the Railway Labor Act, the Supreme Court said, "Congress . . . did not intend to confer plenary power upon the union to sacrifice, for the benefit of its members, rights of the minority of the craft, without imposing on it any duty to protect the minority."[113] In this case the firemen, a majority of whom were white, were represented by the Brotherhood of Locomotive Firemen and Engineers which would not admit Negroes. This union, purporting to act for all employees of the craft it represented, demanded and obtained from the railway an agreement that had the effect of reducing the proportion of Negroes employed and of reducing their seniority. A negro fireman who lost his seniority as a result sought to enjoin the enforcement of the agreement. The Supreme Court observed, "The representative is to act on behalf of all employees which by virtue of the statute it undertakes to represent." If it fails to do this, the only recourse of the minority is to strike, and this act seeks to avoid such interruptions of commerce. "The labor organization chosen to be the representative of the craft or class of employees is thus chosen to represent all of its members regardless of their union affiliations or want of them." In making a discriminatory agreement, it did not act in the interest of all of the employees in the craft it represented.

[111] *Senn* v. *The Tile Layers Protective Union*, 301 U.S. 468 (1937).
[112] Executive Order No. 8802, June 25, 1941, *Federal Register*, Vol. 6, No. 125.
[113] *Steele* v. *Louisville and Nashville R.R. Co.*, 323 U.S. 192 (1944).

Recently the Chairman of the NLRB said:

We have never disbarred a union from running in an election, even though it might be a union which does not admit all races, provided that it is willing to represent all the people in the bargaining unit in negotiating for wages, hours, and other terms and conditions. In other words, we are concerned with its being a genuine representative of all its constituency and not one which, after it has gotten a certificate, will make some agreement which results in the employees of the minority race being deprived of their jobs.[114]

If a union does not consider a man suitable for membership, will it give his interests the same consideration as it gives to those of a union member, especially when a conflict develops between their interests?

Normally the NLRB is not concerned with the problem of the expulsion of members from a union, though a closed shop exists. But in at least one case where there was a closed shop, its decision had the result of reinstating employees in their jobs, after they had been discharged because a union had expelled them from membership. Just before a closed-shop agreement was to expire, the employees withdrew from the union that had made the contract and joined another labor organization. The union expelled these men, and upon its request the employer discharged them. The Board ordered their re-employment on the ground that the discharge was discriminatory.[115]

Where closed-shop agreements exist, the right of the worker to pursue his livelihood might be greatly limited, because unions have an unlimited right to exclude him and practically an unlimited right to expel him. The states, under whose laws the unions are created, have the power to regulate the conditions of union membership, but generally they do not utilize that power. Although the federal government promotes, encourages, and (at times) requires the inclusion of closed-shop clauses in contracts, normally it exercises no control over admission to unions and union discipline.

---

[114] *Labor Department—Federal Security Agency Appropriation Bill for 1945,* Hearings before the Senate Committee on Appropriations, 78 Cong. 3 sess., pp. 114-15; and *Wallace Co. v. NLRB,* 323 U.S. 248 (1944).

[115] *Rutland Court Owners,* 44 NLRB 387 (1942); *The Wallace Corp.,* 50 NLRB 138 (1943), and *Monsieur Henri Inc.,* 44 NLRB 1310 (1942).

*The NWLB does not generally interfere in the
relations of unions to their members.*

In two different ways the National War Labor Board has been confronted with the problem of the relationship of a union member to his labor organization. In almost all maintenance-of-membership clauses, a fifteen-day escape period is provided during which union members can withdraw from the organization. Some union constitutions and by-laws do not permit the resignation of members in that limited time. The Board issued a general order providing that these limitations must be waived or modified to permit such a withdrawal.[116]

Secondly, under a maintenance-of-membership provision, the Board is presented with a problem when an employee who elected to remain a union member contends that he was improperly expelled from the union after the end of the escape period, and that consequently he should not be discharged from his job. In the early maintenance-of-membership clauses, often no machinery was provided to determine the propriety of the union's dismissal of a member.[117] Since the summer of 1942 the Board has included in all such clauses a provision that expulsion from a union is to be treated as a grievance between the union and the employer. If the grievance machinery does not include arbitration as a final stage, the Board on demand will designate an arbitrator to determine the matter finally.[118] This means that the question of the expulsion of the member can be raised only if the employer refuses to discharge him when the union requests it. If the employer acquiesces in the union's request, the employee has no recourse. Unless the employer objects to discharging the employee, the War Labor Board is not concerned with the matter.[119] In one instance the Board has provided machinery to review such an expulsion at the employee's request. Where the Board grants a maintenance-of-membership clause to an organization representing

[116] Release of the National War Labor Board, Nov. 28, 1942.

[117] *Ryan Aeronautical Co.*, 1 WLR 305 (1942); *Federal Shipbuilding and Drydock Co.*, 1 WLR 140 (1942); *International Harvester Co.*, 1 WLR 112 (1942).

[118] *Warner Automotive Parts Division*, 2 WLR 176 (1942); *Buckeye Cotton Oil Co.*, 2 WLR 145 (1942).

[119] Public member Wayne Morse, *To Investigate Executive Agencies*, Hearings before the House Committee on Excess of Power by Executive Agencies, 78 Cong. 1 sess., pp. 1850-51.

writers in the publishing field, an employee expelled from the union for something he has written or said has the right to present all the facts to an arbitrator.[120]

The standard maintenance-of-membership clause used by the National War Labor Board offers no real protection to a worker who is expelled from a union. The handling of such cases through the grievance procedure places the presentation of the employee's case in the hands of the employer. If the employer does not see fit to press the worker's case, the National War Labor Board offers him no protection. An employer trying to get along with a union will not be anxious to antagonize it, by pressing the case of a worker who thinks he was improperly expelled from the organization.

VIII. CONCLUSIONS

The policy of the federal government is now to encourage and promote the closed shop and other forms of union preference except in railroad transportation, where it has prohibited it. This practice is consistent with the government's policy of helping labor to increase its bargaining power, but it is inconsistent with its policy of guaranteeing to workers freedom of organization. Advocates of the closed shop put the need for solidarity in collective bargaining above the workers' freedom to choose their own form of organization.

With the split in the labor movement, the closed shop and other forms of union preference have become weapons of inter-union warfare. Even when the American labor movement was comparatively united, the demand for the closed shop existed. Then it was motivated by the desire to further unionization by forcing nonunion employees to join the organization and by the wish to prevent evasions of collective agreements. The avowed objective of the labor advocates of the closed shop thus was the protection of the interests of the employees.

The A.F. of L.-CIO split has changed the situation. Although closed-shop agreements still serve the purpose of protecting collective agreements and of aiding the growth of unionism, they are often used as a weapon in the fight between the A.F. of L. and the CIO. They are even being used to suppress competition where the rival unions are affiliated with the same major organization. The recent decisions of

[120] *Patriot Co.*, 14 WLR 355 (1944).

the courts and of federal regulatory agencies indicate that more closed-shop disputes arise out of interunion competition than from differences between employers and employees or between union and nonunion workers. Thus the original character of the closed shop has changed; to the usual arguments for the closed shop new arguments have been added.

Although the federal government encourages the development of labor organizations and permits various forms of union preference agreements, it exercises no control over the admission of employees to unions or their expulsion from such organizations. The matters are subject only to state control. Even in designating a bargaining representative, the NLRB and the National Mediation Board take no account of the refusal of the designated organization to admit all employees to membership. This attitude of these two agencies involves difficulties not only where there is a closed shop, but also where it does not exist. Where there is not a closed shop, some may argue that no one has to join the union and therefore no issue of public policy is raised. But since the majority has the exclusive right to bargain collectively for all of the workers, and since individual bargaining has been supplanted by collective bargaining, it is quite possible, even where a closed shop does not exist, that an individual who cannot be admitted to the majority union may not have his interests adequately protected. Where a collective agreement exists, individual bargaining beyond the act of hiring is generally illegal.[121] In addition, where a majority union exists, grievances of individual employees not members of the union can only be adjusted through the union. The employer refuses to bargain if he sets up a procedure to adjust grievances directly with employees, though the collective agreement has no grievance clause. The individual employee can only inform the employer of a grievance; any negotiating beyond that must be done by the bargaining representative.[122]

It hardly meets the issue for the Supreme Court or a member of the NLRB to say that the majority union must represent the interests of nonunion members. It is not entirely reasonable to believe that an organization that does not consider a person to be a desirable member will give full and adequate representation to his interests. Where

[121] See Chap. 3.
[122] *U.S. Automatic Co.* 57 NLRB 124 (1944).

the interests of nonmembers and members conflict, it would be surprising if the union did not favor its members. Further, such an
organization if it is not employer-dominated, and if it represents a
majority of the employees could, if the employer acquiesced, secure
a closed shop that would require the discharge of those employees
whom the union refused to admit. In a dictum in one case the NLRB
admitted that this would present a difficulty.[123]

Thus, although the government permits unions and employers to
establish certain forms of union preference, normally it does nothing
to ensure that all workers have a chance to join and remain members
of a union. Certain special rights are conferred on a union representing
a majority of the employees, but nothing is done to ensure that it will
permit all employees to share in these privileges. Duties commensurate with these rights are not imposed.

[123] *Bethlehem Alameda Shipyard, Inc.*, 53 NLRB 999 (1943).

CHAPTER VII

CONDITIONS OF EMPLOYMENT: WAGES

From 1933 to the spring of 1942, the policy of the federal government was clearly that of increasing the wages of labor. Repeatedly the President asserted that higher wages were desirable.[1] Not until April 1942 did any important government official express the opinion that wages might become too high. From July 1933 to April 1942, according to the Bureau of Labor Statistics, hourly earnings in manufacturing industries increased from 41.1 cents to 82.2 cents. On April 27, 1942 President Roosevelt said: "Wages can and should be kept at existing scales."[2] But in May 1945 hourly earnings averaged 104.3 cents. The efforts of the government to raise wages and to prevent them from rising too high will be considered in this chapter.

Numerous devices—direct and indirect—have been used to carry out these wage policies. The direct method of wage fixing has in general been applied only to minimum wage rates, but recently all wage changes have been made subject to government approval. As for indirect methods of government aid in wage adjustment, the encouragement of collective bargaining has been the method mainly utilized. In discussing the devices used for wage control, an attempt will be made to discover what standards have been used in the process of wage determination.

I. THE DIRECT DETERMINATION OF WAGES

Although the federal government had been importuned to pass minimum wage laws of various sorts prior to 1933, these measures had been of limited and special character designed to protect unorganized workers or those in peculiarly weak economic positions, notably women and children. Only with the passage of the National Industrial Recovery Act, did the government attempt to put a floor under the wages of all workers.

To support the enactment of minimum wage legislation, evidence was presented to Congress at various times, indicating that in some

---

[1] For example, *The Public Papers and Addresses of Franklin D. Roosevelt*, 1934 (1938), pp. 128, 416.
[2] *New York Times*, Apr. 28, 1942.

areas and industries workers were being paid a very low wage. Mr. Sidney Hillman testified that he knew of some cases where a wage of five cents an hour was being paid, and in a few cases as low as two cents.[3] On another occasion he asserted that in one state the average wage paid to all workers was 25 cents an hour.[4] In 1937 the Commissioner of Labor Statistics testified that there were two industries where the average hourly wage of all employees was under 30 cents, and seven where it was less than 40 cents.[5] Mr. Leon Henderson declared that in three industries more than half of the workers received less than 20 cents on hour.[6]

A. The National Recovery Administration

Under the NIRA, minimum wages were fixed either through codes of fair competition or by licenses imposed upon an industry by the President.[7] The codes were formulated by the representatives of an industry sometimes with the collaboration of labor representatives, but however drafted they all had to be approved by the President. Whether codes or licenses were used, the government actually was responsible for the wage provisions applicable to an industry.

Under the NRA there were no
standards for fixing wages.

The NIRA contained nothing to guide an administrator in fixing wages. Of course Section 1 of the act declared that one of its objectives was "to improve the standards of living"; and the President on signing the bill said: "No business which depends for existence on paying less than living wages to its workers has any right to continue in this country. . . . By living wages I mean more than a bare subsistence level—I mean the wages of decent living."[8] He never defined

---

[3] *To Create a National Labor Board*, Hearings before the Senate Committee on Education and Labor, 73 Cong. 2 sess., p. 121.

[4] *Fair Labor Standards Act of 1937*, Hearings before the House Committee on Labor, 75 Cong. 1 sess., p. 950.

[5] The same, p. 338.

[6] The same, pp. 163-64.

[7] Act of June 16, 1933, 48 Stat. 196, 199, Secs. 3 (a), 3 (d), 7 (b), and 7 (c). The codes, of course, had to be approved by the President. The NIRA did not specify directly that the codes of fair competition should contain minimum wage provisions, but under Section 7 (c) the President was given the power to prescribe limited codes of fair competition which would include minimum wages.

[8] *Public Papers and Addresses of Franklin D. Roosevelt*, 1933 (1938), pp. 251-52.

the term "subsistence living," or the "wages of decent living." At no time did the NRA issue an official statement defining its wage policy, or even defining a living wage. "The concept was never defined either in terms of the substantive content of the standard or in terms of how much money it would require to maintain it."[9] Unofficial statements of policy from within the NRA indicated a desire to raise wages as much as possible and wherever possible.[10]

It appears that it was the standard policy of the NRA to regard 40 cents an hour as the normal minimum wage.[11] Close to 50 per cent of the codes called for a minimum wage of 40 cents an hour, and almost as large a percentage provided for minimum wages between 30 cents and 40 cents an hour, but the range in minimum wage rates was from about 12½ cents to 70 cents an hour.[12] It was a general policy of the NRA to maintain existing wage differentials, when a minimum wage was fixed and also to maintain weekly earnings, when hours of work were reduced. But never did the NRA have anything approximating a clearly enunciated wage policy.

B. Wages in Bituminous Coal Mining

When the NRA was held unconstitutional by the Supreme Court in the spring of 1935, many people in the government felt it was necessary to do something to increase wages in bituminous coal mining. Consequently in the Bituminous Coal Conservation Act of 1935, a plan was devised for price control and for the fixing of minimum wages in the industry.

The Bituminous Coal Conservation Act delegated wage determination to private bodies.

Minimum prices and minimum wages were to be fixed by codes, and taxation was used to get producers to comply with them. The legislation divided the country into twenty-three coal-producing districts. If in any one of these districts or in any group of districts,

[9] NRA work materials 45, Pt. C, Sec. 2, *Policy in the Control of Wages under NRA* (1936), p. 42.

[10] Quoted in the same, p. 32.

[11] See quotations from the revised Office Manual of the NRA of June 12, 1935, quoted in the same, pp. 30-31; and confidential document of labor policy group, September 1934, the same.

[12] Leverett S. Lyon, Paul T. Homan, George Terborgh, Lewis L. Lorwin, Charles Dearing and L. C. Marshall, *The National Recovery Administration: An Analysis and an Appraisal* (1935), pp. 317-19.

the wage applicable to two thirds of the coal mined and to one half of the workers employed was fixed by collective bargaining, the wage thus agreed upon was to be the minimum paid to all workers by all employers who operated under the code.[13] Thus the wages fixed by collective bargaining for a part of the workers were to be made applicable to all employees in the district. In the debates on this bill speakers repeatedly said that its major objective was to increase wages.

Actually the determination of wages was placed in the hands of the United Mine Workers of America and the mine owners. The act of 1935 delegated to private agencies the task of wage determination. No standards were set. Thus whatever wage the UMWA could get was to be the minimum wage for the industry. The Supreme Court held the act unconstitutional both because it was a regulation of wages, and because it delegated to private bodies the power to fix wages.[14] Subsequently Congress adopted legislation which provided only for the fixing of minimum prices for bituminous coal,[15] but the primary objective of this legislation was to provide for higher prices so as to make possible the payment of higher wages.

C. The Fair Labor Standards Act of 1938

The Fair Labor Standards Act of 1938 requires the payment of minimum wages to practically all workers who are engaged in the production of goods which are intended to move in interstate commerce. Employees in agriculture and a few other activities are excepted, but generally the production of goods or services intended for interstate commerce has been broadly construed.[16] This act required the payment of a minimum wage of 25 cents an hour until October 1939, and a minimum wage of 30 cents an hour from that date until October 1945, and thereafter a minimum wage of 40 cents an hour. As originally introduced in Congress, this bill provided for a 40-cents minimum wage applicable immediately, but because of a number of pressures, a lower minimum wage was provided during the transitional period. The Administrator of the Wage and Hour Division of the Department of Labor has the task of administering

[13] Act of Aug. 30, 1935, 49 Stat. 991, 1002, Sec. 5 (g).
[14] *Carter* v. *Carter Coal Co.*, 298 U.S. 238 (1936).
[15] Act of Apr. 26, 1937, 50 Stat. 72 and act of Apr. 11, 1941, 55 Stat. 133. This expired in April 1943.
[16] *Kirschbaum Co.* v. *Walling*, 316 U.S. 517 (1942).

the wage provisions of this law. Before October 1945 he was empowered to increase minimum wages to not more than 40 cents an hour in any industry, and after that date he can reduce the minimum wage in any industry to not less than 30 cents an hour.[17]

*Reasons for a 40-cent
minimum are not clear.*

The purpose of the Fair Labor Standards Act was to increase purchasing power by increasing wages. This was a major objective of its minimum wage provisions. President Roosevelt, on May 24, 1937, in requesting Congress to enact this legislation, said:

Today you and I are pledged to take further steps to reduce the lag in the purchasing power of industrial workers and to strengthen and stabilize the markets for the farmers' products. . . . Our nation so richly endowed with natural resources and with a capable and industrious population should be able to devise ways and means of insuring to all our able-bodied working men and women a fair day's pay for a fair day's work. . . .[18]

The testimony of Leon Henderson[19] and the Report of the House Committee on Labor[20] clearly indicate the significance of the purchasing power theory in the development of this legislation.

The report of the Senate Committee on Education and Labor throws some light on why a 40 cents an hour minimum wage was provided.

The Committee feels that a minimum wage of 40 cents per hour, which will yield no more than an annual income of $800 a year to the small percentage of workers fortunate enough to find 50 weeks employment in a year, does not give a wage sufficient to maintain what we would like to regard as the minimum American standard of living. But 40 cents per hour is far more than millions of American workers are receiving today. . . .[21]

Probably one reason for the selection of 40 cents an hour was because a large proportion of the codes under the NRA provided for such a minimum rate.

[17] Act of June 25, 1938, 52 Stat. 1062, Sec. 6 (a).
[18] *Public Papers and Addresses of Franklin D. Roosevelt*, 1937 (1941), p. 210.
[19] *Fair Labor Standards Act of 1937*, Hearings before the House Committee on Labor, 75 Cong. 1 sess., p. 158.
[20] *Fair Labor Standards Act*, H. Rept. 1452, 75 Cong. 1 sess, p. 9.
[21] *Fair Labor Standards Act*, S. Rept. 884, 75 Cong. 1 sess., p. 4.

*The Administrator makes the final
determination of minimum wages.*

The Administrator of the Wage and Hour Division of the Department of Labor, according to the act, is to increase wages to 40 cents an hour as rapidly as possible.[22] In doing so he is to fix the wage for each industry on the basis of a recommendation of an industry committee appointed by himself. These committees must be composed of equal numbers of representatives of employers and employees, and at least one person representing the public interest.[23] In practically all cases the representatives of employees are chosen from among union officials, regardless of the extent of organization of the workers.[24]

The recommendation of the industry committee must be approved by the Administrator. He is directed to do this if the recommendation is in accordance with the law, if it is supported by evidence, and if, after taking into consideration the same factors that are to be considered by the industry committee, he finds that the wages recommended will effectuate the purposes of the act.[25] Since the Administrator must hold hearings before he makes a determination, and since he can set aside the recommendation of a committee if he finds that it does not effectuate the purposes of the act, it can be fairly said that the final determination of minimum wages is in the hands of the Administrator. He practically always follows the recommendations of the industry committee, and in only one instance has he refused to accept its conclusions.[26] The decisions of the Administrator are practically final since the Supreme Court has expressed a disinclination to consider appeals from them.[27]

The Industry Committees are to recommend the highest wage, not exceeding 40 cents an hour, which will not lessen employment substantially, having due regard to economic and competitive conditions. No regional wage differentials are permitted, but classification

[22] Act of June 25, 1938, 52 Stat. 1064, Sec. 8 (a).
[23] Sec. 8 (b).
[24] *Administrative Procedure of Government Agencies*, S. Doc. 10, Pt. 1, 77 Cong. 1 sess., p. 12.
[25] Sec. 8 (d).
[26] Jewelry Industry, Apr. 24, 1941. Here the rejection was on the basis that he refused to agree to the definition of the jewelry industry, and not to the wage rate applied.
[27] *Opp Cotton Mills* v. *The Administrator*, 312 U.S. 126 (1941).

of employers for the purpose of determining different minimum wages can be made on the basis of the following considerations: (1) competitive conditions as affected by transportation and living and production costs; (2) wages established for like work by collective bargaining; and (3) wages paid for work of a like or comparable character by employers who voluntarily maintain fair standards.[28] The decision of the Administrator is to be based on these same standards. The guiding principles contained in the act are exceedingly general, so in order to determine what they really mean, it is necessary to consider their actual application in the decisions of the Administrator. In making his decision the Administrator must determine that the minimum wage fixed does not reduce employment, and that it will not give a competitive advantage to any group in the industry.

The decision of the Administrator is based mainly
on the effect of the wage increase on employment.

The main consideration of the Administrator in practically all cases is whether the proposed minimum wage would tend to reduce employment. In most cases he states that the suggested minimum wage will increase labor costs by a certain percentage, and that the total production costs also will be increased by a given percentage. He has found that an increase in total production costs of 3 per cent,[29] and an increase of 3.2 per cent in total costs, would not affect employment.[30] The Administrator never presents data concerning the comparable effects of other possible minimum rates of pay on total wage costs, on production costs, or on earnings, nor does he present information on high-wage and low-wage plants, or on high-cost and low-cost plants.

In making these determinations of the consequences of a wage increase, the Administrator relies entirely on information contained in the Census of Manufactures and the wage statistics of the Bureau of Labor Statistics. The data contained in the Census of Manufactures is on an establishment basis. Each factory is a separate establishment classified on the basis of its principal product or group of products.

[28] Sec. 8 (c).
[29] Single pants and related products industry, Sept. 12, 1941.
[30] Rubber manufacturing industry, June 27, 1941, especially as related to the southern states.

An establishment producing several products is thus classified as though it were producing only its major product.[31] The Administrator presents no data on specific plants or on high-cost and low-cost plants, or on high-wage and low-wage plants.[32]

In determining the effect of a wage increase on costs, the Administrator does not consider the influence of an increase in the minimum rates on wages that are above the minimum. An increase in the minimum rate of pay will tend to raise wages that were at or above that minimum, because employees are anxious to maintain existing wage differentials. The Administrator summarized the factors that tend to determine how much rates above the minimum will be affected by such an increase as follows:

Among those factors are the bargaining position of labor, the current practice of the industry with regard to profitable operations, the attitude of the management toward the maintenance of occupational differentials of wages, and the extent to which wages of employees are concentrated at a point just above the minimum adopted.[33]

On several occasions he claimed that when the minimum wage was raised, the consequent increase in total wages above it was only about one third of the increase in wages resulting directly from raising those rates which had been below the minimum.[34] But when a minimum wage was first fixed in the textile industry, it was found that the resulting wage increase, that is, the increase of the wages that were below the minimum, would be about 4.4 per cent of the total pay roll.[35] Yet two years later, when the Administrator fixed a higher minimum wage, he found that the original determination resulted in an actual increase of wage payments of 9.2 per cent of the total pay roll.[36] Thus the resulting increase in wages above the minimum was greater than the increase in the wages below the minimum.

In estimating the total increase in wage costs resulting from the imposition of a minimum wage, the Administrator refuses to consider the increase in wages above the minimum, because he asserts that

[31] Sixteenth Census of the United States, *Census of Business,* Vol. 5, pp. 1 and 2.
[32] E. B. Mittelman, "Wage Determination, The Evidence Before the Wage and Hour Division," *Political Science Quarterly,* Vol. 57 (1942), pp. 565, 590, 597.
[33] Knitted and men's woven underwear industry, Nov. 4, 1941.
[34] Knit underwear industry, Apr. 11, 1940.
[35] Decision of Sept. 29, 1939.
[36] Textile industry, June 13, 1941.

it is evident the employer must have the financial capacity to pay such an increase, or he would not have been willing to grant it.[37] The refusal of the Administrator to consider the effect of an increase in minimum wages on wages above the minimum does not seem to be well founded for, as a result, he omits a significant item in wage costs that might have a bearing on total costs, on profits, and thus on employment.

The Administrator has advanced a number of reasons why employers in various industries can afford to pay additional wages without a consequent reduction in employment. He has argued that additional wages can be paid out of profits.[38] But he presents no real data on profits; or on the relationship of net earnings to invested capital for an industry or for any part of an industry. He also contends that the wage increase can be passed on to the consumer in the form of higher prices. He observed concerning the luggage and leather goods industry:[39] "Prices to the consumer may be increased. . . . There may be fewer bargain sales or changes in the quality of goods normally sold at fixed prices, or reduction in the gross margins of distributors."

In some instances the Administrator concluded that style and not price was the determining factor, and therefore the price could be increased without any effect on demand;[40] in others he has asserted that the producer could reduce the quality or quantity of the goods, and consequently a change in the price to the consumer would be unnecessary.[41] He found in the case of seamless hosiery that the wage increase could very readily be passed on to the consumer through an increase in price because no effective substitute exists for the product.[42] He has on occasion recognized that increased wage costs can be avoided by technological changes.[43] In no case were such statements

[37] Pulp and primary paper products, July 18, 1940; buckle and button industry, Sept. 19, 1942.

[38] Drug, medicinal and toilet products industry, June 14, 1941; the clay products industry, Aug. 12, 1941; railroad industry, Aug. 13, 1942.

[39] Dec. 18, 1940, p. 19.

[40] Military goods industry, Dec. 15, 1939.

[41] Wood furniture industry, Oct. 21, 1941; and the embroidery industry, Dec. 28, 1940.

[42] Decision of July 10, 1941, p. 19. In the shoe industry (Oct. 15, 1941) he said it could be passed on to the consumer easily because all prices were rising because of the war.

[43] Single pants and allied products, Sept. 12, 1940; cigars, July 8, 1942.

substantiated by actual data. He thus assumed tacitly that technological changes would reduce labor costs but would not tend to reduce employment.

The act does not in any way define what constitutes a substantial lessening of employment, nor do the decisions of the Administrator. He always asserts that the proposed minimum wage will not substantially affect employment. And there are no comparisons to show the relative consequences of different minimum wages. The reasons a wage increase will not have an adverse effect on employment are divergent. Sometimes the Administrator says that the increase can be paid out of profits—that is, the producer can pay for it. Then again the consumer can bear the increase through higher prices or a reduction in quality. In other instances he has found that the increase in cost might be met through technological changes.

Relatively little consideration is given to the other standard prescribed by the act—the effect of the minimum wage on competitive conditions in the industry. A few opinions contain a little information on comparative labor costs and profits as between the North and the South, but no decision gives any comparison of the results of a proposed minimum wage on different groups of producers. The effect of a given minimum wage on competitive conditions is given little consideration. Consequently the only criterion used is the effect of the minimum wage on employment. It should be remembered that the Administrator has never disapproved of the report of an industry committee on the ground that the wage recommended was improper.

A uniform minimum wage is prescribed for a whole industry.

Under the Fair Labor Standards Act the Administrator cannot make any regional classification within an industry. This means of course that he cannot give a differential to one group as against another on a purely geographical basis. But he can make classifications within an industry based on: (1) competitive conditions as affected by transportation, living, and production costs; (2) wages established for like work by collective bargaining; and (3) wages paid for work of a like or comparable character by employers who voluntarily maintain fair wage standards. Despite this provision of the act the Administrator has never used any classification within an industry, and a uniform minimum wage always has been prescribed for a whole industry.

The Administrator has expressly refused to consider the cost of living as a basis for classification, although the research staff of the Wage and Hour Division once concluded that a 5 per cent differential in cost of living existed between the North and the South.[44] In but few cases has the Administrator considered the possibility of a classification on the basis of wage rates determined by collective bargaining. In the electric lamp shade industry,[45] he pointed out that only one third of the employees were members of a union, and that they were not concentrated on a geographical basis. Therefore he concluded that the union rate would not tend to bring about increases in rates above the minimum in nonunion plants.

The act contains three criteria on which a classification of or a differential in minimum wages can be allowed. First, competitive conditions as evidenced by production, transportation, and living costs might be a logical basis, but the Administrator has never recognized such differences. The second criterion is the wages fixed by collective agreements. This would seem to have little to do with the determination of what is an appropriate minimum wage.

The third method of classification is on the basis of wages paid for work of a like or comparable character by employers who voluntarily maintain fair wage standards. In order to apply this method the Administrator first would have to determine what are fair wage standards. That is what he is doing within certain limits under the act. But the Administrator has not discussed this point in any decision. Consequently this basis of classification does not appear to be a useful guide.

Objective standards have
not been developed.

Reviewing the actions taken by the Administrator under the Fair Labor Standards Act and such reasons as were given for his decisions, it is not evident that there have been developed any clear standards for fixing a minimum wage. As we have seen, the primary test used is

[44] See Report of the Wage and Hour Division on the clay products industry, and Decision No. 24 of the Administrator relative to this industry.
[45] Apr. 30, 1941.

the effect of the given minimum wage on employment. It should be the highest wage possible under the act that will not lessen employment substantially. In making such a determination the Administrator is to have due regard for economic and competitive conditions. As was pointed out earlier, in arriving at these determinations the administrator relies on the generalized data presented by the Bureau of Labor Statistics and the Census of Manufacturers. It is doubtful whether any public service commission could under the Constitution fix rates for a business affected with a public interest on the basis of such meager data.

The standards contained in the law do not constitute a real guide to the Administrator in fixing a minimum wage. Consequently, it is not surprising that he himself has not developed any real standards. The monograph on the Wage and Hour Division prepared by the staff of the Attorney General's Committee on Administrative Law stated:

With the actual functionings of the industry committees there has been somewhat less satisfaction. Observers generally agree that the committee's deliberative process is, in practice, little more than collective bargaining. . . .

. . . .

Wherever the merits may be in the controversy . . . one cannot escape the conclusion that the committees do not function with complete objectivity, nor with the detached intensity that might be supposed to mark a judicial process. Without doubt, horse trading—or collective bargaining—play a not inconsiderable part in the ultimate recommendation.[46]

The chief economist of the American Federation of Labor declared: "There has been a tendency to arrive at wage recommendations blindfolded by drawing lots rather than by careful weighing of all available facts. . . . Labor has felt that only too often wage and hour mediation has been substituted for wage and hour administration."[47] No opinion is here expressed concerning the economic desirability of the standards contained in the law. It is only asserted that under this act no definite and precise standards have been developed for fixing minimum wages.

---

[46] S. Doc. 10, Pt. 1, 77 Cong. 1 sess, pp. 18-19.
[47] Boris Shiskin, "Wage and Hour Administration from Labor's Viewpoint," *American Labor Legislation Review*, Vol. 29 (1939), p. 63.

D. The National War Labor Board

The National War Labor Board has been the only agency that has attempted to restrict wage increases; practically all other establishments engaged in wage determination have sought to increase wages. This Board alone fixes maximum wages; all other agencies fix minimum wages. The National Defense Mediation Board, its predecessor, was primarily concerned with the settling of industrial disputes without resort to strikes.[48] An increase in wages that was necessary to avert a work stoppage was not considered undesirable because of its inflationary potentiality. The National War Labor Board[49] adopted a similar attitude at first, but by the summer of 1942 it had reached the conclusion that it was desirable to limit wage increases. Wages were rising rapidly. Most of the increases were granted voluntarily by employers because of labor scarcity, and because frequently the costs could be shifted to the government under cost-plus contracts. Since the Board could consider only cases where the employer refused to grant increases, whatever principles the Board had were of limited application. Congress felt that wage increases had to be limited if price control was to be effective.[50] Consequently by the act of October 2, 1942 the President was directed to regulate all wages.[51] This act provided that the President should stabilize wages and prices on the basis of levels existing on September 15, 1942. As a standard to guide him in fixing wages the act provides:

No action shall be taken under authority of this Act with respect to wages or salaries (1) which is inconsistent with the provisions of the Fair Labor Standards Act of 1938, as amended, or the National Labor Relations Act, or (2) for the purpose of reducing the wages or salaries for any particular work below the highest wages or salaries paid therefor between January 1, 1942, and September 15, 1942: *Provided,* That the President may, without regard to the limitation contained in clause (2), adjust wages or salaries to the extent that he finds necessary in any case to correct gross inequities and also aid in the effective prosecution of the war.[52]

[48] Executive Order No. 8716, Mar. 19, 1941, *Federal Register,* Vol. 6, p. 1532.
[49] Executive Order No. 9017, Jan. 12, 1942, *Federal Register,* Vol. 7, p. 237 and the act of June 25, 1943, 57 Stat. 163, Sec. 7.
[50] The President first felt no wage control was necessary (Message to Congress, July 30, 1941) and he subsequently felt that any control that was necessary he could exercise without congressional help (Message to Congress, Sept. 7, 1942).
[51] Act of Oct. 2, 1942, 56 Stat. 765.
[52] Sec. 4.

Thus all wage changes were made subject to government control. The President delegated his power to regulate wages of less than $5,000 a year to the National War Labor Board, and control over salaries in excess of $5,000 was given to the Bureau of Internal Revenue. He issued several executive orders setting standards for the Board. The Board generally had final authority to control wage changes; but when an employer asserted a price increase would result,[53] the decision of the Board was subject to review by the Director of Economic Stabilization.[54]

The law, executive orders, and decisions of the Board outlined four major principles on which a wage increase would be granted; to compensate for changes in the cost of living, to correct inequities and inequalities, to correct substandard wages, and to aid in the prosecution of the war.

All workers were entitled to an increase
of at least 15 per cent above January 1941.

In July 1942 the Board said that all workers were entitled to at least a 15 per cent increase in wages since January 1, 1941, and if the employers did not grant it voluntarily the Board would order it. The increase in the cost of living was the justification for this. More specifically it stated in the Little Steel case:

For the period from January 1, 1941, to May 1942, which followed a long period of relative stability, the cost of living increased by about 15 per cent. If any group of workers averaged less than a 15-per cent increase in hourly wage rates during, or immediately preceding or following, this period, their established peacetime standards have been broken. If any group of workers averaged a 15-per cent wage increase or more, their established peacetime standards have been preserved.[55]

From January 1, 1941 to April 1942 the cost of living had increased 15 per cent. The workers involved in this case had received actually general increases of 11.8 per cent from January 1, 1941 to April 1942, when the President said prices and wages should

---

[53] A failure to increase wages as directed may result in the seizure of the employer's plant. Granting an unauthorized increase can be punished by fine and imprisonment (Act. of Oct. 2, 1942, Sec. 11); or the government can refuse to consider any salary increase to be an improper expenditure for income tax purposes. Executive Order No. 9250, Title 3, Sec. 4.

[54] Order of Director of Economic Stabilization, May 12, 1943, 8 WLR XIV.

[55] *Bethlehem Steel Co.*, 1 WLR 325, 334 (1942).

not be increased further. If wages were to keep pace with the increase in the cost of living, the workers were still entitled to a further increase of 3.2 per cent, or roughly 3.2 cents in this case. But the Board actually granted them a wage increase of 5.5 cents. In addition to the 3.2 per cent which was granted on the basis of the increase in the cost of living, an additional 2.3 per cent was granted on the basis of so-called "time equities." By "time equities" the Board meant that if the case had been decided at the time that it was filed, that is, in February 1942, the Board would have given to the workers a larger increase in pay, and it believed the workers should not be made to suffer from the application of new standards. Thus in reality the Board permitted an increase in pay of 17.3 per cent, and not 15 per cent as is generally considered to have been enjoined in the decision.

Some elements in the Little Steel Formula need further explanation. This standard was subsequently imposed on the Board by the Executive Order of April 8, 1943,[56] consequently it could not abrogate or modify the principle directly by its own action. Increases in wages should equal only the increase in the cost of living from January 1941 to April 1942. If the employer had not already granted an increase sufficient for that purpose, the Board would permit an increase equal to the difference between the increase in the cost of living and the actual increase in wages. At the time of the President's "hold the line" statement of April 27, 1942, the cost of living was 15 per cent above the level of January 1941. But since then the cost of living has continued to rise; in June 1945 it was 29 per cent above the level selected. Nevertheless, the Board said, that under the Little Steel Formula it would not permit an increase of more than 15 per cent.[57] Thus the 15 per cent wage increase was not directly related to the change in the cost of living as that has been much more than 15 per cent.

Generally only wage rates and not earnings were considered in the application of the Little Steel Formula. Actual earnings increased much faster than hourly rates, because of the increases in the length of the work week, and because of the payment of higher rates for overtime work. The Executive Order of October 3, 1942 (by which the President empowered the Board to fix wages, not the act

[56] No. 9328, *Federal Register*, Vol. 8, p. 4681.
[57] *Big Four Meat Packers*, 6 WLR 395 (1943).

itself), required that wage rates and not earnings should be considered.[58] Only in one series of cases has the Board considered actual earnings. In the autumn of 1942 the President by executive order limited the payment of overtime in general to not more than one and one-half times the normal rate. Some workers had been getting double time for work beyond the normal work week, hence this order caused a reduction in their total earnings. The Board granted them an increase in the hourly rate so that their total weekly earnings would not be reduced as a result.[59]

Another problem was the question of what constituted a wage increase that was to be offset against the rise in the cost of living. Supposedly such increase must have occurred since January 1, 1941. In some cases the Board held that a wage increase granted before that date, but effective subsequently, was not to be included,[60] and in others it held that such an increase was to be included.[61] Changes in average hourly rates resulting from individual promotions were not considered.[62] To constitute an offset against the 15 per cent, there must have been an actual increase in the rate applicable to a sizeable group of employees, involving at least 10 per cent of the employees at a time.[63]

The "time equity" doctrine advanced in the Little Steel case was a means of granting an increase of more than 15 per cent. In that instance an additional 2.3 per cent was granted on the ground that, had the case been decided immediately when it was brought, a greater increase would have been permitted than at the time it was decided. In the Carnegie Illinois Steel Company case, which arose after the Little Steel Formula was enunciated, the same increase for time equities was allowed, although the wage increase was not requested until after the Little Steel decision.[64]

The Board has not always adhered to the Little Steel Formula with great exactness. In one case an increase of 29.9 per cent was

---

[58] No. 9250, Title II, Sec. 1, *Federal Register*, Vol. 7, p. 7871.
[59] *York Safe and Lock Co.*, 6 WLR 564 (1943); *New Britain Machine Co.*, 6 WLR 565 (1943).
[60] *General Steel Castings Corp.*, 6 WLR 33 (1943).
[61] *New York and New Jersey Wholesale Liquor Dealers*, 9 WLR 713 (1943).
[62] *National Malleable Iron and Steel Co.*, 5 WLR 566 (1942); *Loose-Wiles Biscuit Co.*, 12 WLR 120 (1943).
[63] *Federal Bearing Co.*, 9 WLR 691 (1943); an increase received by 35 per cent of the workers was not considered; *Continental Rubber Workers*, 6 WLR 372 (1943).
[64] *United States Steel Co.*, 2 WLR 453 (1942).

granted,[65] and in another 20 per cent.[66] Where an increase of only 1 cent an hour was in order under the Little Steel Formula, an additional 2 cents was granted to compensate employees for working night shifts, even though some of the workers never had to do such work.[67] Although the workers in an iron mine had already received a 15 per cent wage increase, they got 5.5 cents additional, because they were considered a part of the steel industry.[68] Employees in a bag factory received a 30 per cent increase for inequities as a part of the textile industry, but they were later allowed an additional 15 per cent because of the increase in the cost of living.[69]

When the Little Steel Formula was adopted only about 32 per cent of the employees had not received an increase of at least 15 per cent.[70] Consequently as additional groups were granted such increases, the importance of the Formula declined.[71]

Wages below the average
generally could be increased.

The second major basis for justifying a wage increase was that it was necessary to correct inequities and inequalities.[72] The Board defined inequalities and gross inequities as being "those which represent manifest injustices that arise from unusual and unreasonable differentials in wage rates."[73] Concerning the need for the removal of inequalities the Board said:

[65] *American Smelting and Refining Co.*, 5 WLR 469 (1943).
[66] *Crescent Brick Co.*, 8 WLR 413 (1943).
[67] *Big Four Rubber Cos.*, 8 WLR 537 (1943).
[68] *Lake Superior Iron Ore Cos.*, 7 WLR 53 (1943).
[69] *Golden Belt Mfg. Co.*, 7 WLR 88 (1943). In the *New York Dress Manufacturers Association*, 8 WLR 137 (1943), the workers were entitled to a 6 per cent increase but were granted 7 per cent on the ground that it would be difficult to make the increase retroactive; see also *Hewett Rubber Co.*, 14 WLR 1 (1944); *Pittsburgh Reflector Co.*, 16 WLR 13 (1944); *LaCrosse Rubber Co.*, 15 WLR 224 (1944); *Kelly Springfield Engineering Co.*, 11 WLR 1 (1943).
[70] *Extension of the Emergency Price Control Act of 1942*, Hearings before the Senate Committee on Banking and Currency, 78 Cong. 2 sess., p. 201.
[71] Wage increases designed to stimulate additional production can be granted. Only where both the employer and the employees, speaking through their duly authorized bargaining agents, desire the increase, will the Board permit it; Order of Oct. 2, 1942, 11 WLR XXXIX; *Grumman Aircraft Engineering Co.*, 11 WLR 322 (1943), *Tennessee Coal Iron and R.R. Co.*, 20 WLR 535 (1944).
[72] The latter term has dropped out of general use. See Executive Order No. 9328, Apr. 8, 1943 and Order of Director of Economic Stabilization, May 12, 1943.
[73] "Wage Stabilization Policy of the National War Labor Board," Nov. 6, 1942, 4 WLR XXX.

. . . In our opinion there is no single factor in the whole field of labor relations that does more to break down morale, create individual dissatisfaction, encourage absenteeism, increase labor turnover, and hamper production than obviously unjust inequalities in the wage rates paid to different individuals in the same labor group within the same plant.[74]

Consequently it has required equal pay for equal work for men and women,[75] and for Negro and white workers.[76]

Never did the Board define exactly what constituted an inequity. The mere fact that wages were not equal to the highest comparable rate did not of itself prove the existence of an inequity.[77] The Board stated that there were sound reasons for presupposing that rates below the average represented inequities.[78] In one case where wages were above the average for the industry locally, the Board nevertheless found an inequality existed, because the employees had not received a wage increase that was general in the industry locally.[79]

It stated that it would give consideration only to major inequities.[80] In some cases to determine the existence of an inequity, it considered rates in the trade or craft locally;[81] in others it considered the rates paid in a trade or craft on a regional or national basis.[82] Inequities have been found to exist by comparing rates paid in different industries.[83] But in some cases it refused to make such a comparison.[84]

On occasion the inequity has been caused by the Board itself. For example, it granted wage increases to the employees of the Chicago Surface Lines.[85] As a result it subsequently found that this wage increase resulted in an inequity for the employees of the Chicago Rapid Transit, so it had to increase their wages also.[86] The same thing has happened in several other cases.[87]

[74] *West Coast Airframe Companies,* 6 WLR 581, 594 (1943).
[75] *General Motors Corp.,* 4 WLR 374 (1942).
[76] *Southport Petroleum Co.,* 8 WLR 714 (1943).
[77] *Acme White Lead and Color Co.,* 9 WLR 18 (1943); *Los Angeles Ry. Corp.,* 9 WLR 772 (1943).
[78] *Chrysler Corporation,* 3 WLR 447 (1942).
[79] *Jamestown Steel and Dahlstrom Door Cos.,* 6 WLR 698 (1943).
[80] *Norma-Hoffman Bearings Corporation,* 2 WLR 433 (1942).
[81] *Standard Tool Co.,* 3 WLR 409 (1942).
[82] *Tennessee Coal, Iron and Railroad Co.,* 4 WLR 103 (1942).
[83] *Tyer Rubber Co.,* 4 WLR 368 (1942).
[84] *West Coast Airframes Co.,* 6 WLR 581, 589 (1943).
[85] 7 WLR 623 (1943).
[86] 9 WLR 477 (1943).
[87] *Interstate Steamship Co.,* 6 WLR 263 (1943); *Babcock and Wilcox Co.,* 9 WLR 240 (1943); *Portland Traction Co.,* 13 WLR 138 (1943).

Early in 1943 some government officials felt that unduly large wage increases were being permitted, because the Board generally considered that a wage below the average was evidence of an inequity. So by Executive Order on April 8, 1943, the President prohibited the granting of increases on this basis.[88] But on May 12, 1943 the Director of Economic Stabilization determined that increases could be granted to correct inequities if wages were not raised "above the minimum of the going rates" bracket.[89] "A rate bracket is a range from minimum to maximum, of stable, tested rates for a given occupation in a given labor market." "There should be a bracket for each major job classification studied. Each bracket should be for jobs which are comparable as to the type of work performed." "There is no automatic statistical way of determining the wage rate brackets."[90] The brackets were fixed by the regional war labor boards created as a field organization by the national body, and such determinations were not reviewable by the National Board.[91]

Since the order of the Director of Economic Stabilization says the wage brackets must be set on the basis of a labor market area, it would seem that one single system of brackets could not be set for a whole industry.[92] But in some instances the opinions of the Board indicate that this was done.[93] Although the Board was directed to increase wages only to the minimum of a bracket, except in rare and unusual cases, in a number of cases it ordered that an increase above this figure should be granted.[94] In one decision the Board said: "It is not and never has been the policy of the Board to restrict such comparisons to the minimum of the ranges."[95] An increase to bring wages up to the wage bracket could be given in addition to any increase that was warranted by the Little Steel Formula.[96]

The doctrine of the elimination of inequities (as contrasted with

[88] No. 9328, Sec. 2; *Universal Atlas Cement Co.*, 7 WLR 474 (1943).
[89] 8 WLR XV.
[90] Order of the Board, June 8, 1943, 8 WLR XXIII, Sec. II B, 1, 2.
[91] Order of Apr. 1, 1944; 15 WLR LII.
[92] *Northwest Match Co.*, 13 WLR 133 (1943); *Cotton Garment Industry*, 13 WLR 81 (1943).
[93] *Illinois Powder Co.*, 10 WLR 79 (1943); *United Cork Co.*, 9 WLR 559 (1943); *Southeastern Area Employers Negotiating Committee*, 12 WLR 666 (1943).
[94] *Toledo, Peoria and Western RR Co.*, 8 WLR 663 (1943); *United Cork Co.*, 9 WLR 559 (1943).
[95] *Jenkins Bros.*, 14 WLR 254 (1944).
[96] *La Crosse Rubber Co.*, 15 WLR 224 (1944); *Associated Laundries Cos.*, 9 WLR 147 (1943).

the application of the wage bracket) was confined to the correction
of intra-plant maladjustments and not to the removal of inter-plant
differentials. For the elimination of intra-plant inequities the wage
brackets were not used.[97] At times an increase in some rates on the basis
of the wage brackets has made necessary a subsequent increase in
other rates to eliminate intra-plant inequities.[98]

Logically there are two different ways of correcting wage inequities
(wages below the average); the low-paid employees can be raised,
or the employees getting wages above the average can be lowered.
But only cases involving wages below the average or the bracket
got to the Board. It should be remembered that the Board could
modify a wage only if one or both parties requested it. Also the act of
October 2, 1942 specifically prohibits any reduction below the highest
wage received between January 1 and September 15, 1942.[99] Consequently inequities were corrected only by raising the wages below the
average or the bracket.[100]

The correction of inequities by raising wages to the average or the
bracket had a significant result. The average of this bracket will increase as the wages below it are raised to that level. Consequently the
standard used to correct inequities presented an ever-increasing level.
In one case the Board recognized this, and directed that in computing
new brackets the Regional Board should not use a specific wage increase
that brought the rates concerned far above the brackets.[101]

All wages that were sub-
standard could be raised.

In addition to partial compensation for changes in the cost of
living, and the elimination of inequities and inequalities, the existence
of a sub-standard wage was the third justification for a wage increase.
"The Board has made clear that by substandard wages it means wages
which do not permit of the maintenance of a standard of living of

[97] *Carbide and Carbon Chemicals Corp.*, 16 WLR 114 (1944).

[98] *Spencer Kellogg and Sons, Inc.*, 14 WLR 553 (1944); *Portland Traction
Co.*, 13 WLR 138 (1943).

[99] 56 Stat. 766, Sec. 4.

[100] In only one case was an inequality corrected by reducing wages; see *National
War Agencies Appropriation Bill for 1944*, Hearings before the House Committee
on Appropriations, Pt. 2, 78 Cong. 1 sess., p. 629.

[101] *Boeing Aircraft Co.*, 11 WLR 268 (1943).

health and decency."[102] It refused to define precisely a substandard wage either in terms of money wages or in terms of the physical elements of a standard of living considered by it to be necessary.[103] But it stated that, where the parties agreed, any wage below 50 cents an hour could be raised to that amount without prior approval by it,[104] thus indicating that it considered such a wage substandard under any circumstances. And it stated that in the lumber industry in the Great Lakes area and the South any wage could be raised to 50 cents an hour without prior approval by the Board.[105] In the *Postal Telegraph-Cable Company* case involving many thousand employees, it found an average wage of just under 50 cents an hour to be substandard and ordered a general increase of 12.5 cents and justified it solely on the basis of substandard wages. This action would imply that an average wage of less than 62 cents would be substandard.[106] In another case it held a wage of 64 cents an hour was substandard;[107] but a minimum rate of 78 cents is not.[108] The Board never determined that a specific budget was necessary for the maintenance of a designated minimum standard of living. It said that a wage should maintain a standard of living of health and decency; but it never attempted to demonstrate that the minimum wages it established would yield an income large enough to sustain that level of living.

In many instances the use of the wage bracket made possible a higher minimum wage than the principle of the elimination of substandard wages. But this was not always true in rural areas and the South. Where a higher minimum wage was justified on the bracket principle, the increase was granted on this basis rather than to eliminate substandard wages. The Board fixed a minimum wage of 85 cents an hour for a whole plant on this basis.[109]

---

[102] *General Cable Co.*, 2 WLR 228, 230 (1942).

[103] 4 WLR XXX; see statement of Apr. 8, 1943, 7 WLR IX.

[104] Resolution of the Board of Feb. 26, 1945, 2 WHR 234.

[105] NWLB Release, Aug. 1, 1943.

[106] 8 WLR 644 (1943); 55 cents in *Richmond Engineering Co.*, 12 WLR 421 (1944); and *YWCA*, 12 WLR 441 (1943).

[107] *The Mead Corporation*, 1 WLR 243 (1942).

[108] *General Cable Co.*, 2 WLR 228 (1942).

[109] *Spencer Kellogg and Sons Inc.*, 14 WLR 553 (1944); and 75 cents in *Northwest Match Co.*, 13 WLR 133 (1943). See also resolution of the Board of Feb. 26, 1945.

*Wage increases not justified on other principles
have been granted to aid the war.*

The Board had a fourth justification for a wage increase—that it was necessary for the prosecution of the war. By this statement it meant that higher wages were necessary in order to secure sufficient employees. The wage increase was to prevent employees from leaving the industry and to attract additional workers to it. The decision in the nonferrous metal mining industry in the Northwest was a fine illustration of this principle.[110] The Board said it would not grant such an increase unless the War Manpower Commission requested it.[111] In order to sustain such a request the production of vital and critical goods had to be involved, a vital man-power problem had to be present, a concerted program had to be developed to remedy the situation, an obsolete wage structure had to exist, and it was necessary to show that a wage increase would meet the situation.[112]

But the Board granted increases for this purpose without a request from the WMC, or where these conditions were not present.[113] The reasons for granting such increase were not always evident or logical. The St. Louis team and truck drivers were given a $2.00 a week wage increase on this basis without any explanation.[114] The central states truck drivers got such an increase because the railroad employees had just received a wage increase. The decision did not allege that there was any real wage competition between truck drivers and railroad employees.[115] An increase of pay for the employees of the Boeing Aircraft Company was justified as necessary for the prosecution of the war. Subsequently Chairman Davis explained,[116] the government could not afford to have these employees strike for

---

[110] *Non-ferrous Metal Cos.*, 4 WLR 147 (1942).

[111] Wage Policy Statement, Nov. 6, 1942.

[112] *Industry Wide Fir and Pine cases*, 16 WLR 352 (1944); *Shipbuilding Industry Wage Review*, 10 WLR 237 (1943).

[113] *Owens Illinois Can Co.*, 4 WLR 432 (1942); *Ohio Bell Telephone Co.*, 6 WLR 249 (1942); *Michigan and Wisconsin Lumber Cos.*, 9 WLR 492 (1943).

[114] *Association of Team and Truck Owners*, 14 WLR 32 (1944).

[115] *Midwestern Trucking Operators*, 14 WLR 247 (1944). Despite discussion along this line, the decision finally said it was to compensate for overtime without premium rates under the Motor Transportation Act of 1935.

[116] *Boeing Aircraft Co.*, 11 WLR 268 (1943); and Chairman Davis in *Extension of Emergency Price Control Act of 1942*, Hearings before the Senate Banking and Currency Committee, 78 Cong. 2 sess., p. 219.

higher wages, because they were producing much needed B-29 bombing planes.

The Board has not always followed
literally its announced standards.

Although the War Labor Board generally followed the four principles announced by the President, the Director of Economic Stabilization, and itself, it on occasion granted larger increases than appear to be justified by them. In some instances the Little Steel Formula was disregarded.[117] Sometimes a wage increase under this formula was combined with an increase on the wage bracket basis, to eliminate substandard wages, or to compensate for added production.[118] In one case all employees were given a 2 cents an hour increase for working night shifts although some of them did no night work.[119] When the United Steel Workers of America demanded an increase beyond the Little Steel Formula, they got a wage differential for working second or third shifts.[120] Although the UMWA was told that the Little Steel Formula precluded the wage increase it desired, most of its request was granted in the form of compensation for travel time, payment in lieu of vacations, and a nominal reduction in lunch time.[121] The Board refused to permit a bus company and its employees to increase wages above the minimum of the applicable wage bracket, but it added that if the parties provided for the same increase as a bonus it would be approved.[122]

[117] *Crescent Brick Co.*, 8 WLR 413 (1943).
[118] *LaCrosse Rubber Co.*, 15 WLR 224 (1944), with wage bracket; *Cincinnati Hotels Association*, 10 WLR 33 (1943), combined with elimination of substandard wages (this could not be done after Sept. 20, 1945, 6 WHR 901); *Loose Wiles Biscuit Co.*, 12 WLR 120 (1943), combined with merit raise for increased production.
[119] *Big Four Rubber Cos.*, 8 WLR 537 (1943).
[120] *Basic Steel Case*, 19 WLR 568 (1944).
[121] *Illinois Coal Operators Association*, 11 WLR 687 (1943); *Bituminous Coal Mines*, 12 WLR 64 (1943).
[122] In granting a wage increase the Board will take no account of the ability of the employer to pay the added wages (*New England Textile Operators*, 2 WLR 102, 1942). This is true even though the business is one affected with a public interest and in which consequently the employer might be required to continue operations at a loss (*Detroit and Cleveland Navigation Co.*, 2 WLR 68, 1942). No matter what is the reason for the increase—change in the cost of living (*Acme Mfg. Rubber Co.*, 17 WLR 666, 1943); correction of inequities (*Fairchild Engine and Airplane Corp.*, 6 WLR 81, 1943); or the correction of substandard rates (*Cincinnati Hotels Association*, 10 WLR 33, 1943), the employer's ability to pay is immaterial.

*The Board's actions tended to reduce the
differential between high- and low-wage employees.*

There are several indications that the Board was especially interested in improving the position of the employees receiving low wages. It generally granted a wage increase as a fixed number of cents per hour to all employees concerned. Thus the high paid employees in a plant would get a smaller percentage increase than those paid at lower rates. A raise of 5 cents an hour is a 10 per cent increase for those getting 50 cents an hour and only 3.33 per cent for those paid $1.50 an hour. The correction of substandard wages and the elimination of inequities involved special consideration for low-paid workers. Thus as a result of the Board's decisions, employees receiving less than 40 cents an hour got an average increase of 23.2 per cent, those receiving from 50 to 65 cents got 10.8 per cent, those paid between 80 cents and a dollar got an increase of 10.1 per cent, while the average increase for those receiving more than $1.25 was only 5 per cent.[123]

By way of summary it may be said that definite objective standards were not applied by the Board. The NWLB was not solely to blame for the failure to develop definite principles of decision. Congress and the President were both partly to blame, because in delegating authority to the Board they did not clearly and definitely determine the principles that it was to apply. Nothing here said should be construed to mean that the Board failed to stop undesirable wage increases. It is not within the scope of this study to determine whether the Board has been an effective agency in checking inflation.

II. THE DETERMINATION OF WAGES TO BE PAID ON GOVERNMENT WORK

By several laws Congress requires that government contractors must pay their employees a minimum wage fixed by the government. Employees engaged in public works construction are treated in a different manner from those employed in other types of work. As will be shown in the ensuing discussion different standards are used for fixing minimum wages for these two groups of employees.

[123] Monthly Report of the NWLB for December 1943; and see also its reports for May 1943 and March 1944.

A. Public Works Construction

Several laws regulate the minimum wages to be paid to workers employed on government construction when hired either directly by the government or by contractors. As a rule the statutes provide that the minimum rate of pay on government construction shall be the prevailing rate for the same type of work in the locality concerned.

In effect the union rate is the
minimum wage on public works.

In 1861 Congress first provided for the fixing of wages of laborers in government employ. A law enacted that year required that employees in navy yards must receive at least the prevailing rate of pay.[124] In 1931 Congress, in the so-called Davis-Bacon Act, provided that contractors constructing any public building for the United States that costs more than $5,000 must pay to all workers at least the rate of pay prevailing in the locality. The contracting officer of the government in the first instance was to determine the prevailing rate, but an appeal could be taken from his decision to the Secretary of Labor. If the Secretary of Labor found a higher wage to be prevailing, the corrected rate applied only from the date of the decision of the Secretary; it did not apply retroactively to the beginning of employment under the contract.[125]

This law was enacted primarily because of union pressure. Early in the depression of 1929, wages had begun to fall. Actual wages in the building trades were often lower than the rates provided for in union contracts. Wages below the union rate frequently were paid to workers employed in the construction of buildings that were then being erected by the federal government primarily to alleviate the depression.[126] The unions generally believed that the 1931 act required the payment of the union rate on such work.[127]

In 1935 the act was extended to all public works costing $2,000 or more. The Secretary of Labor was directed to make the original

[124] Act of Dec. 21, 1861, 12 Stat. 329.
[125] Act of Mar. 3, 1931, 46 Stat. 1494.
[126] Thomas Holland, *The Prevailing Minimum Wage Standard in the Public Contract Act* (1939), manuscript in the Department of Labor Library, p. 206.
[127] *Relations Between Employees and Contractors on Public Works*, S. Rept. 332, 74 Cong. 1 sess., p. 3.

determination of the prevailing rate for each skill involved for each specific project.[128] The actual administration of the act of 1931 had been placed in the Conciliation Service, but after these amendments its administration was transferred to the Office of the Solicitor of the Department of Labor.

In determining what constitutes the prevailing rate of pay for a given skill in any locality, the Secretary of Labor has issued a set of rules of decision. These provide that the rate which the Secretary will predetermine shall be: (a) The rate paid to corresponding classes on projects that are similar to the contract work; (b) if no such rate is paid to a majority then the rate paid to at least 30 per cent; (c) if 30 per cent of the workers do not receive any standard rate then the average rate shall be used.[129]

The evidence on which the Secretary's decision is based is important. If the Department has not already made an applicable predetermination, a referee is appointed to hold hearings to take evidence concerning the prevailing rate. The referee is to secure copies of the trade agreements applicable to the specific crafts and skills involved. He is also to supplement this material by securing, (a) information showing the date of adoption of the union rate, the locality in which it applies, and the methods by which it was fixed; and (b) evidence of the proportion of union and nonunion workers in the particular craft employed in the locality.[130] This material is to be considered as evidence, although no effort is made to determine whether the union members actually are paid the rates called for in the agreement.[131]

The few published decisions of the Secretary of Labor under this act indicate that almost universally the union rate is accepted as the prevailing rate.[132] An Assistant Secretary of Labor has testified that the union rate is generally taken as the prevailing rate.[133] A student

[128] Act of Aug. 30, 1935, 49 Stat. 1011.
[129] Code of Federal Regulations of the United States, Title 29, Subtitle A, Pt. 1, 1.2.
[130] The same, Sec. 1.9.
[131] Richard C. Simonson, *The Administration of the Davis-Bacon Law*, manuscript thesis for M.A., American University (1939), p. 192.
[132] Several decisions were published in 1935, *Monthly Labor Review*, Vol. 40, pp. 1549-50. See also Holland, *The Prevailing Minimum Wage Standard in the Public Contract Act*, p. 206.
[133] *Department of Labor—Federal Security Agency Appropriation Bill for 1944*, Hearings before the House Committee on Appropriations, Pt. 1, 78 Cong. 1 sess., pp. 37-40.

who has studied the manuscript decisions of the Department of Labor on the subject concluded:

> Most determinations set the prevailing rates at the same levels as union rates. A leading cause is the fact that union officers are more active in presenting evidence than are non-union employers. The other primary factor is the relation between the definition used and the degree of unionization on construction. Under the definition the union rate normally prevails if it covers thirty per cent of the men employed on work similar to that for which the determination is being made.[134]

The wages fixed under the Davis-Bacon Act supposedly are only the minimum rates that must be paid. On competitive bid contracts the contractor can pay a higher rate if he desires. But on work done under a reimbursable contract, the government will not reimburse the contractor for wages paid in excess of the rates fixed by the Department of Labor.[135] Thus on such contracts, rates fixed under this act are actually the maximum as well as the minimum wages.

The requirement that the prevailing wage must be paid to persons employed on public works would appear to constitute a clear and definite standard. The regulations of the Secretary of Labor identify the prevailing rate with the rate established in union contracts, irrespective of the proportion of employees who are paid that wage. These regulations do not appear to be clearly justified by the law. The TVA Act of 1933 requires the payment of prevailing rates of pay on all TVA construction, but it goes on to provide: "In the determination of such prevailing rate or rates, due regard shall be given to those rates which have been secured through collective agreement by representatives of the employers and employees."[136] Thus this section makes the union rate a basic element in the determination of the prevailing rate. It is not evident from the standpoint of public policy why the union rate, regardless of other factors, should of itself be paid on public works.

B. The Public Contracts Act

A different minimum wage applies to nonconstruction workers em-

[134] Simonson, *The Administration of the Davis-Brown Law*, p. 231; see also p. 80.
[135] Decision of Comptroller General, B-25275, Oct. 19, 1942.
[136] Act of May 18, 1933, 48 Stat. 60, Sec. 3. A comparable situation existed under the PWA, J. K. Williams, *Grants in Aid under the PWA* (1939), pp. 183-94; and the WPA before the summer of 1939, E. A. Williams, *Federal Aid for Relief* (1939), p. 126.

ployed by holders of government contracts. Not until 1936 did Congress attempt to regulate the wages paid to such workers. Then it adopted a new standard for fixing minimum wages.

The prevailing minimum wage must be paid
by employers producing for the government.

The Public Contracts Act of 1935 required the payment of minimum wages to persons engaged in other forms of production for the government. This act provides that the government, in making purchases of materials and supplies costing more than $10,000 must buy only from producers who agree to pay to their workers the prevailing minimum wage as determined by the Secretary of Labor.[137] It does not apply to purchases made in the open market or to agricultural commodities.

The proponents of this legislation rested their case for it largely on the general need for increasing purchasing power. They contended that it was improper and undesirable for the government to let contracts to the lowest bidder without fixing minimum wages, because as a consequence wages might be driven down. It was also argued that the government should set an example in buying from only those who pay proper wages. It was believed that the bill would have some effect also on wages of workers other than those employed on government contracts. Many manufacturers holding government contracts run their business on a continuous process basis. Such employers cannot separate governmental business from nongovernmental business and therefore they would have to pay to all their employees, at least during the period of the contract, the wage required by the order of the Secretary. If they pay such a wage during the period of the contract, the hand of labor will be strengthened to secure such wages regularly. If, on the other hand, the employer pays the prevailing minimum wage only to those working on government contracts, it will create dissatisfaction among the workers not so engaged, and they will demand a comparable increase in remuneration.[138]

---

[137] Act of June 30, 1936, 49 Stat. 2036, Sec. 1 (b).
[138] *Government Purchases and Contracts*, Hearings before the Senate Committee on Education and Labor, 74 Cong. 1 sess.; *Conditions of Government Contracts*, Hearings before the House Committee on the Judiciary, 74 Cong. 1 sess.

Congress has not defined the
prevailing minimum wage.

The "prevailing minimum wage" is a unique idea; only in this law is the expression to be found. The act contains no definition of it, and the congressional committee reports do not indicate what is meant by the term. The debates in the House of Representatives where the language first appeared tend to indicate that certain of the members believed they were providing for a prevailing wage comparable to that required under the Davis-Bacon Act, and that the word minimum was inserted in order to ensure that the wage would be only a minimum wage, not a maximum wage. The debates are far from clear and conclusive on this point.[139]

The statute provides at least four standards that can be used in fixing the prevailing minimum wage. The Secretary may set it on the basis of the wage prevailing in the locality for similar work for the particular industry; for similar industries; or for groups of similar industries.[140] Actually the Secretary of Labor has used wage data only from the particular industry or similar industries as the basis of setting the prevailing minimum wage. The existence of the first standard, that is, similar work, seems to imply that a wage can be set for each particular skill or craft, as is the case under the Davis-Bacon Act, but as a practical matter this has never been done. Since the act provides that the Secretary of Labor shall fix the prevailing minimum wage for the locality where the goods are to be produced, it definitely implies that geographical variations and differentials in wages can be established.

Nor has the Department of
Labor defined it.

The term "prevailing minimum wage" has not been defined with any clarity, either by the Secretary of Labor or the Public Contracts Board, which recommends to the Secretary specific prevailing minimum wages for given industries. The Director of the Public Contracts Division, which was established by the Secretary of Labor to ad-

[139] See "The Determination of the Prevailing Minimum Wages Under the Public Contracts Act," 48 *Yale L. J.* 610 (1939).
[140] 49 Stat. 2036.

minister the act, has said that the determination of a prevailing minimum wage was an exceedingly simple and obvious matter.

. . . The minimum wage section of the statute . . . makes it obvious that the determination is to be made on the existent wages rather than on the basis of what may be considered socially desirable. In other words, the Secretary of Labor has no discretion to set a wage to fix a wage, because her power is limited to the authority to find the wage which is already in existence. In other words, to legalize an existing decent wage practice.[141]

Thus at one and the same time he said no discretion is left to the Secretary, and yet he said "existing decent wage practices" are to be legalized.

The Public Contracts Board in making its recommendations for the dimension granite industry (1937) said:

The Board has confined itself in its consideration of minimum wages to an analysis of the lowest wages received by such a substantial proportion of the workers that in relation to other wages they have superior force, influence and freedom.

Again in the vitreous china case the Board declared:

A prevailing minimum wage within the meaning of the Public Contracts Act is a relative wage. It is derived from a comparison of the number of workers receiving the various wages in the minimum wage brackets of the industry.

The Secretary of Labor stated in the wage determination for the seamless hosiery industry:

The provisions of the Public Contracts Act did not require the Secretary of Labor to determine the lowest wage paid in an industry, or the average of the lowest wages paid in the various plants of an industry. The intent and purpose of the law are rather to have determined the minimum which exists for an outstanding concentration of the workers so that employers paying what is generally deemed to be fair will not suffer from the competition of employers paying unreasonably low wages.[142]

These quotations do not contain any clear statement of how the prevailing minimum wage is to be determined. Where it is identified as the wage paid to a predominant concentration in the minimum wage

---

[141] *Department of Labor Appropriation Bill for 1939*, Hearings before the House Committee on Appropriations, 76 Cong. 1 sess., p. 85.

[142] Decision No. 6, July 28, 1937.

group, the problem of defining the minimum wage group still exists. Neither the decisions of the Secretary nor the recommendation of the Public Contracts Board do that.[143]

In selecting the major concentration of the minimum wage group, the Secretary apparently considered the median or the weighted average wage as the top limit of the minimum wage group. The greatest concentration below this point is used as the prevailing minimum wage.[144]

But this is not a very useful guide in determining what wage the Secretary actually will choose as the prevailing minimum wage. In the decision in the furniture industry case (1939), the Secretary designated 30 cents an hour[145] as the rate, although at least 22 per cent of the workers got less than that. Sixteen and six-tenths per cent of the workers in the small arms industry were getting less than the wage selected as the prevailing minimum wage. In the seamless hosiery case, the Secretary fixed 35 cents an hour as the prevailing wage, although 49.5 per cent were getting less than that. On the other hand, in the photographic supply industry, 40 cents was fixed as the minimum, although the Secretary stated that 1.9 per cent of the workers got less than 39.5 cents an hour, and 6.3 per cent got from 37.5 to 42.5 cents an hour. The Secretary stated that in the die casting industry 25 to 30 per cent of the workers were in the "low-wage group" but this group was never defined in the decision. Miss Perkins then went on to state that the "first substantial concentration of employees is at 50 cents an hour where there are 7.8 per cent of the workers." The prevailing minimum wage was set at 50 cents; no additional information was presented and no further reasons were advanced for the decision. In a number of cases the rate actually selected was considerably above the wage of the largest concentration of workers in the lower part of the wage scale. The seamless hosiery case previously mentioned is an example of this. The handkerchief industry (1938)

[143] In some industries the wages paid to all workers are used in the wage-fixing process. In others only the wages paid to the unskilled or common labor group are considered. No reasons have been advanced for this difference in treatment. (O. R. Strackbein, *The Prevailing Minimum Wage Standard*, 1939, pp. 135-46). The author was a member of the Public Contracts Board.

[144] See recommendations in the explosives industry (1938), recommendations in the airplane industry (1938), and recommendations in the specialty accounting supply industry (1938).

[145] All wages of less than 40 cents an hour have been raised to at least that figure.

and the fuse division of the fireworks industry (1938) are other examples. The wage received by the first major concentration of workers appears to be the standard most nearly in accord with the law. But how large a concentration of workers constitutes a major concentration? Here again the decisions of the Secretary yield no guidance.

On occasion the prevailing minimum wage seems to have been based almost entirely on the average wage paid in the industry. The average was apparently used in the men's clothing case (1937), men's raincoats (1937), work gloves, underwear, and the leather and sheeplined coats cases. The very term "prevailing minimum" would seem to indicate that Congress did not intend that the average wage be used as the basis.

In at least eleven instances, the minimum union rate was used as the basis of the decision.[146] The opinions in these cases do not always show either the proportion of employees who received these rates, or the proportion who were employed under union agreements.

The Secretary's determinations of prevailing minimum wages do not appear to be based on any clearly determined standards.[147] The need for fixing minimum wages for employees engaged in government production is not clear since the enactment of a general minimum wage law applicable to the same employees.

III. FIXING WAGES OF EMPLOYEES OF RECIPIENTS OF GOVERNMENT SUBSIDIES

A third situation in which minimum wages must be paid covers employees of recipients of federal government subsidies. Where the federal government has guaranteed a mortgage on a building to be constructed under the Federal Housing Act, the workers employed in its construction must be paid at least the prevailing rate of pay for the specific skill in the locality. The determination of what constitutes the prevailing rate of pay is made by the Secretary of Labor, in the same manner as the prevailing wage is fixed.[148]

---

[146] *Department of Labor-Federal Security Agency Appropriation Bill for 1942*, Hearings before the House Committee on Appropriations, Pt. 1, 77 Cong. 1 sess., p. 187, and Holland, *The Prevailing Minimum Wage Standard in the Public Contract Act*, pp. 112-13.

[147] Strackbein is not certain that the concept is capable of any precise definition that is generally applicable, *The Prevailing Minimum Wage Standard*, p. 133.

[148] 49 Stat. 793.

The government fixes the minimum wages of seamen on subsidized ships. Operators of vessels that are subsidized under the Merchant Marine Act of 1936 must pay minimum wages to all persons employed on ships for which a subsidy is received. The Maritime Commission is vested with the duty of determining such minimum rates of pay.[149] Mr. Kennedy, when Chairman of the Commission, stated that the Commission's determination was based upon the wage rates established by the existing union agreement in the industry.[150]

Under the Sugar Act of 1937, as amended and extended, the growers of sugar beets and sugar cane who receive benefit payments from the United States must pay their workers not less than the minimum wage set by the Secretary of Agriculture. The basis of the Secretary's determinations are not readily apparent.[151]

IV. INDIRECT CONTROL OF WAGES

Wages are subject to indirect control by the federal government as well as direct control. Chief among these indirect controls is maximum hour legislation.

As will be discussed in the next chapter, the Fair Labor Standards Act of 1938 requires the payment of time and a half for all time worked in excess of 40 hours a week. On February 9, 1943 President Roosevelt ordered all employees in certain areas to work at least 48 hours a week.[152] This executive order did not suspend the overtime requirements of the Fair Labor Standards Act, and it applies to all employers who were not exempted from it, whether or not the demands of their business warranted the longer work week. Because of the requirement that overtime work in excess of 40 hours must be paid at the rate of time and a half, an employee who normally was working 40 hours a week, but who under this order must be employed 48 hours a week, received an increase in average hourly earnings of 8⅓ per cent.

The Employment Service attempts to influence wages indirectly. As was pointed out earlier (Chapter V) the USES instructed the state services that job applicants should not be placed in positions that

[149] 49 Stat. 1992, Sec. 301-a.
[150] *Amending Merchant Marine Act, 1936,* Hearings before the House Committee on Merchant Marine and Fisheries, 75 Cong. 2 and 3 sess., pp. 30, 36-38.
[151] Act of Sept. 1, 1937, 50 Stat. 909, Sec. 301-b.
[152] Executive Order No. 9301, *Federal Register,* Vol. 8, p. 1825.

pay substandard wages. The offices are permitted to list such openings, but they should attempt to persuade the employer to increase the wages offered. An applicant can not be called in to fill such a position, but if he voluntarily appears in the office he can be informed of the opening. Substandard wages are defined as being below the average for the work in the community. When previously substandard jobs are filled at the standard (average) rate, the average rate increases, so consequently this practice might have some tendency to raise wages. The effect of this policy on wages would be conditioned partly by the proportion of the low-wage employers who use the service to recruit workers.

During the past 10 years the federal government has attempted to increase the level of wages by strengthening the bargaining position of labor through encouraging the organization of workers, and by requiring employers to engage in collective bargaining with their employees. The National Labor Relations Act guarantees to most workers the right to form unions; on employers it imposes the duty of bargaining collectively with their employees; and machinery has been established to enforce these guarantees.[153] One of the major reasons for the enactment of this law was the desire to increase wages in conformity with the purchasing power theory. The hearings on the bill, the committee reports, and the debates of both houses, all give ample evidence of this objective.[154] The statement of policy in Section 1 of the act declares "The inequality of bargaining power between employees . . . and employers . . . tends to aggravate recurrent business depressions, by depressing wage rates and the purchasing power of wage earners." The encouragement of collective bargaining does not involve direct government action in wage determination and of course it gives the federal government no control over the level of wages agreed upon by the employer and the union. It provides only for government assistance to labor in order to strengthen its position in the bargaining process. This aid is extended to all employees, irrespective of whether they actually need to have their bargaining power increased.

V. CONCLUSIONS

In practically all of the attempts to regulate wages directly, the

[153] Act of July 5, 1935, 49 Stat. 449, Secs. 7 and 8.
[154] See Chap. 2.

government has failed to develop and apply objective standards. Without standards it is difficult to treat comparable cases in a comparable manner, and it is difficult to be fair to conflicting interests; or if such fairness does exist, it is not easy to convince all parties of its reality. Many friends of labor may contend that the absence of standards is immaterial, since the machinery for wage determination is in the hands of administrators sympathetic to labor. But it should not be forgotten that if the machinery should fall into the hands of persons unsympathetic to labor, the absence of standards would facilitate the use of wage controls to the workers' disadvantage. Only under the Davis-Bacon Act have definite standards been developed—the wage rates fixed by union agreement; but the use of this standard is not specifically justified by the language of the statute.

In addition to the Fair Labor Standards Act which establishes generally applicable minimum wages, a number of separate laws prescribe minimum wages for employees of government contractors or for employees of recipients of government subsidies. In all but one instance (sugar) the employees covered by the specific laws are also subject to the Fair Labor Standards Act. These special laws were enacted before the Wage and Hour Act. If it is argued that the minimum wages established under the Fair Labor Standards Act are too low for employees of contractors or recipients of subsidies, then they are also too low for all employees, since the reasons for special treatment for these groups of employees are not evident. It is doubtful that it is necessary to have these special minimum wage regulations applicable to employees who are covered also by the general law.

CHAPTER VIII

CONDITIONS OF EMPLOYMENT: HOURS, CHILD LABOR, AND SAFETY

In addition to union membership and wages, the federal government has influenced a number of other conditions of employment. Among these are the maximum hours of work, the minimum age of workers, and the existence of safe working conditions. Each of these will be considered in this chapter. An attempt will be made to state the main outlines of the policy that has developed and to indicate its major objectives.

I. HOURS OF WORK

The policies of the federal government concerning the regulation of the hours of work can be considered under three main heads: the general limitation of hours of work; their regulation in specific types of employment; and the determination of maximum hours of work for persons engaged in producing material for the government.

A. General Regulation

The 30-hour week movement. The movement for the adoption of a 30-hour work week is of basic significance in a consideration of the general policy of the federal government in regulating the hours of work. Although the supporters of this movement did not attain their objective, the underlying theory shaped subsequent policy that has been put into effect, for example, the NRA and the Fair Labor Standards Act.

The 30-hour week idea as first presented to Congress by Senator Black in 1932[1] was a product of the depression. His proposal would have prohibited absolutely the employment of anyone for more than 6 hours in any one day, or more than 30 hours in any one week. It contained no provision permitting additional work, even upon the payment of a higher rate of pay for the additional hours worked. It would have applied to all persons employed in producing goods for interstate commerce. The hearings on the bill, committee reports,

---

[1] S. 5267, 72 Cong. 2 sess.

and the debates in Congress all indicate that at least in 1933 the proposal was primarily advanced to alleviate unemployment by sharing the available work among more workers.[2] This bill passed the Senate and, although favorably reported by the House Committee on Labor, the House of Representatives never considered it, mainly because the National Industrial Recovery Act was passed. The proponents of the bill believed that their objective would be attained through the NIRA.

The 30-hour week was proposed to
increase purchasing power.

In 1934 another version of the 30-hour bill was introduced by Representative Connery, but this time it contained a provision for compulsory wage increases. It provided that, when the hours of work were reduced to 30 a week, there would be no reduction in weekly earnings. The proponents of the bill believed that as a consequence the purchasing power of the country would be increased and recovery would follow. There would be an increase in potential demand, because of the added employment required, and the increase in pay rolls resulting from greater employment and higher wages would positively effectuate recovery, rather than merely alleviate unemployment by sharing the work previously available.

Secretary Perkins, in the hearings on Representative Connery's proposal, supported the general idea of the 30-hour week and the theories of its sponsors.[3] In its report on the bill the House Committee on Labor favored it, both because it would reduce relief expenditures as a result of a greater sharing of the work, and also because it would increase employment opportunities through the resulting increase in purchasing power.[4] The bill was not passed by either House.

In reporting favorably another version of this bill the Senate Judiciary Committee stated in 1935:

The 30-hour week, without decreasing wages, would supply jobs and

[2] For example, see *To Prevent Interstate Commerce in Industrial Activities in Which Persons are Employed More Than Five Days a Week*, H. Rept. 124, 73 Cong. 1 sess., p. 4.

[3] *Thirty-Hour Week Bill*, Hearings before the House Committee on Labor, 73 Cong. 2 sess., p. 117.

[4] *Thirty-Hour Week for Industry*, H. Rept. 889, 73 Cong. 2 sess., pp. 2 and 3.

purchasing power; would increase production; reduce costs of production; and raise the living standards of the average American family.

. . . .

. . . Reduction in average weekly hours would be 25 per cent. At the outset, 5,000,000 men and women would be employed, and there would be no decrease in per-capita earnings, but a great expansion in mass purchasing power. This direct employment of millions would indirectly bring about the employment of other millions who would be required to produce all the things necessary to satisfy the wants of those who are now idle and who are now without purchasing capacity.[5]

With the decision of the Supreme Court holding the NRA unconstitutional,[6] the agitation for the adoption of the 30-hour week declined. The movement for the enactment of a federal law directly limiting hours was not revived until the spring of 1937 when it ultimately resulted in the enactment of the Fair Labor Standards Act. But before this act is considered, it is desirable to examine the contribution of the National Industrial Recovery Act and its administration to the formulation of federal policy on the regulations of hours of work.

The National Industrial Recovery Act. This act provided for the general regulation of industry by the federal government, primarily through codes of fair competition arrived at voluntarily by industry and approved by the government.[7] According to the act these codes could regulate the conditions of labor, including the determination of maximum hours of work.[8]

To reduce unemployment and to increase purchasing power the NRA generally adopted the 40-hour week.

Various reasons were presented to justify federal control of the hours of employment. Some proponents contended that depressed labor standards, including both low wages and long hours, had been a significant factor in producing the depression. Competition among employers had taken the form of increasing the hours of work of the employees. If the federal government fixed the maximum hours of work, this form of competition would be ended. Some supporters believed that the depression was a product of overproduction and consequently a reduction of the hours of work would decrease the

---

[5] *Thirty-Hour Work Week*, S. Rept. 367, 74 Cong. 1 sess., p. 6.
[6] *Schechter Poultry Corporation* v. *United States*, 295 U.S. 495 (1935).
[7] Act of June 16, 1933, 48 Stat. 195, Secs. 3 (a), 4 (a), and 7 (b).
[8] See especially Sec. 7 (b).

amount of goods produced.[9] Others believed that by shortening the hours of work more persons would be able to get jobs, and thus the relief load would be reduced.[10] The view was also advanced that by shortening the hours of work without reducing the pay, there would ensue an increase in the purchasing power of workers, and that this additional purchasing power would positively generate recovery.[11] These were the objectives of the proponents of the provisions of the NIRA that permitted the regulation of the hours of work. It should be remembered that the law contained no standards to aid in determining the code provisions on hours.

The policy of the NRA on this problem was evident mainly in the codes approved, about 85 per cent of which provided for a 40-hour work week, about 7.5 per cent for a shorter work week, and an equal proportion for one longer than 40 hours. Approximately 50 per cent of the workers were employed in industries covered by codes providing for a 40-hour work week, 10 per cent were engaged in occupations where less than a 40-hour week was provided by the code, and 40 per cent were covered by codes with a work week longer than 40 hours.[12] About 46 per cent of the workers were covered by codes that permitted overtime at a higher rate of pay.[13] The purpose of this was to discourage employment for longer hours.

How did this policy develop? President Roosevelt seemed to consider that the National Industrial Recovery Act was primarily to bring about re-employment. But he coupled re-employment with the thought that it would be a positive force for recovery, because it would generate additional purchasing power. On the day that he signed the act he declared that it proposed to "our industry a great spontaneous cooperation to put millions of men back in their regular jobs this summer. The idea is simply for employers to hire more men to do the existing work by reducing the work hours of each man's work week and at the same time paying a living wage for the shorter week."[14]

[9] Donald Richberg, *National Industrial Recovery Bill*, Hearings before the House Committee on Ways and Means, 73 Cong. 1 sess., pp. 66-67.

[10] Senator Robert Wagner, the same, pp. 91-92.

[11] William Green, the same, pp. 119, 122.

[12] Leverett S. Lyon, Paul T. Homan, George Terborgh, Lewis L. Lorwin, Charles Dearing, and L. C. Marshall, *The National Recovery Administration: An Analysis and Appraisal* (1935), p. 368.

[13] The same, p. 372.

[14] *The Public Paper and Addresses of Franklin D. Roosevelt, 1933* (1938), p. 252.

The guiding principles of the NRA concerning maximum hours were stated on the day that the organization was set up. At that time the newly established agency declared that the act was "to effect an immediate reduction of unemployment and increase of mass purchasing power." Relative to the length of the work week it asserted the guiding principle in preparation of basic codes, to be: "Consideration of the varying conditions and requirements of the several industries and the state of employment therein." It also specified that "the average work week should be designed . . . to provide for such a spread of employment as will provide work so far as practical for employees normally attached to the particular industry."[15] For the greater part of the life of the NRA, this declaration remained the only formal statement of policy concerning the maximum hour provisions of codes. Later certain officials of the NRA unofficially stated that:

The limitation placed upon hours must necessarily be a compromise between the requirement of reemployment and the ability of the industry to adjust itself to the change in operating conditions. Experience under present codes shows that for the majority of industry forty (40) hours per week is the lowest maximum presently practicable. Accordingly, in the absence of convincing showing to the contrary, no employee will be permitted to work more than forty (40) hours per week.[16]

The labor groups within the NRA were very anxious to establish a 30-hour week. Industry generally desired the continuation of the 48-hour work week prevalent before the depression. The United States Chamber of Commerce was interested in a 40-hour week. The adoption of the 40-hour week in a very large proportion of the NRA codes was a result of a compromise of these different objectives. It was designed to reduce unemployment, both by spreading the available work and by increasing demand by increasing purchasing power.

Fair Labor Standards Act. When the NRA was held unconstitutional, the movement for federal control over the hours of work declined until after the Supreme Court decided, in the spring of 1937, that the federal government had jurisdiction over many labor problems,[17] and that legislation regulating certain basic conditions of em-

---

[15] Quoted in Solomon Barkin, *NRA Policies, Standards and Code Provisions on Basic Weekly Hours of Work* (1936), p. 18; NRA works materials 45, Pt. B.
[16] Contained in the Compendium of Abstracts of Policy and Other Statements Issued by the Policy Group. Quoted by Barkin, the same, pp. 139-40.
[17] *Virginian Railway Co.* v. *System Federation No. 40,* 300 U.S. 515 (1937). *Jones and Laughlin Steel Corp.* v. *NLRB,* 301 U.S. 1 (1937).

ployment would not constitute a deprivation of property without due process of law.[18] Following these decisions, President Roosevelt, on May 24, 1937, recommended the enactment of a federal wages and hours act.

Increasing employment was the
main objective of the act.

The objective was to increase employment both through spreading existing work and through the increase of jobs as a result of greater purchasing power due to increased earnings.[19] President Roosevelt also said that it was desirable to protect our human resources by limiting the hours of work. Most of the major Administration witnesses supported the bill on the premise that it would create jobs directly and indirectly.[20] One reason the Secretary of Labor supported the bill was because an increase in the leisure of the American people was desirable. In justification of the 40-hour work week the Secretary said:

On the matter of hours, I suppose that we have a larger body of knowledge and there is not such an intricate adaptation, and I should say that it should be somewhere between 40 and 30. We have had enough experience on a 40-hour basis in this country to know that it is entirely possible for our industries to produce with great efficiency on a 40-hour basis, and enough of the basic industries have gone to a 40-hour basis to make us quite sure that we are not operating in the realm of the economically unknown when we are on that basis.[21]

To demonstrate the need for regulating hours of employment, the Commissioner of Labor Statistics introduced evidence showing that in 15 industries more than 44 hours actually were worked each week in February 1937, and in one industry more than 50 hours.[22] Mr. Sidney Hillman also testified that a work week of more than 60 hours was not uncommon in the textile industry.[23]

As originally introduced in Congress, the bill contained no definite limitation on hours. As reported by the House Committee on Labor,

[18] *West Coast Hotel Co.* v. *Parrish*, 300 U.S. 379 (1937).
[19] Message to Congress, May 24, 1937, in *The Public Papers and Addresses of Franklin D. Roosevelt, 1937* (1941), p. 209.
[20] See Leon Henderson in *Fair Labor Standards Act of 1937*, Hearings before the Senate Committee on Education and Labor, 75 Cong. 1 sess., Pt. 1, pp. 155-56.
[21] The same, p. 199.
[22] *Fair Labor Standards Act of 1937*, Hearings of the House Committee on Labor, 75 Cong. 1 sess., p. 342.
[23] The same, p. 950.

the bill provided that a board should have the power to fix the maximum work week at not less than 40 hours. The hours provision was justified by the House Committee on Labor:

The Board's jurisdiction, however, does not include the power to declare a maximum workweek of less than 40 hours; but it is the objective of the act to attain a maximum workweek of not more than 40 hours as rapidly as practicable without curtailing earning power or reducing production, and the attainment of a shorter workweek by collective bargaining or otherwise is to be encouraged. . . .[24]

And the Senate Committee on Education and Labor stated:

Similarly, the Committee, in limiting the jurisdiction of the Board to establish a maximum workweek less than 40 hours, recognizes that some industries have adopted and others may be economically able to adopt a shorter workweek. But millions of American workers are now working hours far in excess of 40 hours. Although the committee is desirous that the maximum working hours of the American worker be reduced to not more than 40 hours, the committee realizes that it may not be economically feasible to prescribe at once a 40-hour maximum week for all workers without reducing, instead of raising, their aggregate earning and purchasing power.[25]

The bill as finally enacted provided for a flat 44-hour week during its first year of operation, a 42-hour week during the second year, and a 40-hour week thereafter.[26] The adoption of these provisions seems to have been the result of a compromise between those who wanted no limitation on hours and those who desired a work week of less than 40 hours.

The act establishes a 40-hour
week for most industry.

The act now prohibits the employment of persons for more than 40 hours a week, unless time and a half is paid for all additional time.[27] It also prohibits the shipment in interstate commerce of goods produced in violation of any of its provisions. Three types of sanctions are provided to secure compliance with the law. A fine up to $10,000,

---

[24] *Fair Labor Standards Act*, H. Rept. 1452, 75 Cong. 1 sess., p. 14.
[25] *Fair Labor Standards Act*, S. Rept. 884, 75 Cong. 1 sess., p. 4.
[26] Act of June 28, 1938, 52 Stat. 1063, Sec. 7 (a).
[27] The same, Sec. 15 (a). The time worked is construed in favor of the employee. Travel time when on the employer's property, under his control, and for his benefit is time worked; *Tennessee Coal Train and Railroad Co.* v. *Muscodda Local, No. 123,* 321 U.S. 590 (1944); *Armour and Co.* v. *Wantock,* 323 U.S. 126 (1944).

imprisonment for not more than six months, or both may be imposed upon conviction. The government can also enjoin a violation of the law by an employer, and a person who was not paid overtime as required by the law can sue for double damages for the deficiency in remuneration.[28]

The law covers all employees engaged in the production of goods to move in interstate commerce, or all persons engaged in such commerce. Commerce and the production of goods to move in commerce are defined in very broad terms,[29] and the Supreme Court has construed the language generously. Thus it has held that building service employees (engineers, firemen, electricians, elevator operators, and so forth) in an office building where any tenant is engaged either in interstate commerce or in the production of goods for such commerce, are covered by the act. The Court said that the concerns engaged in interstate commerce could not carry on such commerce without the necessary services of the building service employees.[30] The Administrator has said that persons engaged in the production of a machine tool which was to be sold in intrastate commerce were covered by the act if that machine tool was subsequently to be used in the production of goods to move in interstate commerce.[31] One might logically conclude that the act would cover construction employees engaged in erecting a building that might be used for the production of goods to be moved in interstate commerce.

There are extensive exceptions, but they are strictly construed.

A number of important exceptions to this broad coverage are provided in the act. Thus the act does not cover persons employed in retail or service establishments, in fishing and sponge-gathering, in small rural telephone exchanges, or on small weekly and semi-weekly newspapers, or on local buses and street cars. Apprentices and learners are exempted from its terms, subject to regulations issued by the Administrator. A number of special groups of employees engaged in the

[28] 52 Stat. 1060, Secs. 16 and 17.

[29] The same, Secs. 3 (b), and 3 (j). "Engaged in commerce" refers to those actually so engaged and not to those who merely affect it: *L. McLeod* v. *Threlkeld*, 319 U.S. 491 (1943).

[30] *Kirschbaum Co.* v. *Walling*, 316 U.S. 517 (1942).

[31] *First Annual Report of the Administrator of the Wage and Hour Division*, 1939, p. 17.

actual movement of interstate commerce are not covered. These include seamen, persons engaged in rail transportation, employees of trucking concerns and air transport employees. These are all covered by special statutes.[32]

Agricultural employment is specifically exempted,[33] and the term "agriculture" is defined as including the tilling of the soil, the production, cultivation, growing, and harvesting of agricultural crops, including livestock, bees, poultry, and fur-bearing animals, together with dairying operations.[34] The act also specifically exempts any person engaged in the first processing of milk, or in ginning and compressing cotton, or in the processing of cottonseed. It does not apply to persons engaged in the first processing of an agricultural commodity; including the preparation of meat and poultry. In the area of production any processing of agricultural commodities, including canning and the making of cheese and butter, is exempt.[35]

The Administrator of the Wage and Hour Division is given authority to define the area of production of agricultural commodities. At first the Administrator defined the area of production as any place outside of a town or village with a population of more than 2,500. Under this definition, about 70,000 workers were employed in exempted occupations in areas of production. In April 1941 the definition was changed so that it included only establishments employing more than seven workers, and that handled only materials produced on farms in the general vicinity of the establishment.[36] The Administrator estimated that only about 8,000 workers are exempted under this modified definition.[37]

The Supreme Court held however, that the area of production was geographical in nature. The number of employees of the establishment had nothing to do with its inclusion or exclusion from the area. In fact, the act exempted all plants in the area; consequently the Administrator could not include some and exclude others on the basis of the number of their employees. Therefore the Administrator's definition of area of production was held illegal.[38]

---

[32] 52 Stat. 1060, Sec. 13 (a).
[33] The same.
[34] The same, Sec. 3 (f).
[35] The same, Secs. 7 (c) and 13 (a).
[36] Wage and Hour Manual (1942), Sec. 536.1, p. 394.
[37] Annual Report of the Wage and Hour Division (1941), p. 84.
[38] Addeson et. al. v. Holly Hill Fruit Co., 321 U.S. 607 (1944).

Special exemptions apply to seasonal industries as defined by the Administrator. For 14 weeks a year, 12 hours a day and 56 hours a week may be worked in such industries without the payment of over-time rates.[39] Some thirty-seven types of activity, mainly of an agricultural nature, have been exempted under these provisions concerning seasonal employment.

The act also exempts persons in executive, administrative, and professional positions as defined by the Administrator. In the earlier regulations, administrative and executive employment were lumped in one category and were defined as embracing the employment of any person who received at least $30.00 a week, and whose duties included a combination of management, direction, and the exercise of discretionary powers (including the authority to hire and fire), provided the employee did not devote a substantial proportion of his time to the same work as was performed by those whom he directed. Subsequently this definition was so modified as to exclude from the exemption any person who devotes more than 20 per cent of his time to direct production. The term "administrative" was separated from the term "executive" and was defined as being a person who received more than $200.00 a month and who performed nonmanual work directly related to the formulation of management policy and the performance of business operations and that required the exercise of discretion and judgment.[40]

In some instances premium rates for
overtime can be waived by agreement.

Under certain conditions by collective bargaining agreements, a longer work week without penalty overtime rates can be provided. By such a contract made with a union, overtime could be avoided if it were provided that the workers would be employed not more than 1,000 hours in a period of 26 weeks. Similar agreements can also be made, providing for employment on an annual basis. Thus overtime need not be paid for work in excess of 40 hours per week if the workers are not employed more than 2,000 hours in 52 weeks. This second type of collective agreement differs from those providing for only 1,000 hours in 26 weeks primarily in that the agreement must

[39] "Seasonal" has been defined as relating primarily to climatic seasonality: *Wage and Hour Manual* (1942),Regulations, Sec. 526.3, p. 444.
[40] The same, Sec. 541.1, p. 805.

contain a guarantee either of annual employment or of employment at an annual wage. Under both types of agreement all work in excess of 12 hours a day and 56 hours a week must be paid for at time and a half. The agreements providing for 1,000 hours in 26 weeks are, according to the Administrator, intended to cover primarily seasonal occupations like lumbering and some forms of mining where the work is carried on only for a few months of the year and the employees leave the scene of operation when the work is completed.[41] Agreements providing for one year's employment must be filed with the Administrator. Only 59 valid agreements had been filed with him at the beginning of 1945.[42] Few such agreements have been made for two reasons. The requirement that only 2,000 hours could be worked a year meant less than 40 hours a week. Consequently by the act of October 29, 1941, it was increased to 2,080 hours.[43] In the second place, the Administrator has ruled that if more than 2,080 hours are worked throughout the year, all overtime of more than 40 hours a week must be paid for at time and a half.[44]

Where the weekly wage is above the minimum required by the act, the payment of overtime can be partially avoided by the contract of employment. The act provides that if an employee works more than 40 hours in any one week he must be paid for the excess at $1\frac{1}{2}$ times "the regular rate at which he is employed."[45] In the case of an employee on a weekly wage, what is "the regular rate at which he is employed"? Must it always be determined by dividing the weekly payment by the hours worked, or can the employment contract determine the "regular rate" if above the minimum required by law? The Supreme Court has held that it is legal for an employee and an employer to enter into an employment contract calling for a weekly wage of $40 and an hourly rate of pay of not less than 67 cents and requiring the payment of time and a half for all work in excess of 54 hours a week. It will be seen that under this agreement if the worker is employed more than 40 hours but less than 54 hours a week, he would actually receive more than $1\frac{1}{2}$ times the base hourly rate of 67 cents

[41] "Interpretative Bulletin No. 8," Sec. 16, *Wage and Hour Manual* (1942), p. 562.
[42] 8 WHR 165 (1945).
[43] Act of Oct. 29, 1941, 55 Stat. 756.
[44] "Interpretative Bulletin No. 8," Sec. 29, *Wage and Hour Manual* (1942), p. 566.
[45] 52 Stat. 1060, Sec. 7 (a).

for all time worked in excess of 40 hours. The Court held that as the overtime rate for a work week of less than 54 hours would be more than is required by law, this arrangement was not improper. Although the overtime rate would be variable, the flexibility would not be an evil of itself.[46] But the Court has clearly held that the contract must provide for a definite base hourly rate and also the maximum hours to be worked each week, and that the guaranteed weekly wage must be such as to yield overtime pay at least at the rate of 1½ times the base rate for all work done in excess of 40 hours a week.[47] Thus an employer can avoid the payment of overtime for some work done in excess of 40 hours a week, by making a contract with his employees providing for a guaranteed minimum weekly wage for a maximum work week of a specified number of hours, provided the hourly base rate is above the minimum required by the law.

Despite the wartime man-power shortage, premium rates for overtime still had to be paid.

As a result of the defense emergency and the war, a movement developed for the modification of the 40-hour work week. At the very beginning of the defense program the President declared: "There is nothing in our present emergency to justify making the workers of our nation toil for longer hours than now limited by statute."[48] There was much official opposition to amending the hour provisions of the law, and the Wage and Hour Administrator even argued in his report for 1940 that the act should not be amended because it was desirable to spread work and to increase employment.[49]

But on February 2, 1942, the Secretary of Labor, at a conference to discuss the amendment of state labor laws asserted that a 48-hour work week was advantageous and desirable.[50] On another occasion she stated that a 48-hour work week yielded maximum production, and was desirable.[51] On July 28, 1942 six government agencies issued a

[46] *Walling* v. *A. H. Balo Corp.*, 316 U.S. 624 (1942).

[47] *Overnight Motor Transport* v. *Missel,* 316 U.S. 572 (1942).

[48] May 27, 1940, *The Public Papers and Addresses of Franklin D. Roosevelt, 1940* (1941), p. 237.

[49] *Annual Report Wage and Hour Division* (1940), pp. 2 and 3.

[50] 5 WHR 78 (1942).

[51] *To Permit the Performance of Essential Labor on Naval Contracts without Regard to Laws and Contracts Limiting Hours of Employment,* Hearings before House Committee on Naval Affairs, 77 Cong. 2 sess., pp. 2628-29.

joint statement to the effect that "the 48-hour week approximates the best working schedule for sustained efficiency."[52]

The Secretary of Labor even argued that the Fair Labor Standards Act was never intended to regulate hours. She said:

> The forty-hour law, as I understood it, and as I believe the testimony that I offered during the period when it was under consideration by Congress will bear out, was primarily that it was a minimum-wage law. It was a minimum-wage law which had features which regulated the hours, in order that your minimum wages might not become maximum wages. And it was provided that there should be time and a half over forty hours.[53]

Thus the Secretary was asserting that time and a half for overtime above 40 hours was only a device to prevent the minimum wages prescribed by the law from becoming maximum wages.

This attitude is at variance with the generally accepted view. The Wage and Hour Division seems to have generally believed that the act was designed to restrict the hours of employment for it said in one of its bulletins interpreting the law: "Congress intended to make it economically disadvantageous for an employer to work his employees excessive hours."[54] And the Supreme Court has declared, relative to the act: "Restriction of hours was a part of the plan from the beginning."[55]

The President increased hours without modifying the statutory requirement for premium pay for overtime.

On February 9, 1943, the President ordered all employers in certain labor shortage areas to employ their workers at least 48 hours a week, and the executive order does not modify the requirements of the Fair Labor Standards Act for the payment of premium overtime rates.[56] Thus, while the law provides for the payment of time and a half for all hours in excess of 40 a week (originally designed to discourage long hours of work in order to spread employment), an executive order required that all persons in certain areas were to be em-

[52] 5 WHR 589 (1942).

[53] *To Permit the Performance of Essential Labor on Naval Contracts without Regard to Laws and Contracts Limiting Hours of Employment*, Hearings before House Committee on Naval Affairs, p. 2637.

[54] "Interpretative Bulletin No. 4," Sec. 15, *Wage and Hour Manual* (1942), p. 107.

[55] *Overnight Motor Transport* v. *Missel*, 316 U.S. 572, 578 (1942).

[56] 6 WHR 141 (1943). Revoked Aug. 30, 1945, Federal Register, Vol. 10, p. 1191.

ployed at least 48 hours a week in order to relieve the man-power shortage. The compulsory 48-hour week was extended to the steel industry and to lumbering,[57] wherever they were carried on.

It is obvious that under this executive order the overtime pay provision of the Fair Labor Standards Act really imposed a compulsory increase in pay. Raising the hours of work from 40 to 48 with time and a half for all time in excess of 40 hours resulted in an increase in the average hourly rate of pay of 8 per cent. Thus in a period when we had a man-power shortage and an excess of purchasing power, we still enforced a maximum hours law originally designed to stimulate employment and increase purchasing power.

*The effect of some overtime provisions of
collective agreements was limited.*

By the modification of certain overtime provisions in some collective agreements, an attempt was made to increase the actual hours worked. Many collective agreements provided for penalty rates of pay for work done on Saturdays, Sundays, and holidays, even though the total hours worked were not more than 40 a week. Not only did the agreements provide for the payment of overtime at time and a half, but in some instances they provided that overtime be paid for at double the regular rate. Such provisions were fairly prevalent in the building trades, shipbuilding, and the automotive industry. Some employers hesitated to maintain production on a 7-day week basis under such circumstances. Consequently, by the Executive Order of September 9, 1942, the President declared that on work relating to the prosecution of the war no one should be paid more than 1½ times the regular rate for work done on the sixth day of work in any week, and not above double time for the seventh day in a week. Thus penalty rates were not to be paid for Saturday and Sunday work unless the employment on such days constituted the sixth or seventh day of work in any given work week.[58]

Much labor opposition immediately developed to this order; consequently its application and effect were limited. On September 17, 1942, the President delegated to the Secretary of Labor the authority to interpret this executive order and to grant exemptions

---

[57] The same, Supp. for Mar. 1, 1943.

[58] 5 WHR 705-06 (1942). See also Act of Oct. 2, 1942, 56 Stat. 767, Sec. 5(c). Revoked Aug. 21, 1945, 8 WHR 858.

from it.[59] As a result, building trades, shipbuilding, and sugar refining were entirely exempted from its provisions.[60] The term "war work" was defined in narrow terms.[61] The purpose of the executive order was to make it more attractive for employers to operate their plants seven days a week by removing excessive penalties designed originally to make a long work week unattractive. Very shortly after its issuance, the Secretary of Labor stated that it was not improper for the employer to increase the hourly base rate so that despite the order the employees would secure the same compensation for the scheduled work week as they did before it was issued.[62] In several cases the WLB actually ordered employers to increase the base rate of pay so that the total weekly earnings would be unchanged despite the executive order.[63]

B. Control of Hours in Specific Activities

In a number of specific activities, generally those connected with the movement of interstate commerce, the federal government has regulated the hours of work.

To promote safety and to raise wages, maximum hours are prescribed on interstate carriers.

The first attempt of the government to regulate hours was in the case of employees of railroads engaged in interstate commerce. In 1907 Congress provided that no person engaged in the movement of trains in interstate commerce could be employed for more than 16 hours consecutively, and that after being employed for such a period he could not work again until he had rested for at least 10 hours. An employee who had worked a total of 16 hours out of any 24 could not be employed again until he had rested at least 8 hours. An employee engaged in the direction of the movement of trains by telephone or telegraph cannot be employed for more than 9 hours a day, except in a station that is open only during the daytime when he can be employed for 13 hours.[64]

---

[59] 5 WHR 719 (1942).
[60] 5 WHR 763 (1942), and 6 WHR 227, 357 (1943).
[61] Statement of Secretary Perkins, Sept. 25, 1942, 5 WHR 741 (1942).
[62] Oct. 12, 1942, 5 WHR 785 (1942).
[63] *York Safe and Lock Co.*, 6 WLR 564 (1943) and *New Britain Machine Co.*, 6 WLR 565 (1943).
[64] Act of Mar. 4, 1907, 34 Stat. 1405.

In 1916 in order to get an increase in earnings, railroad labor demanded an 8-hour day, and time and a half for overtime. A strike was threatened to compel the carriers to accept these terms and accordingly Congress passed the Adamson Act, which provided that in computing the pay for persons engaged in the movement of trains in interstate commerce 8 hours should be considered one day's work.[65] Thus this law required that all work done in excess of 8 hours a day should be paid at the regular hourly rate instead of time and a half as demanded by the workers. When the railway employees threatened to strike for a wage increase in 1943, the President granted them a special increase in pay to compensate them for a lack of premium pay for overtime.

By the Motor Carrier Act of 1935, Congress conferred upon the Interstate Commerce Commission the authority to fix the maximum hours of work of any person connected with the movement of interstate trucks and buses, subject to the act.[66] The Interstate Commerce Commission has fixed a work day of 10 hours and a work week of 60 hours, but where carriers operate 7 days a week the work week may be 70 hours. The Commission has made drivers, driver-helpers, mechanics, and loaders subject to these regulations.[67] The primary purpose both of the act and of the Commission's regulations apparently is the maintenance of safety in interstate commerce, because even owner-operators are made subject to these provisions.[68]

The Civil Aeronautics Act of 1938 conferred upon the Civil Aeronautics Authority power to limit the hours of work of air pilots, primarily to ensure the safety of air transport.[69] The rules of the Civil Aeronautics Authority absolutely prohibit all work in excess of the hours provided, and it appears that the purpose is to promote safety. Since 1915 the hours of work of seamen, both officers and members of the crew, have been subject to federal regulation, and the Maritime Act of 1936 establishes a maximum normal work day of 8 hours for both officers and seamen.[70]

[65] Act of Sept. 3, 1916, 39 Stat. 721.
[66] Act of Aug. 9, 1935, 45 Stat. 546, Sec. 204 (a) (1).
[67] See "House of Service: Common and Contract Carriers," Rule 3, *Wage and Hour Manual*, (1942), p. 975.
[68] Sec. 4 of amended rules. See *Wage and Hour Manual* (1942), p. 975.
[69] Act of June 23, 1938, 52 Stat. 1007, Sec. 601.
[70] Act of June 25, 1936, 49 Stat. 1933, Sec. 2.

C. Regulation of Hours of Work on Government Contracts

For several reasons maximum hours are prescribed on production for the government. Some people who believe the government should be a model employer contend that maximum hours should be fixed for persons employed on government contracts.

An eight hour day has been established
on government contracts.

Since 1893 an 8-hour day has been prescribed for federal public works construction.[71] All employment beyond 8 hours a day was prohibited; but this absolute prohibition against overtime was relaxed during the First World War, and since June 1940 overtime has been permitted if time and a half is paid.[72]

The Public Contracts Act of 1936 is a more far-reaching attempt to regulate maximum hours in the production of goods on government contracts. After the NRA was held unconstitutional, some groups desired to retain the NRA standards by imposing them upon persons manufacturing goods for the federal government. It was contended that these standards reduce unemployment by spreading work and would tend to increase purchasing power. The use of such standards on government contracts, it was argued, would make it difficult for the employer to maintain longer hours of employment on other production. Hence, the Public Contracts Act of 1936 was passed. This act provides that a producer of goods bought by the government must certify that he has not employed any person in excess of 8 hours a day, or 40 hours a week. It applies to all purchases of nonagricultural products not made in the open market, provided the cost is more than $10,000. The act grants to the Secretary of Labor the authority to permit work in excess of 8 hours a day,[73] and under this authority the Secretary permits such work when time and a half is paid.[74] The Secretary is given the authority to waive the provisions of the law if the head of any establishment finds that he is unable to secure the product desired under these conditions.[75]

[71] Act of Aug. 1, 1892, 27 Stat. 340.
[72] Act of Sept. 9, 1940, 54 Stat. 884, Sec. 803.
[73] Act of June 30, 1936, 49 Stat. 2036, Sec. 6.
[74] "Rules and Regulations," Sec. 103, *Wage and Hour Manual*, (1942), p. 824.
[75] Act of June 30, 1936, 49 Stat. 2036, Sec. 6.

In several respects this act differs from the Fair Labor Standards Act of 1938. No provision is made for a longer work week in seasonal industries. The Secretary of Labor can remedy this difficulty by granting exemptions to the Public Contracts Act. On a number of occasions, heads of departments have requested the Secretary of Labor to grant exemptions from the provisions of the act, but for several years all such requests were refused. In 1940 Congress authorized the President to grant exemptions from the act.[76] The following year the Secretary of Labor exempted from the hour provision the production of canned goods intended for the armed forces. The exemption permits a work week similar to that allowed in seasonal industries under the Fair Labor Standards Act.[77] The Public Contracts Act originally did not provide for a longer work week where it had been agreed to by collective bargaining as does the Fair Labor Standards Act. An amendment in 1942 made the Public Contracts Act identical with the wage and hour act in respect to agreements for 2,080 hours of work a year or for 1,000 hours in 26 weeks.[78]

The hours of work in one other specific activity are regulated. The Mineral Leasing Act of 1920 provides that in a mine on property leased from the United States only 8 hours of work may be permitted in any one day. It also prohibits the employment of women in underground operations in such a mine.[79] This law probably was enacted because the state laws would be inapplicable, since the contractors are government instrumentalities.

II. CHILD LABOR

Practically all the states have long restricted child labor. Nevertheless there has been a strong demand for federal child labor legislation because some states have lower standards than others.

*Two federal child labor laws were
declared unconstitutional.*

In 1916 Congress forbade the transportation in interstate commerce of goods made by any child under 14 years of age, or by children under 16 who were employed at night or more than 6 days a week or

---

[76] Act of June 28, 1940, 54 Stat. 681, Sec. 13.
[77] 5 WHR 553 (1942).
[78] Act of May 13, 1942, 56 Stat. 277.
[79] Act of Feb. 25, 1920, 41 Stat. 449, Sec. 187.

more than 8 hours a day.[80] The Supreme Court held that this law was beyond the power of Congress, since it was not actually a regulation of interstate commerce.[81] In 1919 Congress attempted to regulate child labor through its taxing power, by placing a 10 per cent tax on goods made by employers of child labor;[82] again the Supreme Court held that this law was not enacted to raise revenue, but was designed to regulate labor and so it was unconstitutional.[83]

A large majority of the NRA codes contained provisions limiting child labor. A minimum age of 16 years was fixed in 444 codes, and in 49 codes a higher age limit was provided. In many codes a higher minimum was provided for hazardous occupations. Compliance with these regulations was very general, and it is commonly believed that they were very effective in reducing child labor.[84]

*Child labor is now regulated
by two federal laws.*

Provisions regulating child labor were included in the Fair Labor Standards Act of 1938. In the hearings on this legislation, the head of the Children's Bureau stated that child labor caused sweatshop conditions because the low bargaining power of children tended to force wages down and to increase hours. The argument that child labor tended to produce unduly long hours and low wages had some validity; but with the enactment of a federal minimum wage and maximum hour law this potentiality is reduced. The Chief of the Bureau argued that although the states have child labor laws, their age standards are low because of interstate competition. She also contended that the employment of children is unusually hazardous, and consequently it is necessary to regulate child labor.[85]

Under the Fair Labor Standards Act, persons below 14 years of age cannot be employed in interstate commerce or in the production of goods for such commerce. Children between 14 and 16 can only be employed subject to rules of the Children's Bureau. The act prohibits

[80] Act of Sept. 1, 1916, 39 Stat. 675.
[81] *Hammer v. Dagenhart*, 257 U.S. 251 (1918).
[82] Act of Feb. 24, 1919, 40 Stat. 1138.
[83] *Bailey v. Drexel Furniture Co.*, 259 U.S. 20 (1922).
[84] Solomon Barkin, *Child Labor Control Under the NRA* (1936), p. 14.
[85] *Fair Labor Standards Act of 1937*, Hearings before the House Committee on Labor, pp. 382-3.

the employment of all persons below 16 in mines and manufacturing establishments that produce goods for commerce. All employment in agriculture and for a parent (except in mines and factories) is exempt. Goods produced by child labor contrary to this act cannot be shipped in interstate commerce, and an employer violating the provisions is subject to criminal penalties.

Under the rules adopted by the Children's Bureau, children between 14 and 16 can be employed not more than 3 hours a day when attending school, and not more than 8 hours a day when not attending school. Their employment at night is absolutely prohibited. The Chief of the Children's Bureau issued only five orders restricting the employment of children between 16 and 18 in hazardous occupations, and the Bureau announced that no more such orders of a binding character would be issued during the war, because of production needs and because boys of 17 were being accepted by some branches of the armed forces.[86]

The Public Contracts Act prohibits the employment of girls under 18 and boys under 16 on work being done on all government contracts subject to the act.[87] Exemptions from this prohibition can be granted by the Secretary of Labor or the President. The Secretary of Labor now permits the employment of girls above 16 in the production of all goods subject to the act. Thus the application of the two laws is now similar.[88]

The inclusion of child labor provisions in contracts for the production of goods for the government is not a very effective method of regulation; especially where we have a general child labor law the desirability of such regulation is less apparent. It is not evident why the standards applicable to such contracts should differ from those contained in the general law.

III. SAFETY

The federal government has regulated safety conditions in interstate commerce to protect both the employees and the persons and goods being transported. Most of these regulations were enacted some years ago, and have not been an issue of current interest.

[86] 6 WHR 78 (1943).
[87] Act of June 30, 1936, 49 Stat. 2036, Sec. 1 (d).
[88] Nov. 14, 1942, Wage and Hour Manual (1943), p. 387.

Only in transportation can the government directly require the maintenance of safe working conditions.

In 1893 Congress required the installation of automatic couplers, and driving wheel brakes on locomotives and all rolling stock used in interstate commerce.[89] Ten years later these requirements were extended to all rolling stock owned by carriers engaged in interstate commerce.[90] All cars must be equipped with hand rails, running boards, and steps as prescribed by the ICC.[91] In 1911 locomotive boilers were made subject to regulation and inspection.[92] Train control devices can be prescribed by the ICC by virtue of the Transportation Act of 1920. (Section 441).

The promotion of safety at sea for members of the crew and passengers alike has been a subject of public concern. Detailed regulations concerning the construction and maintenance of ships have been enacted.[93] Qualifications of the crew are provided.[94] The living space, sanitary facilities, and hospital accommodations for the crew are all regulated by federal laws.[95] In so far as these regulations have been prescribed to protect interstate commerce or the persons engaged in such commerce, they seem to be justified, since state laws are not generally applicable to such employment.

Safety in mines has been approached form several angles. In mines on lands leased from the United States, the Secretary of the Interior can issue rules and regulations governing safety.[96] The maintenance of safe working conditions in mines leased from the United States would not affect the property of the United States, but federal regulations can be justified because state regulations might not be fully applicable. The federal government has long carried on investigations relative to mine safety, and it has equipped and staffed mine rescue cars. Recently the United Mine Workers of America desired the enactment of federal legislation requiring the Bureau of Mines to investigate all mine accidents. In 1941 Congress authorized the Secre-

[89] Act of Mar. 2, 1893, 27 Stat. 531.
[90] Act of Mar. 2, 1903, 32 Stat. 943.
[91] Act of Apr. 14, 1910, 36 Stat. 298.
[92] Act of Feb. 17, 1911, 36 Stat. 913.
[93] 49 Stat. 1380, 1384.
[94] 49 Stat. 1930.
[95] Act of Mar. 4, 1915, 38 Stat. 1165, Sec. 6.
[96] Act of Feb. 25, 1920, 41 Stat. 437, 449, Sec. 187.

tary of the Interior to make general investigations concerning safety conditions in mines and the causes of mine accidents.[97]

*Otherwise only indirect means can be
used to promote safety.*

Under the Public Contracts Act,[98] an employer with a government contract must maintain certain conditions of sanitation and safety. Little was done to carry out this provision, and not until 1942 was a safety code issued by the Administrator of the Public Contracts Division.[99] Even under these regulations conformity with state safety laws is prima facie evidence of compliance with the federal law. The regulation of safety conditions in plants producing for the government can be justified only as an indirect way of promoting safety in general, because the maintenance of safe working conditions does not directly affect the price or quality of the goods bought by the government.

The Division of Labor Standards of the Department of Labor was established primarily to promote the safety of workers. The drafting of model legislation and safety regulations for the states is one of its main functions.[100] It has trained factory inspectors in a number of states.[101] Research in the cause, cure, and prevention of industrial accidents has been pursued.[102] The Division contends that the proper enforcement of safety codes will reduce accidents by only 25 per cent. Consequently it believes that educational work among employers is needed. The man-power shortage in World War II has served as the basis for requests for funds to engage in such safety campaigns among employers, and limited activities are now carried on in this field.[103]

IV. SUMMARY

For various reasons the federal government regulates the maximum hours of work—to reduce unemployment, to increase wages, to in-

[97] Act of May 7, 1941, 55 Stat. 177, Secs. 1 and 2.
[98] Act of June 30, 1936, 49 Stat. 2036, Sec. 1 (e).
[99] *Wage and Hour Manual* (1943), p. 390.
[100] *Annual Report of the Secretary of Labor for 1940*, pp. 58-59.
[101] *Labor-Federal Security Agency Appropriation Bill for 1944*, Hearings before the House Committee on Appropriations, 78 Cong. 1 sess., Pt. 1, p. 59.
[102] *Labor-Federal Security Agency Appropriation Bill for 1941*, Hearings before the House Committee on Appropriations, 76 Cong. 3 sess., Pt. 1, p. 125.
[103] *Labor-Federal Security Agency Appropriation Bill for 1943*, Hearings before Senate Committee on Appropriations, 77 Cong. 2 sess., p. 78.

crease purchasing power, and to promote safety, for example. The limitations, of the hours of work continue, even though the reasons for their imposition no longer exist. One cannot readily discover the criteria used in determining the length of the work day or work week. The exemptions from the general regulations are not always determined by economic or social considerations or on the basis of administrative feasibility.

The regulation of child labor was originally justified because the low bargaining power of children resulted in their exploitation, and their employment at low wages tended to depress the wages of all workers. With the enactment of minimum wage legislation and with the increase in union organization and collective bargaining, these arguments tend to decline in significance. The continuation of the regulation of child labor must be justified now primarily on humanitarian grounds.

Under the Constitution federal efforts to promote safe working conditions must be confined primarily to transportation. In other fields of employment the federal government operates mainly by encouraging desirable state legislation and by assisting in the improvement of the administration of state factory laws.

CHAPTER IX

THE SETTLEMENT OF LABOR DISPUTES

In 1944 government agencies—federal, state, or local[1]—attempted to bring about the peaceful adjustment of almost 60 per cent of all strikes. From 1938 to 1943 the proportion of disputes settled after government intervention almost doubled. The federal government has experimented with various forms of machinery designed to minimize work stoppages resulting from strikes. To a limited extent the government has attempted to remove potential causes of labor disputes, as for example, by the National Labor Relations Act, but generally it has sought to provide machinery to facilitate the peaceful settlement of disputes after they have developed. The jurisdiction of some of the agencies has been restricted to the settlement of disputes arising in one specific type of activity, while in other instances a general jurisdiction embracing all forms of disputes has been granted to the establishment. In some cases the parties are free to utilize the machinery if they so desire; in other instances various degrees of compulsion are employed. The machinery and methods are diverse, and consequently it is illuminating to make comparisons among the various devices used, and the principles applied.

First we shall consider the one attempt to eliminate certain causes of strikes, the National Labor Relations Act. Then the formal agencies for the peaceful settlement of disputes will be examined: the Conciliation Service, the National Mediation Board, the National Railroad Adjustment Board, and the Maritime Labor Board. The informal role of the President in the settlement of labor disputes will then be summarized. The National Defense Mediation Board and the National War Labor Board will be considered in the following chapter.

I. MINIMIZING THE CAUSES OF DISPUTES—THE NATIONAL LABOR RELATIONS ACT

A major purpose of the guarantee to employees of the right to organize and to bargain collectively contained in the National Labor Relations Act is to reduce strikes and thus to free interstate commerce from potential burdens. The preamble of the act states that in order to

[1] *Monthly Labor Review*, Vol. 60 (1945), p. 970.

accomplish this objective, labor is guaranteed the right to organize, and on the employer is imposed the obligation to respect that right.[2] The act assumes that if employees have the right to organize and to bargain, and if machinery is established to enforce those rights, unions will not have to strike to get employers to recognize these rights. The act in no way limits or restricts the right of workers to strike, which of course existed previous to its enactment. It specifically recognizes that the workers have such a right.[3] In fact, it does not place any restraints on the use of strikes by minority unions, which the employer cannot recognize or deal with.

By protecting the right to organize, the National Labor Relations Act reduces the need for strikes to enforce this right.

Under the act it is not necessary for a union to strike to compel the employer to recognize its right to represent workers or to bargain collectively. A labor organization can secure the enforcement of these rights through resort to the NLRB, but it is always free to use the strike for such purposes. Some members of the NLRB have at times believed it more desirable for workers to strike than to use the Board for enforcing the rights guaranteed to them by the act. Thus Edwin Smith assisted the Textile Organizing Committee in carrying out a strike by stimulating a boycott against certain manufacturers.[4] And various employees of the Board in 1937 attempted to bring about strikes in the steel industry.[5]

Although a union can request the Board to certify that it represents a majority of the employees in an appropriate unit, it does not need to do so, and can even go on strike to secure recognition or to promote its organizational activities. Previous to the middle of 1939, an employer was not permitted to request the Board to certify the true representatives of his employees in an appropriate unit, and since then he can request such certification only where two or more labor organizations each claim a majority; but the granting of such petitions is purely discretionary, and the Board has granted them rarely.[6]

[2] Act of July 5, 1935, 49 Stat. 449, Secs. 1 and 8.
[3] The same, Sec. 13.
[4] *Report on the Investigation of the National Labor Relations Board,* H. Rept. 1902, 76 Cong. 3 sess., pp. 13-15; the minority report admits this. The same Pt. 2, pp. 48-50.
[5] The same.
[6] The same, p. 91.

It would seem that in the long run the guarantee of the rights to organize and to bargain collectively would reduce the number of strikes, resulting from the refusal of employers to recognize these rights. But to the extent that the NLRB attempts to promote the organization of labor, the act as administered might tend to increase rather than to diminish industrial disputes, at least during the period of union organization. If the law is administered by a board which feels that its major obligation is to spread unionism rather than to adjudicate rights under the act, then as long as there are any workers remaining unorganized the act possibly will not reduce labor disputes arising from the refusal of employers to recognize the right to bargain. The mere fact that workers have the right to form unions and are organized does not necessarily mean that in the long run the total number of man-days lost in strikes will decline. Some investigations tend to show that strikes are much more prevalent and are of longer duration where the workers are organized than where they are not.[7]

The Board is not authorized
to engage in conciliation.

The National Labor Relations Act[8] clearly prohibits the Board from engaging in conciliation. On signing this law President Roosevelt declared:

> . . . It should be clearly understood that it will not act as mediator or conciliator in labor disputes. The function of mediation remains, under this Act, the duty of the Secretary of Labor and of the Conciliation Service of the Department of Labor. It is important that the judicial function and the mediation function should not be confused. Compromise, the essence of mediation, has no place in the interpretation and enforcement of the law.[9]

II. FORMAL MACHINERY FOR THE ADJUSTMENT OF DISPUTES

There are four federal agencies which provide, or in recent years have provided, formal machinery for the adjustment of labor disputes. These are the Conciliation Service of the Department of Labor, the National Mediation Board, the National Railroad Adjustment Board, and the Maritime Labor Board.

---

[7] Paul Douglas, "An Analysis of Strike Statistics, 1881-1921," *Journal of American Statistical Association*, Vol. 18 (1923), pp. 876-77; and J. L. Griffin, *Strikes, A Study in Quantitative Economics* (1938), pp. 114, 205.

[8] Sec. 4-a.

[9] *The Public Papers and Addresses of Franklin D. Roosevelt*, 1935 (1938), p. 294.

A. The Conciliation Service

Section 8 of the act that created the Department of Labor provides: "The Secretary of Labor shall have power to act as mediator and to appoint commissioners of conciliation in labor disputes whenever in his judgment the interests of industrial peace require it to be done."[10] The first Secretary of Labor in his second annual report explained the nature of mediation: "It should be understood, therefore, that mediation does not mean arbitration, compulsory or otherwise. Nor is it in any other sense a judicial function. The function is one of negotiation. Neither the Secretary nor commissioners of conciliation whom he appoints are arbitrators."[11] The Secretary thus clearly distinguished between conciliation and arbitration, and he took the position that conciliators were not to engage in arbitration. He also asserted that the Department would only intervene in a labor dispute when it was requested to do so. Possibly this position was taken because of a lack of funds. At present the Conciliation Service does not follow its earlier practice of waiting for a request from a party to the dispute before it intervenes. Today even before their assistance has been requested, the conciliators frequently offer their services in a labor dispute that appears to be developing in the industries under their jurisdiction. Since to a limited extent the Conciliation Service is organized on an industrial basis, it is in a position to follow developments in specific industries.

After a slow start conciliation
developed rapidly.

During its first two years the agency handled 75 cases, but in the next two years it handled 608 cases. In its early years, employers did not have confidence in the Conciliation Service and distrusted it; practically all requests for its intervention came from labor unions.[12]

Congress granted the Conciliation Service only small appropriations during its early life. Not until the spring of 1914 did it receive any

[10] Act of Mar. 4, 1913, 37 Stat. 736, 738.

[11] *Second Annual Report of the Secretary of Labor* (1914), p. 46.

[12] John Lombardi, *Labor's Voice in the Cabinet* (1942), p. 102; Alexander Bing, *Wartime Strikes and Their Adjustment* (1921), p. 134. Secretary Wilson admitted in 1915 that it was the policy of the Department for conciliators to urge the closed shop. *Final Report and Testimony Submitted by the Commission on Industrial Relations*, S. Doc. 415, Vol. 11, 64 Cong. 1 sess., p. 10833.

appropriation for salaries, and in the fiscal year 1917 its total appropriation amounted to only $75,000. During World War I the Conciliation Service expandedly rapidly; for the fiscal year 1919 it received an appropriation of $200,000. From 1920 to 1935 the Service operated on an annual budget of approximately $200,000 and had a staff of about 30 conciliators.

The activities of the Conciliation Service have expanded considerably in the past 10 years. Not only does it carry on conciliation work, but it also engages in arbitration both in the negotiation of new agreements and in the interpretation of existing contracts. Its staff will give technical advice in the solution of certain labor problems.

Conciliation is still the main work of the Service. In the fiscal year 1944 it acted as conciliator in 21,900 labor disputes. In 2,843 of these there were actual strikes, and in 2,217 a strike was threatened. In recent years the Service has settled from 90 to 94 per cent of the threatened strikes where it intervened. Previous to the outbreak of World War II most of the disputes handled by the Service involved strikes or threatened strikes. Thus it is evident that the Service to a large extent has mediated disputes after a work stoppage had developed or was imminent. This practice differs from that of the National Mediation Board, which generally will not attempt to adjust a dispute after the workers have declared their intention to strike.

About six years ago the Conciliation Service clearly attempted to build up the good will of employers. At meetings of trade associations, departmental speakers urged employers to invite the Conciliation Service to assist them in the settlement of their labor problems.[13] Requests for the intervention of the Service now are almost equally divided between employers and employees.[14] Several international unions have prohibited their locals from calling a strike until after the Conciliation Service has had an opportunity to settle the dispute, and not infrequently collective agreements contain such a proviso. The good offices of a conciliator at times have been refused by one party or the other, but now refusals seldom occur.

Both the large number of cases that the Service has been able to

[13] *Department of Labor Appropriation Bill for 1939*, Hearings before the House Committee on Appropriations, 75 Cong. 3 sess., p. 9.

[14] Statement of Secretary Perkins, *Department of Labor Appropriation Bill for 1940*, Hearings before the House Committee on Appropriations, 76 Cong. 1 sess., p. 12.

handle on a purely voluntary basis, and the almost universal acceptance of its good offices seem to be significant evidence of the value
of the Conciliation Service. But it is possible that many persons hesitate
to reject its good offices for fear of adverse publicity. The statistics
on the number of strikes settled by its effort are of limited significance.
They do not conclusively demonstrate its value in this field, for strikes
generally have a way of getting settled ultimately. Likewise the fig-
ures on threatened strikes averted have little significance, for it often
is a part of the bargaining strategy of a union to threaten to strike,
although it has no real intention of doing so.

*There have been attempts to coerce
employers to submit disputes to mediation.*

Supposedly employers have the right to refuse to accept the good
offices of the Conciliation Service. The National Labor Relations
Board has attempted to compel employers to accept mediation if the
Service intervenes on its own initiative or at the request of employees.
When an employer refused to meet with a Commissioner of Conciliation during a dispute concerning the terms of a proposed agreement,
the Board held that the refusal constituted a failure to bargain.[15]
The Supreme Court reversed the Board and held that the employer
did not have to treat with a conciliator seeking to settle the dispute if
he were not actually the agent of the employees.[16] Nevertheless the
Board subsequently has held that an employer's refusal to accept
mediation constituted a failure to bargain.[17]

When first organized, the Department of Labor took the attitude
that it was desirable to use the force of public opinion to compel the
parties to a dispute to agree to proposals that a conciliator considered
to be reasonable. If one party refused to agree to such proposals, not
only were the alleged facts of the dispute to be made public, but if
it were the employer who declined to co-operate, his profits during

---

[15] *Columbian Enameling Co.*, 1 NLRB 181 (1936); *Columbia Radiator Company*, 1 NLRB 847 (1936).
[16] *NLRB* v. *Columbian Enameling and Stamping Co.*, 306 U.S. 292, 297, 299 (1939).
[17] *Reed and Prince Manufacturing Co.*, 12 NLRB 944 (1939), and see decision of Circuit Court of Appeals, 8 LRR 250 (1941).

previous years were to be called to the attention of the public.[18] However, the Service soon abandoned the idea of using unfavorable publicity to force a settlement.

For two reasons there are difficulties in a policy of giving publicity to the facts of a labor dispute. When the Conciliation Service intervenes in a dispute, it always contends that the acceptance of its good offices is purely voluntary. If the parties accept its assistance voluntarily, the subsequent use of the threat of publicity to secure compliance with its recommendations will hardly stimulate confidence among either employers or employees. The second difficulty is that the qualities that make for a good mediator do not necessarily produce a good fact-finder. A successful mediator must be an agreeable, diplomatic person, who easily wins confidences. He must be a person who easily can discover a practical method of compromise. A fact-finder must be skeptical, critical, and able to weigh and evaluate evidence. It seems that the discovery of the truth does not necessarily have a significant role in the conciliatory process.[19]

The peaceful adjustment of disputes, and not
the terms of settlement, is its main concern.

The basic principle of the Conciliation Service is the settlement of disputes with a minimum stoppage of work. The Secretary of Labor observed: "Our duty as conciliators is to get the stoppage of work over and get in production again."[20] The Department takes the attitude that public policy requires the settlement of the dispute with a minimum work stoppage, regardless of the terms of settlement. Thus Secretary Perkins has stated that in settling a defense strike the Conciliation Service would urge the payment of higher wages, without taking into consideration the fact that the United States government would have to pay for the wage increase, under the terms of a cost-plus fixed-fee contract.[21] The Conciliation Service apparently assumes

---

[18] Lombardi, *Labor's Voice in the Cabinet*, pp. 106-07.

[19] William R. Leiserson in *Conciliation Act of 1941*, Hearings before the Senate Committee on Education and Labor, 77 Cong. 1 sess., p. 89.

[20] Statement of Secretary Perkins, *Inquiry as to National Defense Construction*, Hearings before the House Committee on Military Affairs, 77 Cong. 1 sess., Pt. 2, p. 152.

[21] The same, p. 163.

that the terms of settlement of the controversy (if not illegal) can
never be as bad for the public as would be the cessation of production.

*The Conciliation Service has considered
itself the special representative of labor.*

William Wilson, the first Secretary of Labor, saw no need for impartiality in conciliation:

In administering this authority I have regarded it as contemplating a
development of diplomatic duties with reference to labor disputes analogous
to those of the Department of State with reference to international controversies. As it is the duty of the Department of State to represent our
Nation with fairness toward all other nations, so it is the duty of the
Department of Labor to represent wage-earning interests with fairness
toward all other industrial interests.[22]

And on another occasion he said: "Primarily the Department of Labor
must conserve in industrial disputes the interests of the wage earners
of the United States."[23]

It should not be forgotten that by its organic act the Department
of Labor was charged with the task of being the special defender of
labor. The first section of that law declares: "The purpose of the
Department of Labor shall be to foster, promote, and develop the
welfare of the wage earners of the United States, to improve their
working conditions, and to advance their opportunities for profitable
employment."[24] A department seeking to carry out this objective will
almost inevitably give special assistance to labor. A large segment of
the staff of the Service consists of ex-trade union officials. In a recent
year more than one third of the conciliators were former union officials.[25]

But apart from the background of the conciliators, the fundamental
principle of the Service tends to operate somewhat to the advantage of
labor. As has been shown, the Service takes the position that its most
important objective is the reduction of work stoppages. In an era when
the lockout has practically disappeared, labor is generally the party
that threatens the overt act that would result in a stoppage.[26] If the

[22] *Third Annual Report of the Secretary of Labor* (1915), pp. 7-8.
[23] *Second Annual Report of the Secretary of Labor* (1914), p. 21.
[24] Act of Mar. 4, 1913, 37 Stat. 736, Sec. 1.
[25] *Department of Labor Appropriation Bill for 1939*, Hearings before the House
Committee on Appropriations, pp. 70-74.
[26] Of course it is possible for the employer to act in such a way as to force the
employees to take the initiative and strike.

avoidance of work stoppages is the main objective, then an advantage is frequently given to the party threatening the stoppage, since conciliators will tend to believe he must be placated if that is necessary to attain the objective. Consequently under present circumstances this attitude of the Service gives some assistance to the workers when it is attempting to conciliate disputes.[27]

The Conciliation Service now engages in arbitration.

The attitude of the Service toward arbitration has changed. In its formative period it vigorously urged the use of arbitration in the settlement of disputes, but it refused to permit its commissioners to act as arbitrators. Now it not only urges the use of arbitration, but it will designate members of its staff to act in that capacity. It has an arbitration division with a sizeable staff; but frequently conciliators act as arbitrators.[28] Most of this work consists of the interpretation of existing agreements and not in arbitrating disputes concerning the terms of new agreements. No charge is made for the use of members of the staff as arbitrators. Over 50 per cent of the trade agreements on file with the Conciliation Service contain clauses providing for the arbitration of all disputes arising under them, and about 17 per cent of these agreements provide that the Conciliation Service shall designate the arbitrator.[29]

This inclusion of arbitration work in the Conciliation Service in the Department of Labor raises an important question. If the same organization intermittently operates as an arbitrator and a conciliator, can it perform either function successfully? For at least two reasons, there would be difficulties. First, the type of person who will make a good conciliator will not necessarily make a good arbitrator. An arbitrator should have a judicial temperament; he should be able to determine the facts objectively and then select the principles that cover the existing fact situation. A conciliator need not be interested in the

[27] See also, H. S. Kaltenborn, *Government Adjustment of Labor Disputes* (1943), p. 225.
[28] The Service attempts to keep the two functions separate; J. R. Steelman, *Mediation, Arbitration, and Conciliation*, Department of Labor Press Release, July 25, 1940. But it does not always succeed in this; Kaltenborn, *Government Adjustment of Labor Disputes*, p. 34.
[29] *Department of Labor—Federal Security Agency Appropriation Bill for 1941*, Hearings before the House Committee on Appropriations, 76 Cong. 3 sess., pp. 93-94.

actual facts involved or in the appropriate principles for the solution of the controversy. He is primarily interested in a solution that is acceptable to the parties, and he is not concerned with the most desirable solution in terms of the pre-existing standards applicable to the dispute. The arbitrator, on the other hand, should decide cases on the basis of principles. Second, if the same organization intermittently operates as an arbitrator and as a conciliator, it may lay itself open to criticism. If it applies the same standards in conciliation that it uses in arbitration, it will hardly be acting as a conciliator, and one party or the other may allege that it is prejudiced. But if it does not apply in conciliation the same standards that it uses in arbitration, one party or the other might call the Service inconsistent. On the other hand, if in arbitration it acts without any regard to principles, as is its practice in conciliation, its inconsistent determination of comparable cases will inevitably lead to charges of bias, prejudice, and inconsistency. Consequently, if an agency is going to maintain the confidence of all parties, it will be difficult for it to act both as conciliator and as an arbitrator.[30]

B. The National Mediation Board and the Emergency Boards

The Railway Labor Act of 1926, as amended in 1934, provides machinery for the settlement of railroad labor disputes without resort to strikes.[31] This machinery consists of the National Mediation Board, special emergency boards, and the National Railroad Adjustment Board.

The Railway Labor Act provides mediation
as a first means to settle disputes.

The Railway Labor Act requires that all carriers and their employees shall give each other at least 30 days' written notice of any intended change in a labor agreement. Criminal penalties are imposed upon the carriers for failure to give such notice; no penalties are imposed upon the unions.[32] Within 10 days after such notice is given the parties shall agree upon a place for holding the meetings to discuss

---

[30] William R. Leiserson, *Conciliation Act of 1941*, Hearings before the Senate Committee on Education and Labor, p. 89.

[31] Act of May 20, 1926, 44 Stat. 577; Act of June 21, 1934, 48 Stat. 1185.

[32] Act of June 21, 1934, 48 Stat. 1185, Secs. 2 (sixth, seventh, and tenth) and 6.

such changes. In case a dispute over the terms and conditions of employment is not settled by direct conference between the parties, the National Mediation Board has jurisdiction to attempt to mediate the controversy.

The present National Mediation Board was established by the act of 1934 and is composed of three persons appointed by the President by and with the advice and consent of the Senate.[33] No more than two of its members can be of the same political party. Either party to a dispute can bring it to the Board, or the Board can assume jurisdiction on its own motion when it believes an emergency situation exists. If mediation fails, the Board is directed to offer arbitration. Both parties must agree before a dispute can be submitted to arbitration. If arbitration is refused, the jurisdiction of the Board is exhausted.

Thus the Board attempts to mediate or to facilitate the arbitration of disputes before a strike or a threat of a strike develops. It does not attempt to mediate strikes. During the period in which the Board has a case before it and for 30 days thereafter, neither party to the dispute can change the working conditions or terms of employment.[34] If the Board does not secure a settlement by any of these means, and if an emergency is threatened by the possibility of a strike, the President may appoint a special emergency board to report on the facts of the controversy. The terms and conditions of employment cannot be changed for 30 days after the case has been submitted to a special emergency board, nor can such a change be made for 30 days after the Board has rendered its report. Again, penalties can be applied only against the carrier for changing the terms of employment in violation of the act.[35] There is nothing in this act that in any way limits the right of employees to strike.[36] But in at least one instance the Board told striking employees who had not exhausted the procedures of the act that they could not secure the benefits of the act while on strike.[37] The significance of this warning is not readily apparent.

The objective of the act is to delay any change in the terms of

[33] The same.

[34] Sec. 2 (seventh and tenth) and Sec. 5. Sec. 5 (first b) imposed this obligation on both carriers and employees; but a failure to comply involves penalties *only* for the employer.

[35] Act of May 20, 1926, 44 Stat. 586, Sec. 10.

[36] The same, Sec. 2 (tenth).

[37] *Third Annual Report of the National Mediation Board* (1937), p. 4.

employment that is desired by the carrier and opposed by the workers, so long as any possibility of peaceful settlement exists. By preventing the parties from modifying the terms of employment by unilateral action, the act seeks to avoid the possibility that mediation may be interrupted by a strike, while there is any possibility of arriving at a peaceful settlement.

*Mediation has been preferred
to arbitration.*

In its first nine years of existence, the National Mediation Board has had before it 1,590 mediation cases. Over half of these (843) were settled by agreement arrived at through mediation. The proportion of cases successfully settled by its mediation has increased from 35 per cent in 1935 to more than 53 per cent in 1944.[38] Five hundred and twenty-three cases were withdrawn prior to or during the mediation process, thus indicating that some form of settlement had been secured before the Board had brought its work to completion. Thirty-seven cases were settled by arbitration, and 42 cases were settled only after the creation of emergency boards.[39]

Under the Railway Labor Act the parties do not appear to be obliged to submit a dispute to arbitration. But the Supreme Court has held that if a carrier refuses to submit a dispute to arbitration at the request of its employees, the railroad cannot subsequently secure an injunction restraining the striking employees from damaging its property.[40] The Norris-LaGuardia Anti-Injunction Act of 1932 provides that no injunction can be issued unless a complainant has made every reasonable effort to settle the dispute, either by negotiation or with the aid of available government machinery for mediation or voluntary arbitration.[41] The courts held that the arbitration provisions of the Railway Labor Act fall within the category of available governmental machinery for voluntary arbitration.

Arbitration is not widely used as a method of settling disputes under this act. When the Board fails to persuade the parties to accept its

[38] *Tenth Annual Report of the National Mediation Board* (1944), p. 13.
[39] The same.
[40] *Brotherhood of Railroad Trainmen* v. *Toledo, Peoria and Western Ry. Co.*, 321 U.S. 50 (1944).
[41] Act of Mar. 23, 1932, 47 Stat. 72, Sec. 8.

mediation, it is directed to urge arbitration. Boards of arbitration may consist of three or eight members, divided equally between representatives of each party and neutral members. If the disputants cannot agree upon the neutral members, the National Mediation Board can name them. The award of the arbitrator is final and enforceable in the United States district courts. In the past nine years arbitration has been proposed by the Board 165 times, but only 37 cases actually have been settled by this method. The carriers have refused arbitration in 81 cases; the unions declined in 11, and in 36 instances both parties have refused to arbitrate. It may be significant that a very large proportion of the arbitration awards have been in favor of the unions.[42]

Emergency boards have
prevented strikes.

Since the present Railway Labor Act was enacted in 1934, only 38 emergency boards have been created. If the National Mediation Board fails to mediate a dispute, and if the parties refuse to arbitrate it, the Board can, if it desires, certify to the President that the dispute threatens to deprive a substantial section of the country of essential transportation. If he desires, the President then can appoint an emergency board. The board is directed only to investigate and to report to the President concerning the dispute.[43] Nothing in the law makes the recommendations of a board binding on either party, but seldom have the parties disregarded them. For the duration of the war, the President created in 1943, a continuing emergency panel of nine men capable of serving on emergency boards.[44] The Presidential order provided that if a dispute were not settled by the procedures established by the Railway Labor Act, the representatives of the employees could inform the chairman of the panel of this fact, and if he felt the dispute was likely to interfere with the prosecution of the war, he could appoint an emergency board consisting of three members of the panel. Thus during the war it was not necessary for the employees to threaten to strike before an emergency board could be set up.

Since the present National Mediation Board was established, there

[42] Data gathered from the annual reports of the Board.
[43] Act of May 20, 1926, 44 Stat. 586, Sec. 10.
[44] Executive Order No. 9172, May 22, 1942, *Federal Register*, Vol. 7, p. 3913.

have been seven strikes on rail carriers (only one of these was a Class I road) one in an express company, and one on an airline. But in only one of the nine strikes had the dispute been referred to an emergency board. In another case it was referred to the National War Labor Board.

The recommendations of emergency boards are not always based on the merits of the controversy. At times the boards are guided by what is needed to placate the parties and settle the dispute without a strike. Thus in one case where a carrier offered the workers an increase in the hourly rate in return for the relaxation of certain rules that it believed to be onerous, the board observed: "The result of these rules has been to interfere seriously with the most practical and economical operation of the railroad in the rendering of reasonable service to its patrons." But nevertheless the board opposed the proposal because it meant "a complete breakdown of many years of organizing effort."[45]

Another comparable recommendation was made in 1938. The carriers desired a general wage reduction, and the unions opposed it. The emergency board refused to recommend any wage reduction. The Board said that it was not interested or concerned with the earnings of the carriers. It also stated that it would not consider a decline in the cost of living a justification for wage reductions.[46]

Although determinations of emergency boards are only advisory, seldom have the parties disregarded them. But within the last few years, neither labor nor the government has considered the recommendations to be conclusive. In 1941 the operating unions desired a general wage increase, and ultimately an emergency board was appointed. This board granted a large part of the demands of the unions. It stated that it was granting these demands as a matter of "temporary expediency." Nevertheless the unions threatened to strike, and President Roosevelt requested the emergency board to take additional evidence. The board, after taking more evidence, finally settled the case by mediation, and the workers secured practically all their demands.[47]

In 1943 emergency boards were used in the dispute between the

[45] *Decision of emergency board in the Kansas City Southern Railroad Case*, Oct. 12, 1933.
[46] *Atchison, Topeka, and Santa Fe Ry. Co. Case*, Oct. 29, 1938.
[47] *Report of Emergency Board Appointed Nov. 5, 1941.*

carriers and the nonoperating employees and also in the controversy involving the operating unions. In the case of the nonoperating employees the board appointed on February 20, 1943, recommended an increase of approximately 8 cents an hour.[48] The Director of Economic Stabilization opposed this increase, because it was too large. Although the workers thought it was too small, they were willing to accept it.[49] As a consequence the President created another board to consider the case.[50] This board gave the employees increases of from 4 to 10 cents an hour.[51] The employees objected, took a strike vote, set a date for a strike, and then the President intervened. He finally granted them increases of from 9 to 11 cents an hour, although he had opposed the recommendation of the emergency board that gave them an increase of 8 cents an hour. The President also gave increases of approximately the same amount to the operating employees, although an emergency board had recommended a much smaller increase.[52]

The National Mediation Board was set up at the joint request of the carriers and the unions. In rail transportation there has been a long tradition of collective bargaining, and the unions know that public opinion would not favor a major strike on any significant interstate carrier. The workers also have not been anxious to strike, because of the fear of a loss of seniority, which is very important under the operating rules. But the workers are in a position to get a large part of their demands without making good a strike threat. Under the present system of industry-wide bargaining, a strike would tie up almost all railroads. The National Mediation Board has apparently been very successful in settling peacefully labor disputes arising out of the negotiation of new contracts. This success has been achieved primarily through mediation rather than arbitration or the use of emergency boards. The railroads' freedom from strikes probably has been at some cost to the public, because of increased wages and uneconomic working conditions on the carriers. What this additional cost has been is difficult to assess.

[48] *Report of Emergency Board Appointed Feb. 20, 1943.*
[49] George B. Harrison in *Railway Wages*, Hearings before the Senate Committee on Interstate Commerce, 78 Cong. 1 sess., p. 108.
[50] Executive Order No. 9388, Oct. 16, 1943, *Federal Register*, Vol. 8, p. 14105.
[51] *Report of Emergency Board Appointed Oct. 16, 1943.*
[52] *Monthly Labor Review*, Vol. 58 (1944), p. 611.

C. The National Railroad Adjustment Board

For the final settlement of disputes arising out of existing collective agreements between railroads and their employees, the Railway Labor Act of 1934 provided for the establishment of a National Railroad Adjustment Board.[53] This Board consists of 36 members, 18 of whom are chosen by railroad labor unions, and a like number by the carriers. The members of the Board are employees of the group they represent, and not of the government. The Board sits in four divisions, on each of which the carriers and the unions are equally represented. Each division has jurisdiction over specific types of employees. If the division is evenly divided in any case, it can appoint a neutral member to sit with the regular members to determine the case. If it fails to agree upon a neutral member, the National Mediation Board can appoint one.[54]

*The Board engages in
compulsory arbitration.*

This Board is the only permanent agency actually engaged in compulsory arbitration in the United States. Its jurisdiction can be invoked by either party. The Board issues binding judgments, enforceable in the courts against the defendant, though he never accepted the jurisdiction of the Board. It can consider all grievances and controversies arising out of the interpretation and application of agreements. The Board early held that it would not consider any grievances that did not arise out of existing agreements, although the act would seem to indicate that it was to have jurisdiction over such grievances.[55]

There is some question concerning the exact function of the Board. The labor members contend that its function is one of adjustment rather than adjudication. They argue that its work is at least primarily the settlement of disputes by negotiation and adjustment. It is their

[53] The Railway Labor Act of 1926 provided for the creation of system adjustment boards and a National Adjustment Board. The National Adjustment Board never was set up because the carriers opposed its creation for several reasons. First, the creation of a national adjustment board as against system adjustment boards would have facilitated the creation of national railroad labor unions as against system-wide labor unions. In the second place, the carriers with small profits did not care to see a national board established for fear it would give encouragement to rules and practices that would be more costly than they believed they were able to afford.

[54] Act of June 21, 1934, 48 Stat. 1189, Sec. 3.

[55] The same, Sec. 3 (first) (1).

contention that a division of the Board does not become an arbitral body until a neutral member has been added. The carriers contend that its functions are only adjudicative. The Board itself has not been too clear on this question. The word "adjustment" in its title would give some weight to labor's contention. The procedures used and type of proof required tend to indicate either that the Board gives some support to labor's claim or that it has not clearly envisaged the problem.[56] The jurisdiction of the Board is not exclusive. Labor can always strike in order to attempt to enforce its interpretation of a contract, and instead of bringing a case before the Board, either side can sue in the courts.[57] But once a proceeding has been brought before the Board by one party, the other cannot seek to have it adjudicated in the courts.[58]

Over 80 per cent of the cases considered by the divisions have been brought by the unions, and close to 20 per cent have been brought jointly by the carriers and the unions.[59] Rarely does a carrier bring a case of its own volition. Possibly the explanation of the small number of cases brought by the carriers lies in the fact that over 67 per cent of the judgments of the several divisions of the Board are in favor of the employees.[60]

Individual employees cannot bring cases before the National Railroad Adjustment Board.

It is almost impossible for an individual employee to bring a case before the Board. Practically all cases are brought by unions, although the act does not limit the jurisdiction of the Board to cases brought by unions. Generally when a case is brought by an individual workman, the labor members of the division refuse to take jurisdiction, the employer members vote in favor of considering it, the division is equally divided, and consequently does nothing.[61] The refusal of the

---

[56] *Administrative Procedures in Government Agencies*, S. Doc. 10, 77 Cong. 1 sess., Pt. 4, pp. 5-6.

[57] *Moore* v. *Illinois Central R. R.*, 312 U.S. 630 (1941).

[58] *Washington Terminal Co.* v. *Boswell*, 319 U.S. 732 (1943).

[59] S. Doc. 10, Pt. 4, p. 11.

[60] W. H. Spencer, *The National Railroad Adjustment Board* (1939), pp. 50-51, and *Department of Labor-Federal Security Agency Appropriation Bill for 1946*, Hearings before the House Committee on Appropriations, 79 Cong. 1 sess., Pt. 1, p. 473.

[61] S. Doc. 10, Pt. 4, p. 7. In one case a district court issued a mandamus to compel a division of the Board to take a case brought by an individual, *Patterson* v. *Chicago and Eastern Illinois Railroad Co.*, 7 CCH Labor Cases 61, 768 (1943).

Board to consider cases of individual employees does not seem to be in accord with the law. There is nothing in the act to justify it, and the agreements or rules and regulations that the Board applies govern all employees, whether or not they belong to a union.[62] Of course the labor members of the Board are all chosen by trade unions. It is possible that these members have adopted this policy in order to make union membership more attractive.

The carriers cannot themselves
appeal from the decisions of the Board.

The decision of the Board can be enforced by a judgment of a district court, and in such enforcement proceedings its awards are considered prima facie evidence of their own validity. This enforcement proceeding is the only method of appealing the decision of the Board to the courts. Only if the carrier refuses to obey the award, and if the union seeks to have it enforced judicially, can the carrier get the decision reviewed by a court. But if the carrier refuses to comply with the award, labor rarely uses the enforcement method provided in the law; instead the union generally threatens a strike and ultimately secures the appointment of an emergency board to consider the matter.[63] Thus practically there is no judicial review for the carriers. Unless the unions desire to enforce an award through the courts, the carriers cannot get judicial review in any case.

It appears that the Board has performed its function in a reasonably satisfactory manner. It has been used more frequently than has the procedure for the arbitration of disputes as to interests.

D. The Maritime Labor Board

In 1936 when Congress sought to revitalize the merchant marine by a new program of subsidies, labor relations in the shipping industry were in a chaotic condition. There were several rival unions existent, and each had a noticeable lack of discipline over its workers. Quickies and sit-down strikes were prevalent. The United States Maritime Commission stated:

Labor conditions in the American merchant marine are deplorable.

[62] Sec. 3 (first) (i) which refers to disputes between an employee or a group of employees and a carrier seems to lend support to this view.

[63] Spencer, *The National Railroad Adjustment Board*, pp. 55-58; and S. Doc. 10, Pt. 4, p. 6.

Unless something is done to reduce interunion friction, to increase the efficiency of our crews, and to restore order and discipline upon our ships, all Government efforts to develop a strong American fleet will be futile. . . .
. . . .

Order and discipline have in many cases disappeared. . . . Vessels have been delayed by the frequent use of the "sit down" and "quickie." . . .
. . . .

The present situation is complicated by conflicts now raging between the different unions. . . .[64]

More than 1,100,000 man-days were lost annually in strikes in the shipping industry in both 1936 and 1937.[65]

The Maritime Commission urged Congress in 1937 to bring the shipping industry under the Railway Labor Act of 1934, but neither the shippers nor the unions looked with favor upon even the moderate form of compulsion provided by the act.[66] Consequently as a compromise Congress in 1938 created the Maritime Labor Board. This Board was composed of three members appointed by the President by and with the advice and consent of the Senate. It was given the tasks of encouraging collective bargaining and of mediating labor disputes in the maritime industry. The Board could intervene on its own initiative, or it could be called in by either party.[67]

*The composition of the Board and the nature of
its powers made it ineffective.*

The President appointed to the Board three men each of whom had a very definite labor background. Louis Bloch had been Industrial Commissioner of California, and he had been endorsed for the position by both John L. Lewis and Harry Bridges.[68] Another member, C. E. Seehorn, had been president of the Railroad Firemen's Union for a number of years. Robert Bruere, the chairman, had a long record as a social worker, and his sympathy for trade unionism was well known. Partly as a consequence of its membership, the Board

[64] United States Maritime Commission, *Economic Survey of the American Merchant Marine* (1937), pp. 43, 46, 47.
[65] *Report of the Maritime Labor Board* (1940), p. 249.
[66] *Amending Merchant Marine Act 1936*, Hearings before the House Committee on Merchant Marine and Fisheries, 75 Cong. 2 sess., pp. 13-17.
[67] Act of June 23, 1938, 52 Stat. 967, Secs. 1001-10.
[68] Statement of Commissioner Bloch, *Maritime Labor Board*, Hearings before the Senate Committee on Commerce, 77 Cong. 1 sess., p. 91.

did not have the full confidence of the employers, the A.F. of L. unions, and the independent labor organizations.

Its primary task was to encourage collective bargaining. It was also empowered to attempt to mediate disputes, and if mediation failed, it was to urge arbitration. All labor agreements in the maritime industry had to be filed with the Board. When an agreement was about to expire, the Board sought to intervene in the process of negotiating a renewal and attempted to bring the parties together before any dispute actually arose.[69] Its authority to mediate in no way limited the jurisdiction of the Conciliation Service; the two agencies exercised concurrent jurisdiction.

In three years it considered 195 mediation cases. Only 34 of these were referred to it by the employers, 91 were referred by unions, 16 were jointly submitted, the Board took action on its motion in 39 cases, and 15 were referred to it by other bodies. During this same period, the Conciliation Service handled 326 disputes in the shipping industry or almost 70 per cent more than the Board.[70]

There is reason for believing that parties to disputes sometimes shopped around between the Board and the Conciliation Service, to see which would offer the more attractive terms of settlement.[71] The Conciliation Service had been active in this field before the Board was established, and it is natural that more disputes would be brought to it than to the new agency, especially when the latter did not have the full confidence of all parties.

This Board incurred the enmity of the shipping industry in a number of ways. In the San Francisco shipping clerks' strike in 1939-40, the Board publicly blamed the shipping companies for causing the dispute.[72] On the other hand, the Board refused to reprimand unions for calling quickies and sit-down strikes in violation of contracts.[73] To increase the workers' bargaining power the Board recommended the repeal of the mutiny laws which limited the right to strike.[74]

[69] The same, pp. 14-15.
[70] The same, p. 90.
[71] *Extension of Certain Provisions of Title X, Merchant Marine Act, 1936*, S. Rept. 457, 77 Cong. 1 sess., p. 23.
[72] Statement of Commissioner Bloch, *Maritime Labor Board*, Hearings before the Senate Committee on Commerce, pp. 55 and 91.
[73] The same.
[74] The same, p. 17.

The employers did not seem to trust the Board. Twenty-two agreements between the shipping associations on the Pacific Coast and labor unions provided for the arbitration of all disputes under them by an arbitrator to be designated by an outside body. No one of these agreements provided for the designation of arbitrators by the Maritime Labor Board.[75] Twenty of them provided for the designation of arbitrators by the Department of Labor; two provided for their selection by local organizations.

Its failure to win the full confidence of both the employers and the employees was a major difficulty with the Maritime Labor Board. There were three reasons for this lack of confidence. It was charged with the tasks both of promoting collective bargaining and of mediating labor disputes in the maritime industry. A mediation agency was directed to promote collective bargaining. By performing this function the Board built up the bargaining power of the workers, and it is not surprising that the employers considered this activity to be disadvantageous to them. Consequently, since the Board was charged with the performance of these two tasks, it was difficult for the employers to view it as impartial. Secondly, in selecting the members of the Board, the emphasis appears to have been on its function of promoting collective bargaining rather than on mediation. This emphasis tended to reduce the employer's confidence in it. Another factor working in the same direction was its practice of publicly blaming employers for failing to settle disputes in conformity with its wishes, while refusing to do the same where a union refused to follow its recommendations.

Originally the Board was created for only a three-year period, which ended in 1941, but it sought to become a permanent agency. The House of Representatives voted to extend its life without added powers. The Senate, however, regarded its mixture of authority to mediate and to encourage collective bargaining as being in conflict with impartial mediation.[76] As a result, its existence was extended for only one year, and it was given no power to mediate labor disputes. In July 1942 its life ended.

III. THE PRESIDENT AND LABOR DISPUTES

Although the President's role in the settlement of labor disputes

[75] The same, p. 56.
[76] S. Rept. 457, p. 3.

cannot be evaluated at present because of a lack of published data, President F. D. Roosevelt was much more active in this field than any of his predecessors.[77] He intervened in no less than four labor disputes each year after 1933. Presidential intervention has taken three main forms: (1) he has attempted to mediate disputes himself or through specially selected agents; (2) adverse publicity has been threatened against parties who were unwilling to engage in peaceful settlements; and (3) he has sought to facilitate arbitration, or on his own initiative he has stated what he considered a proper solution of a controversy. These major methods used by the President are not entirely separable; several of them have been used in adjusting a single dispute.

*Attempts at conciliation
have had some success.*

The early action of the President in the Pacific Coast Longshoremen's dispute in 1934 is an example of an attempt to urge the parties to continue to negotiate and to refrain from striking. Despite such urgings, a strike ultimately occurred and further steps were required.[78] He did not secure any better results with these methods in the automobile strike in 1937.[79]

When the contract between the UMWA and the bituminous coal producers was about to expire at the end of March 1943, President Roosevelt urged the parties to extend the existing agreement indefinitely, to continue negotiations, and to make retroactive any changes in wages.[80] The parties agreed to extend the existing agreement for only one month.

In a steel strike in 1934 the President first designated Secretary of Labor Perkins to mediate the dispute,[81] and when she did not get results, he appointed a special Steel Labor Relations Board to settle the matter. This was helpful in settling the dispute.[82] In the "Little Steel" strike in 1937, he appointed a special mediation board headed by Charles P. Taft.[83] Before he set up this mediation board the

---

[77] Edwin Berman, *Labor Disputes and the President of the United States* (1924).
[78] *The Public Papers and Addresses of Franklin D. Roosevelt, 1934* (1938), p. 157.
[79] *The Public Papers and Addresses of Franklin D. Roosevelt, 1937* (1941), p. 20.
[80] *New York Times*, Mar. 30, 1943.
[81] *The Public Papers and Addresses of Franklin D. Roosevelt, 1934* (1938), p. 305.
[82] The same, p. 310.
[83] *The Public Papers and Addresses of Franklin D. Roosevelt, 1937* (1941), pp. 270-71.

President expressed his opposition to the employers' stand;[84] consequently this board's lack of success is not surprising.

With the expiration of the bituminous coal collective agreement at the end of March 1939, a coal strike occurred. In the negotiations which continued during the strike, the main issue was the miners' demand for a union shop. When the negotiations appeared to be breaking down, the President got both parties to confer jointly with him, and on the day following this meeting the producers signed a contract containing the union shop provision demanded by the miners.[85]

The threat of unfavorable publicity has not always had the desired results.

Only a few examples of the use of unfavorable publicity for one or both parties to a dispute will be given. In the sit-down in the General Motors plants in 1937, the Department of Labor asked Mr. Sloan, the head of the corporation, to come to Washington to meet with union leaders and representatives of the Department; but Mr. Sloan said he would do it only if the President asked him. The President then stated at his press conference: "I was not only disappointed in the refusal of Mr. Sloan to come down here, but I regarded it as a very unfortunate decision on his part."[86] When the "Little Steel" companies, in June 1937, refused to make a written agreement with the Steel Workers' Organizing Committee, the President stated at a press conference that those who made agreements should be willing to put them in writing.[87]

When a railroad strike was threatened in December 1943, the President asserted that if labor were not reasonable in its demands, he would make a radio broadcast giving them a tongue lashing, and if the carriers would not yield, he would seize the roads. Although the carriers were willing to accept his offer to arbitrate, and although many of the unions were not willing to do so, he never made a speech attacking the unions, but he did seize the roads.

During the bituminous coal strikes in 1943, he attacked the coal miners and their leaders in a number of public statements.[88] Nevertheless the miners won most of their demands.

[84] *New York Times,* June 16, 1937.
[85] *The Public Papers and Addresses of Franklin D. Roosevelt, 1939* (1941), pp. 304-05.
[86] *The Public Papers and Addresses of Franklin D. Roosevelt, 1937* (1941), p. 20.
[87] *New York Times,* June 16, 1937.
[88] *New York Times,* May 3, and June 24, 1943.

The President has urged arbitration
or himself acted as arbitrator.

Several times the President practically insisted that the parties to a dispute submit it to arbitration. When the National Defense Mediation Board refused to grant a union shop in the captive mines, John L. Lewis threatened a strike. The President stated during the controversy that the United States would never compel a man to join a union.[89] Consequently it was not surprising that when the President urged arbitration, Mr. Lewis declined. Only when the President suggested Mr. J. R. Steelman, the head of the Conciliation Service, as the arbitrator, did Lewis agree to the proposal. Mr. Steelman rendered a decision in favor of the union shop.[90]

To settle the railroad strike threatened in November 1941, the President insisted on the use of arbitration. On the ground of "practical expediency" the President's emergency board had recommended a wage increase. This increase in wages was not as large as the workers desired, so they threatened to strike. The President finally got both parties to submit the dispute to the emergency board again. The board finally secured a settlement that was more favorable to the workers than the original decision.[91]

In the settlement of the railroad wage dispute in December 1943, the President insisted upon arbitration and actually acted as arbitrator himself. In the case of nonoperating unions, the Director of Economic Stabilization had set aside a recommendation of an emergency board for an 8-cents an hour increase on the ground that it was inflationary. A second emergency board justified a smaller increase, which the workers refused to accept, and they then voted to strike. The operating unions also voted to strike, because of an unsatisfactory decision of an emergency board relative to a wage increase. On the day before the National Mediation Board was going to intervene, the President called all the parties to a meeting at the White House. After several days of negotiating, the President proposed that he personally be authorized to arbitrate the dispute. On December 23 two of the operating unions agreed to have him arbitrate it, while the others

[89] *New York Times*, Nov. 14, 1941.
[90] The same, Dec. 8, 1941.
[91] The same, Dec. 2, 1941.

refused. Exactly what was to be arbitrated was never clear to all parties. The President gave these two unions increases of from 9 to 11 cents an hour, plus a week's vacation with pay, and on the same day (December 27) he took over the railroads.[92] Subsequently the other unions called off the strike, and they ultimately got terms comparable to those given to the first two unions. They thus secured a wage increase greater than the one which the administration denied them because it was inflationary.

In the bituminous coal strikes in 1943, President Roosevelt intervened several times to compel the UMWA to submit to the jurisdiction of the National War Labor Board and to abide by its decision. After four strikes, the seizure of the mines on two occasions, and several statements by the President criticizing the miners, they got from the government most of the demands that the National War Labor Board originally refused to grant.

The President attempted on several occasions to suggest what he considered a proper solution of a dispute. In September 1933 a controversy arose concerning the application of the bituminous coal code to the captive mines. The President declared that the code applied to the mines and that the union shop and the check-off should be granted.[93] Ultimately a contract was signed embodying these terms.[94]

The 1934 automobile strike involved the question of the exclusive bargaining rights of a union representing a majority of the workers. The President insisted on a settlement on the basis of minority representation. Although the A.F. of L. vigorously opposed it, this settlement was adopted.[95]

The railroads and the unions agreed in 1933 to a 10 per cent wage reduction to last until June 30, 1934. When this agreement was about to expire, the union wished to terminate it, thus restoring the previous wages, while the carriers desired a 22½ per cent wage reduction. On at least two occasions the President urged both sides to continue the

---

[92] What constitutes a week's vacation with pay is not simple in the case of the operating unions because of the nature of their members' employment. In the case of some unions they got seven days with pay, and others got the earnings during a seven-day period, *New York Times*, May 18, 1944.

[93] *The Public Papers and Addresses of Franklin D. Roosevelt, 1933* (1938), p. 383.

[94] The same, p. 439.

[95] The same, pp. 166-68.

existing 10 per cent reduction.[96] Finally, the President announced an agreement providing for the gradual termination of the reduction by April 1, 1935.[97]

In order to permit Congress to pass the National Bituminous Coal Act in 1935, President Roosevelt urged the mine operators and the unions to continue until September 16, 1935 their contract that expired on March 31, 1935. This was done, thus averting a strike, and after the passage of the act a new contract was made providing for a wage increase.[98]

Thus it appears that in recent years the President has exercised a considerable personal role in endeavoring to settle labor disputes. On occasion he intervened before the exhaustion of all other peaceful remedies established by Congress. The President relied more upon his personal prestige than upon any definite grant of constitutional or statutory authority. From this discussion it is evident that any President, if he is so minded, could through personal expression of opinions or through his influence on officials of regular government agencies influence the settlement of labor disputes to a greater or less extent.

The following chapter will deal with the special machinery created during World War II, to assist in the peaceful settlement of labor disputes. That discussion will be followed by a general summary of the policy of government toward the peaceful adjustment of industrial disputes.

[96] *The Public Papers and Addresses of Franklin D. Roosevelt, 1934* (1938), pp. 97-98, 187.
[97] The same, p. 201.
[98] *The Public Papers and Addresses of Franklin D. Roosevelt, 1935* (1938), pp. 306-07.

CHAPTER X

MACHINERY FOR THE ADJUSTMENT OF WARTIME LABOR DISPUTES

After the development of the defense emergency in 1941, two major agencies were established to facilitate the peaceful settlement of labor disputes, the National Defense Mediation Board and the National War Labor Board. Furthermore some of the agencies concerned with war production developed their own staffs to facilitate the maintenance of good industrial relations between war contractors and their employees. The War Department, the Navy, and the War Production Board had such units.[1]

In the process of advising on industrial relations these organizations sometimes engaged in conciliation, and consequently there was some overlap between their work and that of the Conciliation Service.[2] But the methods of these new agencies differed from those of the permanent Conciliation Service. The units operating in the field of war production generally participated in the adjustment of a dispute before a strike or a threat of a strike developed, whereas the Conciliation Service normally is called in only after a strike has been threatened.[3] In addition the war agencies were in a position to exercise a certain amount of subtle coercion on both parties to a dispute. Recalcitrant employers could be threatened with the potentiality that their contracts might be canceled if they refused to accept suggestions for a solution. The Army and Navy largely used officer personnel in their industrial relations work. One reason for their utilization was the belief that suggestions coming from a uniformed officer might carry added weight with the workers.

I. THE NATIONAL DEFENSE MEDIATION BOARD

A wave of strikes in the early part of 1941 stimulated congressional demands for legislation to curb work stoppages in defense industries.

[1] *National War Agencies Appropriation Bill for 1944*, Hearings before the House Committee on Appropriations Pt. 1, 78 Cong. 1 sess., pp. 1170-71.
[2] *Department of Labor-Federal Security Agency Appropriation Bill for 1946*, Hearings before the House Committee on Appropriations, Pt. 1, 79 Cong. 1 sess., pp. 86-90.
[3] *National War Agencies Appropriation Bill for 1945*, Hearings before the House Committee on Appropriations Pt. 1, 78 Cong. 2 sess., p. 691.

Consequently on March 19, 1941, by executive order, President Roosevelt created the National Defense Mediation Board.[4] It was composed of 11 members: 3 representing the public, 4 representing industry, and 4 representing labor.

This Board could take jurisdiction only over such disputes as were certified to it by the Secretary of Labor. The Secretary of Labor was directed to certify to the Board any dispute between employers and employees that threatened to obstruct or burden the production of materials for national defense if it could not be settled by the Conciliation Service. The Board was given the authority to attempt to settle such disputes by any available means. It could offer conciliation or voluntary arbitration, and if these efforts failed, it was empowered to take testimony and make public recommendations. If a case was one that should be considered by NLRB, the National Defense Mediation Board could urge that agency to consider it at the earliest possible moment.

The Defense Mediation Board engaged in
both mediation and arbitration.

While the Board actually considered conciliation its major function, it was directed to make recommendations for the final determination of a case if mediation failed. This latter method of settlement actually amounted to arbitration.[5]

The relative significance and effectiveness of conciliation and arbitration is partly revealed by the number of cases settled by various means. Final settlements were secured in 96 of the cases that came before the Board from March 1941 to January 1942; 10 cases were disposed of before they went to hearing; and of the 86 cases settled after a hearing was held 22 were terminated by contracts voluntarily entered into by the parties without the assistance of the Board; 23 were settled by an agreement after some help from the Board; 30 were concluded by recommendations from the Board; and 11 were settled by other means.[6] It is not easy to distinguish between the 23 cases settled by a contract formulated with some aid of the Board, and

[4] Executive Order No. 8617, *Federal Register*, Vol. 6, p. 1532.
[5] Bureau of Labor Statistics, *Report on the Work of the National Defense Mediation Board*, Bureau of Labor Statistics Bulletin No. 714 (1942), p. 19. This was prepared by employees of the Board at its request.
[6] The same, p. 14

the 30 cases that were concluded on the basis of recommendations from the Board. Although the Board asserted that it would not inform the parties in advance of the recommendations it intended to make in a case, it would nevertheless tell them what it would not recommend.[7] Consequently, the dividing line is not easily discernible between the cases settled by an agreement with some help, and those in which a recommendation was made. Probably the 23 closed by an agreement made with some aid from the Board represent those settled by conciliation, and the approximately 41 cases settled by recommendations of the Board and other means represent those where conciliation failed. Thus conciliation was successful in about 26 per cent of the cases heard by the Board.[8]

No principles existed to guide the Board in making recommendations.

Neither in conciliating nor in making recommendations did the Board have any standards or rules on which to base its decisions. Neither Congress nor the President enunciated any principles for the settlement of disputes. And the Board itself did not develop any standards.[9] When acting as a conciliator, the lack of standards was not so significant, because the settlement was essentially something the parties themselves developed and ratified. But in arbitration the determinations were made by the Board, inconsistencies were apparent, and the responsibility for them was on the Board.

In cases involving the problem of union security, this lack of principles caused difficulty, for the board could not make up its mind whether to grant the union shop or merely the maintenance of union membership as a means of solving a specific case. In one case the Board granted a union shop,[10] and as a result unions demanded it in other cases. When the United Mine Workers of America did not get a union shop in the captive mine case in November 1941,[11] the CIO members withdrew from the Board. Concerning the reasons for this lack of standards the report on the Board's activities observed:

[7] The same, p. 22.
[8] H. S. Kaltenborn, *Government Adjustment of Labor Disputes* (1943), p. 93.
[9] See quotations in the same, pp. 23-33.
[10] Bethlehem Steel Co., Shipbuilding Division, No. 37, *Report on the Work of the National Defense Mediation Board*, p. 160.
[11] Bituminous Coal Operators, Captive Mines, No. 20-B, the same, p. 118.

. . . It was the opinion at least of the majority of the members, that the Board itself, being primarily a mediatory Board, could not consistently adopt a set policy upon a matter concerning which there was basic disagreement between employers and employees. To some extent this attitude was a true reflection of the mediatory nature of the Board. . . . The tri-partite composition of the Board explains much. It had not only to solve the controversy before it but to do it without disaffecting the Board members. The difficulty arose where it was called upon to take positions which seriously offended one or the other group and which could not be fortified by a reference to a well-established governmental policy. . . .

It is probably correct to state that the Board did not adopt a fixed or inflexible attitude toward demands for the union shop or union maintenance. Any such attitude would have excluded from consideration the intangibles which were important in a process in which mediation played so large a part: the relative strength of the opposed parties, the intensity of their attitude with respect to union security, the importance of the industry's operations for national defense. . . .[12]

Defects of organization and a lack of
power impaired the Board's effectiveness.

The jurisdiction of the National Defense Mediation Board was limited to such cases as were certified to it by the Secretary of Labor. Shortly after the Board was established, an informal committee was set up to recommend to the Secretary of Labor the specific cases that should be certified to the Board. The Conciliation Service, the Labor Division of the Office of Production Management, and the National Defense Mediation Board were represented on this committee. The Secretary of Labor acted upon its recommendations.

All eleven members of the Mediation Board were part-time employees. Normally a case was considered by a panel of three members: one public, one labor, and one employer member. Since these part-time members normally regarded their job on the Board as secondary to their major employment, the Board had difficulty in securing the active participation of many of its members. In one instance, four successive labor members sat on one panel considering a specific case.[13]

A report on the operations of the Board prepared by members of its staff stated that the employer and employee members were not expected to be impartial.[14] Thus Philip Murray, while a member of the

[12] The same, pp. 24, 28.
[13] *Report on the Work of the National Defense Mediation Board*, p. 7.
[14] The same, p. 21.

Board in April 1941, left its sessions, put an alternate member in his place, and went to Pittsburgh to call a strike of the United Steel Workers of America in a case then pending before the Board.[15]

Under the executive order the Board could in the last resort only recommend what it believed to be a proper solution of a case. It was given no power to compel either party to obey its recommendations. It did not have marked success in persuading the parties to follow these recommendations. In almost 30 per cent of the cases, strikes occurred after the Board took jurisdiction. In almost 20 per cent of the cases that the Board decided by formal recommendations, the union refused to abide by the determination. In several other instances the employers did not abide by the recommendations. In at least two instances the Board brought about compliance with its order by threatening to secure the cancellation of war contracts. On three occasions, compliance with the Board's order was secured by action of the President in taking over the employer's plants. In one of these cases the President took the plant away from the employer, even though he was not the party who failed to comply with the Board's recommendations. In the case of the captive bituminous coal mines, the United Mine Workers of America refused to accede to the recommendations of the Board. The CIO members of the Board withdrew and the President appointed a special board of arbitration to settle the case. This board finally decided the case in favor of the union. In at least a dozen instances, unions refused to abide by a recommendation of the Board, but no action was taken to get them to obey.[16]

The Board was not entirely successful in preventing strikes in cases that came before it. Eighty-five separate strikes occurred in 72 cases out

[15] *New York Times*, Apr. 6, 1941. Judge Charles E. Wyznski, formerly a public member of the National Defense Mediation Board and one-time Solicitor of the Department of Labor, advanced the following argument against partisan members of such boards: "Then there are more fundamental objections which tend actually to weight the scales in favor of labor. The labor representatives are more conscious of their identity with the labor litigant than the management representatives are conscious of their identity with the employer litigant. The labor representatives also ordinarily are more skillful than the employer representatives in the arts which prevail in the arbitration tribunals: they know the terms better, they talk better on their feet or around the conference table, they know more of parliamentary or statutory law, frequently they have greater experience and wider contacts in the government. Also they are likely to have a program, whereas the employer representatives, if they have a program at all, are likely to have a negative one." *Public Policy, III* (1942) edited by C. J. Friedrich and Edward S. Mason, p. 192.
[16] *Report on the Work of the National Defense Mediation Board*, pp. 15-16.

of a total of 111 cases certified to it.[17] In 61 disputes strikes were in progress when the controversy was referred to the Board. Twenty-four strikes occurred in cases after the Board had secured jurisdiction. Since strikes were in actual progress in more than 55 per cent of the cases certified to the Board, it often was confronted with a difficult situation for which it was not fully responsible. It will be recalled that the Board could take only cases certified by the Department of Labor. It would be natural for that Department to be hesitant to refer a case to the Board, since that would involve a confession of failure. Consequently it is possible that delay in certification might have made the task of the Board more difficult.

II. NATIONAL WAR LABOR BOARD

The usefulness of the National Defense Mediation Board ended upon the withdrawal of the CIO members after its decision in the captive coal case early in November 1941. When it appeared that Congress might enact anti-strike legislation a labor-management conference was called by the White House on December 17, and this conference supposedly reached an agreement on certain phases of wartime labor policy.[18] One item of this alleged agreement was that the President should establish a National War Labor Board.

The War Labor Board was set up by the President but subsequently was authorized by Congress.

On January 12, 1942 by executive order, the President created a National War Labor Board composed of twelve members (four public, four labor, and four management), appointed by himself.[19] It was given jurisdiction over all controversies that might affect war production. Subsequently, by the Executive Order of October 3, 1942, issued pursuant to the Price Stabilization Act of October 2, 1942, the President gave it authority to approve all wage increases where the

[17] In a number of cases more than one strike occurred.

[18] The labor members offered the following proposal: no strikes during the war, peaceful settlement of all disputes, and the creation of a war labor board. The employers proposed these three points with an addition: that the closed shop be not subject to arbitration. The labor members refused to support the employers' resolution, and the employer members refused to support the labor resolution. Despite this deadlock, the President announced that the conference was agreed on the three points of the labor proposal: *Memorandum on Deliberations of the War-Labor Conference called by the President on December 17, 1941.*

[19] Executive Order No. 9017, *Federal Register*, Vol. 7, p. 237.

total annual remuneration was below $5,000.[20] Dispute cases were to be referred to the Board by the Conciliation Service, but the Board could take a case on its own motion without such a referral.[21] In the solution of any controversy the Board was directed to use mediation or voluntary arbitration, and if these failed it could resort to compulsory arbitration. The executive order provided that the Board was to settle finally all cases that come before it, but it said nothing concerning how the Board was to enforce its decisions.

Congress gave statutory approval to the Board by the act of June 25, 1943.[22] This law provided for the continuance of the Board as created by executive order.[23] The Board was given authority to settle finally any dispute likely to cause substantial interference with the war effort. In such cases it was empowered to prescribe all conditions of employment, including wages and hours.[24] It was given the power to subpoena witnesses.[25] Even under this legislation, the Board received no direct power to enforce its decisions. But the President was given the authority to seize any war plant where production was interrupted by a labor dispute.[26] The act also required that where a labor dispute threatened war production, the employees should give notice of the existence of the dispute to the Secretary of Labor, the National Labor Relations Board, and the National War Labor Board. For thirty days after such notice, neither party could change the conditions of employment. And a strike could occur only after the National Labor Relations Board had taken a poll of the workers.[27]

Under the executive order and the statute, the Board in effect had jurisdiction over all labor disputes affecting war production. The Board held that it could consider a labor dispute in any activity that might involve a strike. It said that it

. . . takes judicial notice of the fact that any labor dispute of whatever nature which threatens to result in a strike or a lockout does, in fact, affect the prosecution of the war on the home front.

[20] Executive Order No. 9250, *Federal Register*, Vol. 7, p. 7871.
[21] Only a very few cases have been taken by this means: W. H. Davis, *National War Agencies Appropriation Bill, 1945,* Hearings before the House Committee on Appropriations Vol 1, 78 Cong. 2 sess., p. 247.
[22] 57 Stat. 163, 166, Sec. 7.
[23] The act prohibited a member from sitting in any case in which he had a direct interest. The same, Sec. 7 (c).
[24] The same, Sec. 7 (a) (2).
[25] The same, Sec. 7 (a) (3) (4).
[26] The same, Sec. 3.
[27] The same, Sec. 8.

. . . Thus a strike in a so-called non-essential industry, such as one of the service industries, is likely to have very serious consequences on industrial relations in the community. . . .[28]

Organization and procedures have
added to the Board's difficulties.

Only the public members were full-time employees; the labor and industry members were only part-time employees, who drew most of their remuneration from their ordinary employment. Under such circumstances it was not surprising that the nonpublic members considered themselves as the special representatives of their respective groups. And Mr. R. J. Thomas, a labor member said: "I don't consider my job on the Board as working for the government. I am there to represent labor."[29]

Chairman Davis attempted to justify this attitude: "You don't have a tripartite board unless you expect the labor members to represent the views of labor and the industry members to represent the views of industry. Representing these views we expect them to vote in the public interest."[30] In the light of this attitude the impartiality of the Board was not clearly established.[31]

A procedural difficulty led workers to strike against the Board. Because its docket was crowded, decisions were sometimes long delayed. Workers sometimes struck in order to get the Board to decide their case ahead of others.[32] A strike often had the desired result. If the

[28] *Reuben H. Donnally and Co.*, 7 WLR 198, 205 (1943).
[29] *New York Times*, July 29, 1944.
[30] *The Daily News* (Washington, D.C.), Mar. 23, 1944.
[31] One may raise the question of the impartiality of Chairman Davis, who is a public member. "Mr. O'Neal: Would you say that one side more than the other side had a decision rendered in its favor by your board? Mr. Davis: Well, I think in all labor disputes there are more decisions in favor of the workers than there are in favor of the other group. . . . Mr. O'Neal: But that does not mean the man is necessarily always correct. Mr. Davis: . . . After all people, over all, do not manufacture the grounds for all of the complaints, if you see what I mean; there is usually some basis for the complaint." *(First Supplemental National Defense Appropriation Bill for 1943*, Hearings before the House Committee on Appropriations, Pt. 1, 78 Cong. 1 sess., p. 307). The general policy of the Board of granting a wage increase retroactively to the date of the employees' request indicates that the Board assumes that any delay in the bargaining process was due exclusively to the employer. In *Jenkins Bros.*, 14 WLR 254, decided in August 1944, an increase was made retroactive to November 1942, although it was based on regulation of the Director of Economic Stabilization issued on May 12, 1943.
[32] *National War Agencies Appropriation Bill, 1945*, Hearings before the Senate Committee on Appropriations, 78 Cong. 2 sess., p. 128, and *Ninth Annual Report of the National Labor Relations Board* (1944), p. 73.

Board had put such a case at the bottom of its docket rather than give it special preference, the utility of such strikes would have disappeared.

The policies actually applied by the Board already have been considered in detail.[33] They related to two major problems: wage determination and union security. It may be pointed out that the National War Labor Board was no more successful in clearly enunciating and consistently applying policies than its predecessor.[34] Neither Congress nor the President clearly determined the principles to be applied by the Board.[35] Thus the Board has been in the position of having to make policy itself.

The National War Labor Board engaged in mediation, arbitration, and regulation.

The Board represented a mixture of mediation, compulsory arbitration, and regulatory action. In fixing maximum wages in voluntary wage adjustment cases, where it was acting under power conferred upon it under the act of October 2, 1942, it performed a regulatory function. In all dispute cases where its function was primarily arbitral, the Chairman testified that the Board first attempted to mediate the case.[36]

The type of mediation used by the Board deserves at least brief consideration. Generally it attempted to mediate a dispute that the Conciliation Service was unsuccessful in settling. Practically all dispute cases considered involved strikes or threats of strikes. In this respect again it resembles the Conciliation Service, and it differs from the National Mediation Board, which attempts to facilitate the settlement of disputes only before a strike or a threat of a strike has developed. In mediation by the National War Labor Board there was always the possibility that if a party was unwilling to accept a solution

---

[33] See Chaps. 6 and 7.

[34] The lack of principles is evident from the following: "Mr. O'Neal: What is the basis upon which a decision is made? . . . Is it primarily to get the work done, irrespective of whether there is a just or unjust claim? Is the primary purpose to get them back into war production? Mr. Davis: I think that is a fair statement." *First Supplemental National Defense Appropriation Bill for 1943*, Hearings before the House Committee on Appropriations, Pt. 1, 77 Cong. 2 sess., p. 306.

[35] By Executive Order No. 9328, Apr. 8, 1943, *Federal Register*, Vol. 8, p. 4681, some standards relative to wage determinations were given to the Board.

[36] *To Investigate Executive Agencies*, Hearings before the House Special Committee to Investigate Executive Agencies, 78 Cong. 1 sess., p. 1483.

offered by the NWLB or its employee, the Board could subsequently settle the case by compulsory arbitration. The potentiality of the Board's imposition of its solution made a party more willing to accept its mediatory advice than he would be to accept the same solution proposed by a commissioner of conciliation of the Department of Labor. Thus conciliation as carried on was not voluntary like that offered by the Conciliation Service.

The consequences of combining mediation and arbitration in the same agency were discussed previously. Because of these resulting difficulties, the performance of both functions tends to be impaired.[37] The regulatory function—that is the fixing of maximum wages—could hardly be separated from its arbitration function, since wages were involved in most dispute cases which it arbitrated. Although this merger of arbitration and regulation might appear to be peculiar, members of the Board did not believe that it was feasible to separate them. Generally it would not have been practicable to have two separate agencies fixing wages for the same type of work, because it might have led to a divergent treatment of a comparable situation depending on whether it arose in a dispute case or in a wage approval case.[38] In one situation Congress has provided that wage approval cases are to be handled by a different agency than the one considering wages in dispute cases. By the 1944 amendments to the Price Control Act, in dispute cases, wages of employees subject to the Railway Labor Act can be determined by the National Mediation Board and the special emergency boards. But the approval of voluntary wage changes for these employees still remains in the National War Labor Board.[39]

Only the President enforced
the Board's orders.

When the National War Labor Board reached a decision, it issued an order directing the parties to make a contract embodying the terms of its directive. As the Chairman of the Board said: "We substitute our volition for his" [the employer's].[40] And the employer could not insist

---

[37] William L. Leiserson, "Labor Faces a Crisis," *American Magazine*, January 1945, pp. 20-21.

[38] *To Investigate Executive Agencies*, Hearings before the House Special Committee to Investigate Executive Agencies, p. 1463.

[39] 58 Stat. 632.

[40] *To Investigate Executive Agencies*, Hearings before the House Special Committee to Investigate Executive Agencies, p. 1469.

that the contract include a clause stating it was made under duress.[41]

Neither the executive order creating the Board nor the War Labor Disputes Act provided any direct means of enforcing its orders in dispute cases. The United States Court of Appeals for the District of Columbia held that neither the executive order creating the Board nor the War Labor Disputes Act made the Board's decisions enforceable. Consequently the court refused to review or enjoin the enforcement of these orders.[42] It asserted the Board was only advisory to the President, and if it referred a case to the President because a party refused to comply with its determination, he did not have to follow its recommendation. The act of June 25, 1943[43] authorized the President to take over plants needed for the prosecution of the war, or in which war production had ceased because of a labor dispute. It was the policy of the Board to inform the President if any party to a controversy refused to carry out an order of the Board. The President then took over the property of the employer irrespective of which party failed to comply. In at least 12 instances the property of the employer was taken by the President where it was the workers who refused to obey.[44] The Board also secured compliance with its determinations through the cancellation of war contracts.[45]

Rarely were sanctions
applied against unions.

Although President Roosevelt stated that he would not require a labor union to comply with a decision of the Board,[46] he did confer upon the Director of Economic Stabilization the authority to take limited steps against a union to secure compliance. The President had the right to sequestrate union funds temporarily, to withhold dues collected by the check-off, and to cancel union preference clauses in contracts where a union failed to abide by a decision of the Board, but

[41] *Montgomery Ward Co.*, 11 WLR 1720.
[42] *NLWB* v. *Montgomery Ward and Co.* 144 Fed. (2d) 528 (1944) and *NWLB* v. *U. S. Gypsum Co.* 145 Fed (2d) 97 (1944).
[43] 57 Stat. 163, 167, Sec., 8; see also act of Oct. 16, 1941, 55 Stat. 742.
[44] *Report of Executive Director to the National War Labor Board*, Jan. 12, 1945, p. 5.
[45] *To Investigate Executive Agencies*, Hearings before the House Special Committee to Investigate Executive Agencies, p. 1514-15. See also the case of *E. A. Laboratories*, 15 LRR 822 (1945).
[46] *New York Times*, July 10, 1943.

only after the government had confiscated the employers' property.[47] Only once were these sanctions used.[48]

As a part of the supposed labor-management agreement of December 23, 1941 that led to the Board's creation, labor pledged itself not to engage in any strikes in defense production. The Board refused to grant maintenance of membership to a union that engaged in a strike, either before or after the dispute was referred to the Board. According to the Board, the union demonstrated its irresponsibility by striking in violation of its pledge and thereby abrogated its claim to security.[49] The Board knew of no case where an international union punished a local for striking in violation of the no-strike agreement.[50] As a result of this failure to apply sanctions against a labor organization, a strong and determined union could often defy the Board and get what it wanted.[51] The United Mine Workers of America and the American Federation of Musicians illustrate this.

III. SUMMARY OF PEACEFUL ADJUSTMENT OF LABOR DISPUTES

The federal government has made two approaches to the problem of minimizing labor disputes: it has attempted to prevent them from arising, and it has established machinery to facilitate their settlement when they arise. The guarantee of the worker's right to organize and to bargain under the National Labor Relations Act is an example of an attempt to prevent disputes by removing a significant cause. The remedial approach consists of either conciliation or arbitration. Agencies that have engaged in conciliation are the President, the Conciliation Service, the Maritime Labor Board, the National Labor Relations Board, and the National Mediation Board. The National Railroad Adjustment Board and the National War Labor Board engage in arbitration.

Most of the agencies attempting to settle disputes take the attitude that the maintenance of industrial peace is their primary objective. They generally assume that any concession, not illegal, is justified if

---

[47] Executive Order No. 9370, Aug. 16, 1943, *Federal Register*, Vol. 8, p. 11463.
[48] *California Metal Trades Association*, 16 LRR 733, 812 (1944).
[49] *Monsanto Chemical Co.*, 2 WLR 479 (1942).
[50] *National War Agencies Appropriation Bill, 1945*, Hearings before House Committee on Appropriations, Pt. 1, 78 Cong. 2 sess., p. 281.
[51] Leiserson, "Labor Faces a Crisis," *American Magazine*, January 1945, pp. 20-21.

by granting it a work stoppage can be avoided. It is implicitly assumed that no concession, not illegal, can have consequences more undesirable than a work stoppage. The Conciliation Service and several railway emergency boards have adopted this attitude. As a result of this policy an advantage is given to the party threatening to disrupt the industrial peace. Since lockouts and concerted activities by employers are illegal, it is only the employees who can threaten to break the peace by overt acts. Consequently the policy that the maintenance of industrial peace is all-important gives an advantage to labor.

Not all of the agencies engaged in conciliation approach it in the same manner. The National Mediation Board mediates disputes only before the threat of a strike has developed. It generally does not mediate strikes. On the other hand the Conciliation Service and the National War Labor Board primarily mediate disputes only after a strike or threat of a strike has developed. The Conciliation Service and the National War Labor Board have sanctions available to compel the parties to accept their suggestions. The National War Labor Board and some of the industrial relations sections of war agencies had indirect sanctions that in some cases could be used against parties who were unwilling to accept suggestions for settling a dispute.

Arbitration may be compulsory or voluntary. Arbitration under the Railway Labor Act is completely voluntary; it depends on the consent of both parties. But a dispute within the jurisdiction of the National Railroad Adjustment Board can be submitted to it by either party; the Board's jurisdiction then is obligatory on the other party. The National War Labor Board could assume jurisdiction that was compulsory over any dispute that might affect the war effort, even though neither party desired it.

Disputes submitted to arbitration are of two types—as to rights and as to interests. Arbitration of rights consists of the determination and application of the terms of an existing agreement to a specified dispute. The work of the National Railroad Adjustment Board, as well as most of the arbitration activities of the Conciliation Service, are of this type. The arbitration of interests is the determination of the terms of a new contract by the arbitral body when the parties cannot agree upon them by themselves. This type of arbitration is obviously more difficult than the settlement of disputes as to rights. In the latter case the arbitrator has the contract of the parties as a standard on which to base his decision. In settling a dispute as to interests there are no pre-existing standards to guide the arbitrator in determining what should be the terms of the new agreement. The National War Labor Board determined primarily disputes as to interests.

Several agencies have attempted to combine conciliation and arbitration. If the same agency is given both of these functions, it is difficult for it to perform either one effectively. In conciliation the aim is to bring about a settlement of the dispute; almost any terms that will produce a settlement are desirable. In arbitration, the aim should be a sound settlement of the dispute on its merits. If the arbitrator follows the conciliation techniques, he may be charged with inconsistency; if the conciliator attempted to adhere to the principles he applied as an arbitrator, some might charge him with being prejudiced in advance.

Various types of sanctions have been used to compel compliance with the decisions of the agencies engaged in facilitating the peaceful settlement of disputes. The decisions of the National Railroad Adjustment Boards and the voluntary arbitral boards provided for under the Railway Labor Act can be enforced by court action. The Conciliation Service and the Maritime Labor Board have attempted to use publicity as a sanction; but the use of any sanction, even publicity, tends to destroy the voluntary nature of the process, and it would also reduce the willingness of parties to accept the good offices of the agency. The President also tried to use publicity to secure compliance with his recommendations in conciliation, and the results were not very good. Public opinion is the only sanction the railroad emergency boards have had, and until 1941 it was successful. If either labor or management refuse to accept a recommendation of the National War Labor Board, the primary sanction used was the seizure of the employer's property by the President.

CHAPTER XI

MAJOR TRENDS

From this survey of statutes, administrative activities, and judicial decisions that relate to labor problems, it is evident that the federal government does not have a labor policy that can be regarded as a coherent and integrated system.[1] The systematic arrangement and presentation of the material in this study might convey to the reader an erroneous idea concerning the degree of systematization that actually exists. Since the Constitution does not confer on the federal government any direct authority to regulate labor relations or the conditions of employment, and since the fundamental law reserves to the exclusive jurisdiction of the states many powers that impinge upon any labor program, under our constitutional system it has not been easy to develop a well-rounded labor policy. Conversely, the lack of any systematic labor policy has been a factor contributing to the piecemeal nature of federal labor legislation.

Nevertheless, among the maze of federal statutes, rules, regulations, and decisions in this field, it may be possible to distinguish the basic objectives of our labor policies and some of the major principles that are used to attain those objectives. The purpose of this book, it will be recalled, has been to see what are the objectives and practices and not to discuss their merits and defects. In recent years the major objective of the government in this field has been to secure for labor a larger income with shorter hours of work.[2] It has sought to facilitate the attainment of this goal primarily through the bargaining efforts of the workers themselves. Only where they cannot attain desirable wages and working conditions by their own efforts, does the government directly set minimum conditions of employment.

An effort will first be made to summarize the principles that have been developed in the process of aiding workers to improve conditions of employment by their own efforts. Some of the interrelationships of these principles and the conflicts involved in their application will be indicated. Then an attempt will be made to summarize the efforts

[1] Leo Wolman, "Labor Policy and the Volume of Employment," *Proceedings of the Academy of Political Science*, Vol. 18 (1940), p. 404.
[2] The same, p. 405.

of the government to set minimum standards of employment where the workers have not been able to attain these objectives themselves.

Assisting workers to increase earnings and improve working conditions. Three basic principles have been evident in the process of assisting workers to increase their earnings and to improve their working conditions. They are: (1) the government encourages workers to engage in concerted action; (2) the government protects the workers' right to organize in their own way; and (3) the government seeks to promote the peaceful settlement of labor disputes.

Concerted action is encouraged to facilitate employees to make collective agreements with their employers. Since by collective action the bargaining power of workers is increased, and consequently better terms of employment are secured, the government requires the employer to engage in collective bargaining if the workers desire it. To facilitate the attainment of increased bargaining power, the right to organize, to strike, to picket, to boycott, and to bargain collectively is protected, and employers are prohibited from interfering with workers who are exercising these rights. To give added assistance to organizing activities and to increase the bargaining power of workers, unions and employers are encouraged to enter into various kinds of union preference contracts; closed shop, union shop, preferential shop, and maintenance of membership agreements are all permitted where the negotiating union represents a majority of the employees. Of course employers and workers covered by the Railway Labor Act cannot enter into such agreements.

Very few limitations are imposed on the workers' use of strikes, pickets, and boycotts. These instruments of self help can be utilized even if such use imposes considerable restraints on the free movement of goods in interstate commerce. A minority group of employees, with whom the employer is forbidden to bargain, can use these weapons to interfere with the rights granted to another labor organization that represents a majority of the workers in a bargaining unit. Although the representatives of a majority of the employees have the exclusive right to bargain for all employees, minority groups or unions, even though they have no members employed in a plant, have in effect an unlimited right to use boycotts, strikes, and pickets to attempt to coerce the employer to deal with them. Where a majority of the employees has selected a bargaining agent, it is illegal for an employer to bargain with any other group of workers. Nevertheless it is not illegal for other groups to use these weapons to coerce him to commit an unfair labor practice that is prohibited by the National Labor Relations Act.

As a part of the concerted activities encouraged by the government, workers have the right to bargain collectively, and employers have a corresponding duty to bargain with them. To determine whether the employer properly performs this duty, the National Labor Relations Board attempts to discover whether he bargained in good faith. In some instances it has been held that an employer has demonstrated his bad faith if he refused certain demands of his employees or if he requested the inclusion of certain clauses in an agreement. As thus applied, these tests have been to labor's advantage; but in the hands of an agency manned by a staff unfriendly to labor, comparable tests of good faith could be used to labor's disadvantage.

The final objective of the various forms of concerted action is the formulation of collective agreements by employers and employees. But several aspects of the government's labor program run contrary to the attainment of this objective. It is often difficult for employers to enforce effectively collective agreements made with labor unions, because many obstacles stand in the way of a suit against a labor organization. Some friends of labor argue that it is not desirable for union funds to be used to pay a judgment arising out of a breach of an agreement with an employer.[3] Even though the workers contract not to engage in strikes, picketing, or boycotts, labor is not prevented from using such concerted activities to compel a modification of the agreement or to attain any other objective. One reason an employer makes an agreement with his workers is to free his establishment from interruptions resulting from strikes and boycotts. Many employers see little to be gained from a collective agreement if they do not secure such enforceable advantages from it.

Another fundamental principle of our labor policy is that workers have a right to form their own labor organizations. The employers are precluded from doing anything that interferes with the right of workers to organize and to bargain collectively. But the practical application of this principle involves a contradiction. For the employer to know with which group of his employees he must bargain, some

[3] Edwin S. Witte, *The Government in Labor Disputes* (1932), pp. 148-50.

government agency must exist to determine the appropriate bargaining unit and also to discover which group represents the majority of the employees in the unit. Since such an agency of the government must select the unit as a practical matter, it inevitably will interfere with the free right of workers to choose their own form of labor organization. Since the nature of the bargaining unit is significant in determining what organization will be chosen as the representative of the majority, any government board that selects the bargaining unit will influence the choice of the workers in selecting their representatives. This is especially true when, as is often the case today, rival unions exist.

Finally, the third major principle the government follows is that it desires to facilitate the peaceful settlement of labor disputes. Various types of machinery have been set up to mediate, investigate, and arbitrate labor disputes. In practically all instances labor has a free right to choose whether or not it will use this machinery designed to make work stoppages unnecessary. But in no case is its right to strike really limited or restricted in order to encourage its use of the machinery. In some cases indirect sanctions are used to encourage employers to utilize such devices.

Occasionally there are direct conflicts between the protection of the employees' right to engage in concerted action and the encouragement of the peaceful settlement of labor disputes. Even though administrative agencies exist to protect labor's right to organize and to bargain, if workers feel that these rights have been transgressed, the employees can use measures of self help (strike, boycott, and so forth) at their own discretion, or they can call upon the government to enforce their rights. Nothing is done to make it more attractive for employees to utilize the administrative or judicial machinery set up to protect these rights. Further, if labor feels its rights under a contract have been violated, it can engage in self help to enforce its own interpretation of the agreement, or it can bring an action in a court to secure compliance or damages. Here, again, nothing is done to make the use of direct action unattractive.

When labor uses government machinery for the peaceful settlement of disputes, actually it does not thereby place itself in a disadvantageous position. The major objective of the agencies engaged in the peaceful settlement of disputes is to avoid a work stoppage, and the party threatening to breach the industrial peace has the advantage, for there would be a tendency to believe that its demands must be appeased if it is to be dissuaded from its threat. Since almost any lockout by an employer is prohibited, most disputes involve the employees' threat of a strike, and workers generally make the direct threat to disturb the industrial peace. As a result labor suffers no significant loss of bargaining power by submitting to conciliation. Further, although the workers agree to conciliation or arbitration, they are still free to strike if the settlement proposed should be too displeasing to them. This potentiality of the ultimate use of the strike further tends to condition the outcome of the proceedings.

Conflict of objectives. The protection of the right of self-organization and the efforts to increase bargaining power are interrelated. All workers have the free right to organize, but only the group that represents a majority has the right to bargain. Putting the right to bargain exclusively in the hands of the majority union of course tends to increase the bargaining power of this group of workers, because it gives to the union representing perhaps only a bare majority of the employees just as much bargaining power as though it actually represented all workers. As a consequence of this principle, the bargaining power of the majority group of the workers is strengthened.

The relationship of the increase of bargaining power to the right of self organization can be illustrated in a number of other ways. Generally, the larger the bargaining unit the smaller is the actual right of the individual employee to engage in self organization. Groups of workers with specialized skills and problems have a more effective method to express their separate interests in small units than in large units. But small units tend to have less bargaining power than large ones. In designating bargaining units, the NLRB always has these two objectives before it—the protection of the workers' right to organize, and assisting workers to increase their bargaining power. It has generally favored larger bargaining units, specifically because they have more bargaining power.

As a further illustration of this tendency, workers with a free right to organize may join either local organizations or units affiliated with national bodies. A local union supported by a national organization will tend to have more bargaining power than an unaffiliated union, because the affiliated union can engage in concerted action on a wider plane, and because it has more power and resources at its disposal. The government in several different ways tends to favor the development of national organizations over unaffiliated local organizations. Thus, here again, the attainment of increased bargaining power is placed above the protection of the workers' right of self determination.

The union preference agreement also trenches on the employees' right of self determination. If workers are hired on the basis of union membership and discharged if they cease to remain members in good standing, it can hardly be said that they have the right of self determination. They are not free to determine the union that they wish to join, and they are not free to leave it when they see fit to do so. Of course as a result of union preference, the bargaining power of the workers is augmented both as a consequence of the increase in the size of the labor organization, and because the union will tend to have a more monopolistic position concerning the labor supply.

Thus generally when the government's desire to increase the bargaining power of employees clashes with the protection of their right of self determination or with the desire to facilitate the peaceful settlement of disputes, the efforts to increase bargaining power prevail over the other two. It is immaterial whether or not this tendency is a result of a conscious effort on the part of the government. The desirability of this trend is not questioned in the present study. The only point being made here is that the increase in bargaining power is considered more important than the protection of the right of self determination or the maintenance of industrial peace.

The determination of terms of employment. As was said at the beginning of this chapter, the government has sought to help labor secure a larger income and shorter hours of employment. To accomplish these objectives, the federal government relies primarily on the worker's own efforts with government assistance to increase bargaining power, and it does not generally rely on the direct determination of the conditions of employment by the government. Only where labor by its own efforts has not secured the desired minimum conditions of employment, has the government fixed minimum wages, maximum hours, and other conditions of work.

Minimum wages have now been fixed under various separate laws and even maximum wages are being set, but only as a wartime measure. No real standards have ever been developed and applied in the process of determining either minimum or maximum wages. Diverse and dissimilar standards exist: the prevailing wage, the prevailing minimum wage, the highest wage that will not adversely affect employment, and a number of others. The administrative agencies concerned have given no real objective substance to these standards. In the Fair Labor Standards Act, Congress has set one general standard for the determination of minimum wages, but the National War Labor Board employed another one. Although the Fair Labor Standards Act contains a minimum wage standard of general application, Congress has established a higher minimum wage standard applicable to employees of government contractors and to persons employed by recipients of certain government subsidies.

Maximum hours of work are regulated, but it is not easy to discover the logical principles on which these regulations are based. Forty hours a week is the maximum for general employment, 60 to 70 hours a week is the maximum for motor transportation, and on railroads 8 hours a day is used for pay purposes, and 16 hours a day for purposes of safety. Separate maximum hour regulations apply to employees of government contractors. Spreading employment, increasing purchasing power, and the promotion of safety are among the objectives of these maximum hour laws. Even in a period of a labor shortage, the government still considered as desirable the payment of time and a half for all work in excess of 40 hours a week, though the requirement originally was adopted to spread work during a period of unemployment. The only logical basis for this requirement was that the higher rate of pay would encourage employees to work longer hours.

The sole objective of this study is to describe the labor policy of the government. Whether or not that policy succeeds in attaining its objectives has not been considered. Nor has the desirability of its basic objectives been within the scope of this undertaking.

INDEX

INDEX